IN SEARCH OF THE PERFECT JOB

12 Proven Steps for Getting the Job You _Really_ Want

Clyde C. Lowstuter

David P. Robertson

McGraw-Hill, Inc.
New York   St. Louis   San Francisco   Auckland   Bogotá
Caracas   Lisbon   London   Madrid   Mexico City   Milan
Montreal   New Delhi   San Juan   Singapore
Sydney   Tokyo   Toronto

Dedicated to the personal power within you to fully discover and manage your limitless talents, skills, and abilities. May you achieve all that you commit to while enjoying the process.

Especially to our families who love us, inspire us, and help us enjoy the journey:

Carolyn, Nathan, and Cammie Lowstuter
Marian, Dan, and Jim Robertson

 This book is printed on recycled, acid-free paper containing a minimum of 50% recycled de-inked fiber.

Library of Congress Cataloging-in-Publication Data

Lowstuter, Clyde C.
    In search of the perfect job : 12 proven steps for getting the job
you really want / Clyde C. Lowstuter, David P. Robertson.
        p.   cm.
    Includes bibliographical references and index.
    ISBN 0-07-038880-6 (hc) :   —ISBN 0-07-038881-4 (pb) :
    1. Job hunting. I. Robertson, David P. II. Title.
HF5382.7.L69   1992
650.14—dc20   92-6888
                                                    CIP

    7 8 9 0 **DOH DOH** 9 8 7 6 5

ISBN 0-07-038880-6 {HC}
ISBN 0-07-038881-4 {PBK}

The sponsoring editor for this book was Betsy Brown, the editing supervisor was Caroline Levine, and the production supervisor was Donald F. Schmidt. It was set in Garamond Light by North Market Street Graphics.

Printed and bound by R. R. Donnelley & Sons Company.

CONTENTS

Step 4
BUILDING AND MANAGING YOUR REFERENCES   138

Step 5
USING APPLICATION FORMS TO YOUR ADVANTAGE   153

Step 6
IN SEARCH OF THE PERFECT EMPLOYER   166

Step 7

USING THE TELEPHONE TO CAPTURE LEADS
AND LAND INTERVIEWS

200

Step 8

INTERVIEWING POWERFULLY
Beating Out Your Competition

221

Step 9
KEEPING YOUR JOB SEARCH "ON TRACK" AND "ON FIRE"

265

Step 10
TURNING AROUND REJECTION, STRESS, OR A STALLED SEARCH

278

Step 11
IN SEARCH OF THE PERFECT OFFER
Creating What You Want Through Effective Negotiations

291

Step 12
LOOKING BACK AND MANAGING FORWARD
Ensuring Success in Your Perfect Job

311

FOREWORD

If you have never before read *In Search of the Perfect Job* or heard of Clyde Lowstuter or Dave Robertson, then you are in for a pleasant surprise. Be prepared for fast-paced reading and insights on every page.

As management consultants specializing in career development and outplacement counseling, Clyde, Dave and their team have helped thousands of displaced employees throughout North America develop and pursue career choices. So, they really *do* know what they're talking about. They have put together a highly practical book which equips people to uncover and explore career options unique to their situation, while guiding them through the often bewildering process of job hunting. What really makes *In Search of the Perfect Job* perfect is Clyde's and Dave's ability to institute sound career search strategies from the vantage point of honest-to-goodness human beings.

I felt I was walking in the shoes of someone whose life's fabric had been suddenly torn asunder, felt all the attendant stress, fear, and rejection, insight, positive expectations, and joy of success. Both authors have personally experienced the pain of involuntary separation and the gain of effectively putting their lives and their careers back on track.

I am sure you will enjoy experiencing a proven blueprint for job-changing success as you work through the thought-provoking questions and results-producing exercises. If you utilize this book as it was intended, you will undoubtedly pick up some new ideas, become reacquainted with familiar but unused actions, and put other recommendations on the shelf for later retrieval. Nowhere do Clyde or Dave suggest that you do every single exercise to gain value from their book. Far from it. However, your progress will be accelerated if you follow the "12 Proven Steps for Getting the Job You _Really_ Want" in sequence.

This well-written, user-friendly book shows great insight, a caring nature for people, and, most of all, a practical path to follow to restore one's hopes and dreams. I do not know whether to call it a novel or a text, but it is one of the finest business publications I have ever read.

Edward J. Noha
Chairman of the Boards and Chief Executive Officer
CNA Insurance Companies

A SPECIAL NOTE

When I Got Zapped—Migraines and All

In 1974 I left the organizational consulting firm with whom I was employed in Chicago to join a $120 million manufacturer in the northern woods of upper Wisconsin. I wanted to have the practical experience of executing that which I was recommending as a consultant.

Three weeks after we moved north, Carolyn, my wife, gave birth to our son, Nathan. As you might imagine, things were quite chaotic: new job, new baby, new area of the country, new friends, and no family in the immediate area. In addition, Carolyn's mother had recently died.

I don't think at the time we could have endured many more changes in our lives. Although I tried to keep my work and personal life balanced, my workaholic nature seemed to get the best of me. There were never enough hours in the day to get it all done. Shortly after I arrived at the company I was asked to provide human resources support to the chemicals division, which was in transition with a new management team and lagging profits.

On one project, I worked numerous 90-hour weeks researching and preparing a comprehensive affirmative action plan which was the key to the pending sale of one of the company's business units. I was under a lot of pressure to complete the work quickly yet accurately. Carolyn thought I had kept crazy hours previously, but this was ridiculous. I would arrive at the office at 7:00 a.m. and seldom leave work until after 1 a.m., six days a week. My motivation? I was told that the company depended upon me to help it sell this one strategic business unit.

In the midst of all of this, my division needed some streamlining. One morning after I had heatedly hammered out some additional severance concessions from my boss to more appropriately support some recently hired senior contributors, he turned to me and said, "By the way Clyde, you're fired too." I laughed, thinking it was merely "gallows humor," given the conversation we were having. But only after seeing his pale, waxy complexion did I realize that he was serious. I remember sitting back down in a lump, feeling the rush of emotions: shock, hurt, anger, fear, vengefulness, bitterness; most of all I felt violated and used.

"Excuse me, but you must be thinking of another Clyde Lowstuter. I'll go get him because you can't be referring to me! I've got a graduate degree, I was not the most recent hire, and given my consulting work throughout North America, clearly I was the most broadly experienced."

(I stopped short of saying that I was both the best looking and the most intelligent. I probably couldn't have pulled that one off even if I had tried!)

My emotional roller coaster was predictable: a prolonged disorientation alternating between red-hot anger and profound sadness. I blamed my boss: I thought he was the jerk and I was the victim. I was so ticked I couldn't see straight. I also found something else about organizations which I had not realized before: No matter the extent of the support and endorsement you had inside the company, once you get zapped, the organization closes ranks and isolates whoever got terminated. Granted, there may be a lot of sympathy, but rarely is there sufficient hue and cry to overturn the decision. It's not personal, rather it's a form of survival instinct. As hard as it was for me to realize it, the company needed to operate like this to keep on moving so it did not grind itself to a halt agonizing over these kinds of decisions once they were made.

I'll never forget the sights, sounds, and sensations as I drove up the small hill leaving my office with some of my personal effects. Everything seemed so hazy, yet incredibly vivid. The barber, in his small two-chair shop at the top of the hill continued to cut hair in the fifties' style for which he was known, and a young boy was filling his bicycle tire from the air pump at the corner gas station. It looked like a scene out of a Norman Rockwell painting. I had my window half-way rolled down ready to scream out, "The bomb has dropped! Run for your lives and take cover!" only to catch myself. The bomb had indeed dropped. On me, though, not on anyone else. My life had suddenly been turned upside down, yet no one else seemed to be affected. Strange. Very strange. It was one of the most surreal experiences of my life.

Within a matter of days, the projects I was working on got absorbed by others or dropped. Interestingly enough, it was as if the projects which were deemed to have a high priority several weeks ago now seemed to be contaminated, as if to imply that anyone assuming responsibility for this work would suffer the same fate. Consequently, there was no passion or commitment to see these programs through to completion.

It was a rough time for me. I thought of myself as confident, assertive, and competent, yet all that was shaken to the core. I got migraines, gained weight, lost weight, and fiddled away the modest six weeks of severance, with no outplacement. It wasn't for the lack of trying, I was just badly beaten up in the process, not unlike being run over by a truck and living to tell the tale. Sure, my boss could have terminated me more effectively (and compassionately), but I'm convinced he didn't because he was frightened of how I might react.

So in effect, I got exactly what I had created in the relationship; I wrote the script and my boss played out his role. I'm convinced that he did not see me endorsing him, so why should he endorse me with a more generous severance package or a longer notice? Before my termination, my boss was probably as frustrated with me as I was with him. It's a shame neither one of us had the foresight to stop the destructive cycle. Unfortunately, the termination of our relationship was unnecessarily messy, on both of our parts. The more adverse reaction my boss received internally from his peers, the more he tried to justify his actions, which made me even more angry when I heard about some of his explanations. I only wish I had been able to create the much-needed emotional distance to put my upset in perspective.

Clearly, I was stuck. It was only through the tireless loving support from my family and friends that I was able to survive and get back on track. The ownership of my dismissal went through some distinct cycles, not unlike my emotional roller coaster. My boss fired me. I thought he was wrong, myopic, inflexible, and had difficulty sharing authority. Clearly, he did not know how to handle high-energy, creative professionals. I blamed him. I also blamed myself for confronting him openly in staff meetings and for falling asleep in every windowless, smoke-filled production meeting. (What can I say? It was hot and stuffy and I was up all night with a kid with colic.)

Once I pushed through all the blame, I realized that there was much more personal power in my accepting complete responsibility for how my career and life looked, rather than rationalizing my termination by assessing fault. The "context" of fault requires that someone be wrong, that blame be levied, and that roles of victim and persecutor be assigned. I didn't want to blame anyone anymore.

When I finally worked this out for myself, I realized that I had wasted a lot of energy making my old boss wrong and me right. In the final analysis, I was disruptive to what he wanted and needed for his department, regardless how talented I felt I was. Although he had made a business decision, it felt deeply personal. He wasn't wrong, he was right to terminate me if there wasn't a fit. I'm only sorry neither one of us had the courage or insight or skills to candidly discuss the status of the relationship. Had we been able to do so, a tremendous amount of trauma and years of recrimination would have been avoided.

This book reflects the lessons I personally learned from this experience as well as from our work with over 15,000 displaced employees in the past 11 years. As you read this material you may find yourself being described in the examples or you may relate personally to some of the people mentioned. All names of people and organizations have been altered to maintain confidences. Any resemblance to actual people is strictly coincidental.

Clyde C. Lowstuter

PREFACE

This Book Is for You If . . .

- You have ever wished for more control in your career or knew you could advance to greater heights, if only given the chance.
- You have ever felt that you have the talent, skill, values, and personality to enjoy a truly rewarding personal life, yet it keeps slipping out from your grasp before you have the opportunity to fully master it.
- Your career seems to be stalled, stuck, or not moving quickly enough.
- You aren't "politically connected."
- Your company is undergoing change, possibly due to increased or decreased sales, a merger or acquisition or stiffer competition.
- You have been terminated, or you suspect that your job is in jeopardy.

If you can identify with any of these, then keep reading; you've found the right book. Please do not be intimidated by its size—it really is easy reading. If you skim the contents, you'll notice that a number of Worksheets help you accomplish what you want; here we avoid a "cookie cutter" approach to job-changing success. The exercises are critical to bettering your understanding of yourself and your career. In addition, a number of sample scripts in the book serve to "coach" you through particularly sensitive encounters.

In Search of the Perfect Job was written to enable individuals like yourself to take control—to more effectively manage your careers and personal lives. Unfortunately, countless people sleepwalk through life, unaware of their marvelous talent and potential. And if they get a glimpse of their potential, they more than likely become frightened at the prospect of greater success. Many unconsciously sabotage those efforts which could lead to a more exciting and richer life and career.

This book will help you unlock your potential and discover those areas of your life which "roadblock" you as well as those that empower you. Through a series of interactive exercises you will create a focus for your career and identify those organizational environments and working relationships which are best for you and those in which you will flourish. This book is a road map for how to achieve your career dreams, one that you can tailor to meet your own unique needs.

Zero In on What You Need at Your Own Pace

"The 12 Proven Steps for Job-Changing Success" have been designed to work together or separately, if you want to zero in on one particular section ahead of another. For instance, although you may not have your résumé as powerfully written as you'd like, you have an opportunity to interview for an important job. Turn to Step 8, "Interviewing Powerfully," and study up on how to effectively manage the interview by taking a proactive position, asking penetrating questions, and volunteering information that uncovers data not normally revealed in the interview.

In addition, you will learn how to handle stressful interviews and how to recover gracefully and confidently when you've "blown it." In effect, we help you "peel back the layers" of a prospective employer so you can accurately assess if this is the right fit for you while clearly distinguishing yourself from other job candidates.

So, utilize *In Search of the Perfect Job* in a way that works for you. Read this book like you would a newspaper—initially skimming those topics of greatest interest to you. Then, go back and study in detail each section you feel you can benefit from.

If you want to . . .	Then study and work on . . .
Get a better handle on what you want to do with your life and your career	Step 2: In Search of Who You Are: Uncovering Your Talents, Skills, and Career Options
Develop a powerful result-oriented résumé which prompts companies to call you for an interview	Step 3: Writing a "Knock-Out" Résumé and Marketing Letters That Get Read!
Find out where the right jobs are and how to talk to the hiring manager	Step 6: In Search of the Perfect Employer
Learn how to interview better, increase your confidence, and create offers	Step 8: Interviewing Powerfully: Beating Out Your Competition

How to Use This Book

Instead of chapters, each major section of this book has been written as a Step. Each Step contains materials, exercises, and challenges which will provide you with the effective tools for job hunting and a well-organized process that works. These are to be considered *steps for getting the job you* really *want*.

Acknowledgments

It is difficult to identify all the people who have helped make this book a reality, because so many people have influenced our thinking and contributed to us.

Thanks go to our families who encouraged us, provided suggestions, and offered support when writing at even the most bizarre hours.

Rod Deighen first gave us our start in this form of consulting full time, for which we are forever in his debt. Our friend, George Morrisey, author or coauthor of 14 books, was always steadfast in his support of this project, offering ideas, critiquing materials, and providing reality checks. Thanks also to our many colleagues whose testimonials you read, for their input and guidance. It was much appreciated.

Deep-felt appreciation and love to the entire consulting team at Robertson Lowstuter whose perspectives you engage in as you complete exercises or read text: Ann Collins Baker, Win Gould, Patt Reed, Tom Moffat, and Scott Anderson. To Kenna Washington who reassured and educated us regarding computers and to Cynthia Arnold and Dorie Schultheiss for their typing support. A special thanks to Ginny Hilgart-Roy upon whose shoulders this project rested. It was through her tireless and gracious typing and administrative skills that this book came into being. Jill Novak graciously provided the artwork for some of the models presented.

We deeply appreciate Betsy Brown, McGraw-Hill Senior Editor, and her faith in our work, as well as Ted Nardin, Publisher, and Caroline Levine, Senior Editing Supervisor, for their ongoing efforts to make publication of this book possible. In addition, we would like to thank Phil Crosby who graciously introduced us to the folks at McGraw-Hill which steamrolled into a great relationship.

We are indebted to our client organizations and the thousands of individuals they entrusted to our care and with whom we were privileged to serve.

A special thanks goes to the rest of our team at Robertson Lowstuter, Inc., who helped create an organization where innovation, service, compassion, humor, and results are the standard.

Clyde C. Lowstuter
David P. Robertson

About the Authors

Clyde Lowstuter and **David Robertson** are principals of Robertson Lowstuter, Inc. (RL), a leading management consulting firm in Chicago which specializes in equipping organizations and individuals to operate more effectively. Through breakthrough approaches in the field of career development, performance improvement, and organizational change, RL empowers individuals to create and explore options in their lives, both on and off the job. They and their team help individuals through the trauma of termination, getting them quickly back on track, launching successful, well-organized job searches. In addition to their corporate-sponsored outplacement, two RL programs, *Living in a Changing Organization* ℠ and *Career Enhancement* ℠ revitalize valuable people, avert termination, and strengthen organizational effectiveness.

RL's client list reads like a Who's Who in publicly traded and privately held manufacturing, service, and nonprofit organizations throughout North America. During the past ten years, the authors' distinctive approaches to careering have enabled over 15,000 people to make rewarding and fulfilling career moves.

For more information about Robertson Lowstuter's capabilities, resources, and programs, or to order the audio cassette, "Empowering Your Career," developed by Clyde Lowstuter, call toll free 1-800-398-2665.

IN SEARCH OF THE PERFECT JOB

Mastering Your Emotions and Regaining Control

Michael Commons: Zapped While the Sun Was Shining

Friday afternoon at 4:15, Mike Commons's world fell apart. At age 50, with 23 years with TCA Corporation, he was out. Although he knew TCA was experiencing financial difficulties, he never thought that his job was in jeopardy. Granted, budgets had been steadily cut in the last 18 months, and all nonessential programs or projects were either eliminated or severely scaled back. Even Mike's department, Sales and Marketing, had experienced the financial squeeze. Despite Mike's strong protests, his department's advertising budget was dramatically cut even though the company needed to promote its products, services, and capabilities.

Mike's boss expressed deep appreciation for the years of faithful service and contribution and then informed Mike that his job, along with several others, was being eliminated—effective immediately. Mike's manager indicated that TCA's budgetary problems were so severe that it was critical to downsize quickly. And because sensitive people issues always seem to have a way of "leaking out," management felt that it was important to tell the affected people once the decision was made to downsize.

Whammm, bammm! Unfortunately, no chance for appeal to his old friends, many of whom were now in executive positions. "I'm sure everyone is scrambling to survive at a time like this," thought Mike. What was really upsetting was that his last year's performance review was deemed excellent. And now! Nothing, except sudden and perfunctory dismissal with zip opportunity for appeal. Mike understood that this was a business decision, but it felt deeply personal. Intellectually, Mike knew that TCA had done everything in its power to survive, but the odds were stacked against it. He also knew that the senior managers, many of whom he had known for more than 20 years, did not make termination decisions lightly. Nonetheless, he still felt

1

crushed, angry, embarrassed, and scared. This was not like the old days where you could count on people to support you through thick and thin.

Mike was dimly aware that his boss, Huddy Brown, was trying to make him feel OK about the decision and that Huddy seemed to be hurting, as well. Huddy was a number of things to Mike: boss, colleague, friend, and now, bearer of terrible news. Huddy's voice sounded distant, almost like an echo or a bad telephone connection.

Mike noticed that his head throbbed with a scratchy tingly sensation which quickly developed into a thunderous roar, drowning out Huddy's explanation of the severance benefits and what the company wanted him to do with regard to his current programs and projects. Mike felt the rush of tears come to his eyes and the need to remain strong overshadowed the emotion. As he lowered his head to conceal the humiliation and rage, Mike noticed with mounting alarm that he could not feel his fingers nor move his arm. "Oh Lord," Mike silently prayed, "let this not be a stroke! I have just been fired and to top it off, I'm going to be carried out on a stretcher. What a way to go out! I am not going to give anyone the satisfaction of being able to tell others that I had outlived my usefulness and was too old to handle the pressure." Mike could almost imagine his dear, sweet wife, Emily, murmur, "Pride goeth before a fall, dear," and the numbness in his limbs made him cry out.

"What company will hire a paralyzed sales and marketing manager?" Mike thought. He felt nauseous and could taste the bile rising in his throat. Mike knew he had to regain control of his mind and body so as to fully understand the details of his severance package.

He stumbled out of Huddy's office clutching the carefully worded severance letter with only "legalese," and facts and figures about months of pay, and benefit conversion stuff. There was nothing about the many years of faithful service filled with contribution and sacrifice. Mike felt himself floating in slow motion in a sea of flashing and blinding lights filled with alien shapes and sounds.

Not used to what his body was doing, Mike jerked and shuffled awkwardly down the hall to his office. He knew several people looked at him funny, but he couldn't respond very well. In fact, because Mike's vision was impaired by an acute stress and anxiety attack, he found he could not actually make out the features on people's faces. Everyone looked like they walked out of a 3-D movie, all wavy and distorted.

He groped for his office door, felt the cool metal of the jamb, and pulled himself into familiar terrain, almost unrecognizable for the pain and the flickering lights. "Mike, what's wrong?" he heard his secretary cry out in alarm, somewhere in some distant echo chamber. Mumbling, "Nothing Jean—it's OK, I'll talk to you later," he swung his chair around to face the parking lot and, beyond that, the woods where his kids played. "All that is changed now," he mused. "I dedicated myself to the company for 15 years, traveling around the country, working long hours, missing countless dinners and band concerts." Emily was always very supportive and understanding, and, as the kids grew older, they stopped asking him when he was coming home to dinner. Mike could not honestly remember the last time he and Charley, 17, and Ann, 15, sat together and had a meaningful conversation. "I cast their childhood away for the company, for more money, more responsibility, power, prestige, and authority. Sure, I enjoyed what I was doing and would probably work the same kinds of hours again, but I certainly didn't expect to be out of a job even though other long-service employees are also being zapped."

Buoyed by his love for his wife and his two growing children, Mike reached for the phone. As Emily answered in her bright and cheery voice, "Commons's!," he knew he would survive.

Taking Charge of Your Life . . . and Your Career _____

Unreal, you say? Perhaps, overdramatic? Not at all. In fact, the Mike Commons story is under-told, if the truth be known. What Mike Common experienced is not at all uncommon. Thousands of individuals are caught unaware when their careers end abruptly in termination or when they face forced early retirement. Thousands more anxiously "sleepwalk" through their jobs, denying the potential of an untimely exit. Even though Mike had seen quite a few "warning signs" that indicated, in hindsight, that his job was in jeopardy, he chose to ignore them because he did not know how to effectively look for and land the right job for himself. It was less scary for him to stay at TCA (and ultimately get terminated) than it was to launch an uncertain career search, perhaps with a flawed strategy.

Tragically, it is often during these desperate and confusing times that once-excellent performers are ignored or criticized for sloppy and incomplete work. They may even be told to "pay attention" or that "you should know better!" Concern about previously terminated employees may be expressed, and seasoned managers may volunteer that their desire is to make it to retirement or get vested. The work may no longer be fun and exciting, rather, it is drudgery. The work may even feel like involuntary servitude or slavery. People have acknowledged going through the motions of work as if they have been "chained to their desks."

The interesting questions that you might be posing may very well be: "If people really truly feel that way, why don't they just change jobs or careers and get their lives back on track? Why would normal people hang around in a job or in a company where they no longer feel that they are contributing? Don't they know that when they stop 'playing the political game' they have already left the organization, though they still remain?" Good questions. The point is that we are dealing with normal individuals in somewhat abnormal times. If you are feeling out of control in your job while watching other less competent people take charge and gain favor, you may feel you are in a weakened position. Making a commitment to revitalize your career in the face of what you may feel is rejection by your boss requires an exceptional amount of personal power and strength. Ironically, the time when we need to feel most confident is the time when we feel the weakest and the most unsure of ourselves. Besides, we don't always know when we are in trouble.

Who is Michael Commons? He is you and me. He is all of us who have ever been anxious about the stability of our jobs or have ever lost our jobs, for whatever reason. He represents each one of us who have been committed to our careers and interested in moving forward, while being fearful, stymied, or road-blocked in our efforts.

Although all the names of the individuals, organizations, places, and events in the Michael Commons story have been changed, the events have actually occurred. The recommendations presented are a composite of practical strategies and tactics that hundreds of actual clients have successfully used for more than 10 years. As you read through this book and complete the worksheets, you may find yourself relating to Mike's plight. Who knows, you may even recognize yourself as Mike Commons.

Changing Jobs: It's Simple, Though Not Easy

As you probably already know, or have heard, the job of changing jobs is a full-time job. Changing jobs is also a process, often described as a process of becoming—a journey, rather than a final destination. You will find you have already been engaged in your search for the perfect job and that your search will continue throughout your career. Although the steps referred to here are specifically geared to job changing, they also relate to the ongoing management of your career.

Dos and Don'ts of Your Search: The Early Days

If You Have Been Separated, DO . . .

- **Tell your close friends and your family of the situation, and talk it out with them.** Assume responsibility for your separation, to the extent possible. Operate with a positive attitude, since people will be reassured by this.

- **Even though you may be angry or deeply hurt and feel your separation is very unfair, try to remain positive and confident.** It's OK to acknowledge that you are upset *while* keeping an optimistic frame of mind. People will take their cues from you. If you are OK, they will be also.

- **Help people support you by allowing them to be with you, provide contacts, leads, etc.** This is not a time to retreat or go it alone, no matter how independent you feel you are; rather it is a time to aggressively "tackle" the immediate problem of career and life planning.

- **Be aware of emotional swings commonly experienced by a sudden job loss.** Feelings such as anger, mourning, hurt, excitement, frustration, relief, disbelief, sadness, grief, acceptance, fear, and disappointment are all normal and are to be expected. Do not be upset if you find yourself on this emotional, up-and-down roller coaster. Just keep working your career plan.

- **Be alert to how you feel about being pulled off projects and the sensations of not having "any" job responsibilities.** It is quite common for people who have been involuntarily terminated to feel both a significant emotional upset as well as a profound loss of your sense of personal worth, as once-meaningful projects are summarily stopped or turned over to someone else and you are not allowed to manage the "handoff." (Worksheet 7 is a specific exercise which helps you address this situation and helps to reestablish your well-being.)

- **Begin financial planning.** Review your budget or develop one to accurately assess your financial situation. Know exactly what your separation package is from your company and how long you are able to sustain your current lifestyle without significant changes. You may need to temporarily cut back or cut out certain activities until you are once again employed.

- **Become deeply and actively involved in your job campaign and return to a professional worklike life pattern of getting up early, showering, and getting dressed as if you are going into work.** Now is *not* the time for a vacation or extended holiday.

- **Create a sense of positive expectancy.** Expect the best, even in the worst of times.

If You Are Still Employed, DO . . .

- **Lighten up.** If you approach every discussion as one which will make or break your career, you run the risk of living in continual upset or worse, manipulating others to get what you want. You may be tak ing yourself way too seriously. Ask yourself, "Am I the only person who is acting emotional?" If you are, you are probably creating your own problems.

- **Rebuild your relationships, if you have damaged any of them.** If you are going to confidentially conduct an effective search for your perfect job, you need to maintain as much endorsement from others as you can. Now is not a time for people to take cheap shots at you.

- **Recommit yourself to excellence.** Do the best job you possibly can with the kind of enthusiasm and confidence you had on your best day at work. You will be surprised at how much more complete you feel.

- **Look for ways to contribute to your boss and add value to his or her job, on a *daily basis*.** If you can't think of any ways, go ask, "I would like to help, how may I?" It is amazing how a shift in language will affect your attitude and behavior.

- **Begin to strengthen your portfolio of knowledge and skills.** Critically assess your credentials (like your boss might) and identify those areas that might make you more valuable if you had these skills. Find people who are skilled in these areas (preferably, persons in your own company) and go "pick their brains." Caution: Do not neglect your own job, and do not become a nuisance.

- **Volunteer for challenging, high-visibility assignments, commit to being successful, and then go achieve it.** Seek out help and guidance from others who have effectively managed complex projects, study their traits, and model their successful way of managing.

- **Commit to working on your search campaign daily.** Even though you might not be able to conduct an aggressive job search while employed, you can still find the time to make one call, jot down one new strategy you are committed to, and you can write one letter. If you feel overwhelmed, break your campaign strategy into smaller bits of activity.

- **Begin to network *now*, building solid, permanent relationships while you still have a job.** Become known within search firms and professional associations. Make your acquaintance with your peers in other companies, as many of them could refer bona fide openings or personal contacts to you if they are not interested in changing companies at this time.

If You Have Been Separated, DON'T . . .

- **Panic.** A common reaction to being involuntarily separated from your company is "fight or flight." You may find yourself alternating between anger and sadness, confidence and depression, acceptance and vindictiveness, attack and withdrawal, certainty and confusion.

- **Tell everyone.** Inform and involve only close friends and relatives in the initial stages of your career plan. You will have plenty of time to effectively tell others in a manner that helps your job search. If you tell a wide array of business contacts or acquaintances of your separation too soon after leaving, you may inadvertently damage networking possibilities because you are still upset.

- **Blame others.** Unfortunately, position eliminations, personality clashes, and organizational downsizing are increasingly becoming a way of life, worldwide. Your separation may hurt tremendously, but try to view this situation as a "no-fault" divorce, where neither party is really to blame. Blaming others puts you in a victim role, and, as a victim, you are powerless.

- **Make major decisions which dramatically shift the way you are currently living.** Do not make major purchases (to feel happy) or significant cash withdrawals (to finance your search, unless you really need to, of course). Guard against putting your house on the real estate market before you have a better feel for what you are going to do and where you will be employed.

- **Get into behavioral swings that are not typical of your lifestyle, such as overeating, overdrinking, excessive spending, or wild living.**

If You Are Still Employed, DON'T . . .

- **Start behaving as if you have already left.** Perform your duties to the best of your abilities with good humor and good cheer.

- **Become disruptive to your boss, peers, or subordinates.** It is too easy to create yourself unemployed once you have made the conscious (or unconscious) decision to leave. Reinforce your commitment to your organization and the people who count on you. When you do, magical things happen.

- **Tell people that you are looking—even in confidence.** Your leaving will start to be visible soon, no matter how hard you try to conceal it. Besides, you didn't keep your secret, why should someone else?

- **Disappear for long periods of time without prior approval and a good cover story.** Wearing your best suit and having a three-hour lunch looks awfully suspicious after a while.

Bill Robbins changed jobs every five to eight years, whenever his old boss, Fred Dee, would call on Bill to rescue Fred in his new company. Bill's reputation as a troubleshooter was well deserved, as he was one of the nation's best in turning around troubled operations in his industry. Bill moved from one troubled hot spot to another, dragging his wife and four children around, trying to ignore their protests and tears. Unfortunately, Bill had trouble saying no to his bosses. Following orders and frequent relocations had became second nature to Bill and his wife, Helen, after 20 years in the military. After retiring with his stripes, Bill "knocked around" for 18 months trying unsuccessfully to find employment. Then Fred Dee materialized and opened up for Bill a whole new realm of skills and possibilities. Although Fred didn't mention it outright, both he and Bill knew that Bill "owed him."

On this basis, Bill heeded the call each time Fred needed him. Bill was comforted by the military style in which he and Fred operated. Fred got the assignment, went in advance to scout out the terrain, and then called for Bill to come in to "kick butt and mop up," as they'd often say. Bill didn't mind doing the "dirty work." Bill was a self-taught industrial engineer who got more satisfaction from working with his hands and machinery than from working with the "suits," even though he now carried the title of director of Manufacturing and Engineering. So far, Bill had followed his old mentor and boss into action three times, faithfully executing what needed to be done.

Bill handled the manufacturing and engineering, and Fred handled the company politics and the career moves for the two of them. When Bill's recent recommendation to modernize the plant encountered stiff opposition, Fred reassured him, "Don't worry, you're with me. I'll take care of everything. This old guard has got to go." Little did Bill perceive the seriousness of Fred's political infighting until Bill made a major presentation and realized that he had no positive support. After he finished his remarks justifying the cost of an operational expansion, he was viciously attacked. As several people continued to hurl stinging insults, Bill looked at Fred for support, only to see Fred doodling on his pad of paper.

Only when the reality of his vulnerability sank in did Bill finally realize that Fred had repeatedly caved in to the more powerful, politically connected old guard. Deeply disappointed, Bill reluctantly admitted that Fred had misled him and sold out Bill to save himself. In the same moment of feeling tremendous betrayal, Bill also understood that he was alone in his career—for the first time. Being alone was both frightening and exhilarating. Bill knew he and not his boss was ultimately responsible for his career and his life. It dawned on Bill that he only knew how to change jobs by saying yes to his old friend, even though doing so had jeopardized his career and damaged his family more than once. For Bill, this rude awakening was truly a beginning, for he was on his own for the very first time in 20 years. He had suffered a painful but very necessary "push out of the nest." Based on insights gained in this meeting, Bill began to formulate the strategy in search of his perfect job.

Learning to Market Your Talents Effectively

Like Bill in search of his perfect job, you will learn things in this book that will make your skills and abilities stand out to a potential employer. Perhaps for the first time in your life, you are going to have to market yourself like a company markets a product—using every appropriate tool and resource to gain attention and respect in the marketplace.

If you thoroughly read the material in this book as if you were using a workbook, complete the worksheets, and risk practicing the recommended action, you will be on your way to creating a positive distinction between you and your competition in the marketplace.

> **The person who is hired is not necessarily the person who would be best at doing the work but is the best at getting the job.**

Where Am I Now?

Chances are pretty good that either you can't wait to get connected or you don't wish to look for a new job. Let's face it, job changing is a hassle. You have to put together a powerful résumé, locate potential employers, contact your friends explaining why you're looking for a job, and relearn how to interview from the other side of the desk. Granted, this may not be a pleasant situation for you, and you may be asking "What's going to happen to me now?" and "Where do I go from here?" You may alternate from feeling stressed about looking for a job to being enthused and relieved to be finally getting your search moving.

At this moment, your life has probably taken on several new dimensions. Even though you might still be an employee of your company, you have "turned the corner" in your career. You are now also working for yourself—finding a new job. **Your job is to get a job.**

This means *you will have to manage your resources as if you were a business*. The way you handle your time, energy, creativity, finances, and motivation has taken on new importance. Building up and maintaining your self-confidence will be the key to your success.

What kind of opportunity are you looking for? Probably one that can utilize your skills and abilities to their maximum, bring you a fair wage, and allow you to be happy. Finding this special job may be tough, perhaps even one of the most challenging goals you've ever set for yourself. However, only you can determine if you're worth the effort.

Pushing Through Your Psychological Roadblocks

Hunting for a job can be very lonely and, often, frustrating. You interview for positions which are perfect for you and you find it impossible to convince the interviewers of your capabilities. In addition to these normal challenges that confront every job seeker, you will find that you have a number of psychological roadblocks to your own success, roadblocks of your own making. These roadblocks are rooted in what you believe to be true. It does not matter whether anyone else believes your perception, rather it is how you perceive things. If you believe you are too old, then you are. If you believe that no companies are hiring now, then they won't.

When the search takes three times as long as you'd like and seems to require four times the amount of patience you thought you had, it is easy to erect the roadblock which says, "I will never get a job again." It is no wonder that people's searches take so long.

It is not uncommon to feel that you will never make it, that you will be unemployed forever. Thoughts of suicide are not all that uncommon. You may feel that you are better or worth more dead, given your insurance policy, than you are alive. Do not believe that for a second! Of the hundreds of clients we have worked with, a number of them contemplated some form of life or career suicide at least once during their campaign. In each and every case, the individual's depression was handled through some form of planned action, for example, building on small successes every day, or therapy. When in doubt, get help from your physician or area crisis center. Having your career search stall out on you is no big deal; everyone experiences it.

If you diligently follow the guidelines in this book, you eventually pull out of the tailspin. However, you can become deeply stuck when you don't believe in yourself anymore and you don't have faith in the action plan you laid out for yourself.

Sometimes when you get rejected "one more time," your resolve can crack, and you begin to doubt if you will ever land the right job. Granted, you may have to accept a position which may not be to your liking initially but which may position you for advancement opportunities later. Conversely, you may accept a position with a company merely to put "bread on the table" until something more suited comes along. That's OK; it happens all the time. There is dignity in all kinds of work, though the work you may accept on an interim basis is less challenging than you have been used to, and not your ultimate goal.

If you are currently employed and are actively looking, you may feel like the right job is ever alluding you, almost within grasp. . . . At times, the sensation of life's circumstances being stacked against you can be overwhelming—whether on your job, in your career search, or in your personal life.

If you believe in yourself and deem yourself to be worthy, if you are committed to your personal success and trust your skills, you will assuredly find the strength and courage to successfully get through this complex process we call "careering."

Managing Your Emotional Roller Coaster

Whether you have recently been "let go" or are merely beginning to contemplate a career change, you may have a number of conflicting feelings: fear, anger, shock, disbelief, self-doubt, denial, betrayal, guilt, depression, shame, or maybe even a feeling of freedom or excitement. Relief is an emotion people experience, as well. People often report to us that they feel as if a "50-pound weight has been lifted off" of their shoulders.

Millions of people experience and feel what you are feeling (and have felt) when they find themselves in your situation. What you feel is normal and common to all of us. A respected psychologist, Dr. Elisabeth Kubler-Ross, found that people living through periods of uncertainty or trauma (such as job loss) usually go through a series of emotional stages (Figure 1-1).

Do not worry about being discouraged or anxious about feeling out of control emotionally; most people experience a wide range of emotions. These emotional swings are normal and they do shift. It is like being on an "emotional roller coaster" with many ups and downs. But don't let these emotional "moods" control you or paralyze you for an extended period—you can be defeated when you most need your courage and determination to come out of this situation as a winner.

If you were zapped, the moment you became aware of your changed status your first and natural reaction may have been, "This can't be true. This isn't happening!" (*denial*).

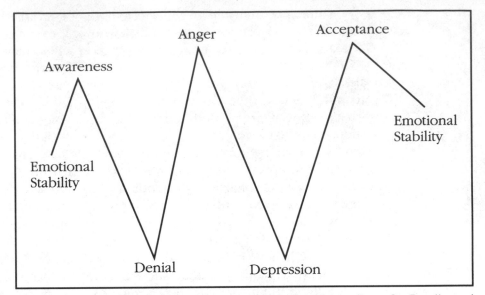

Figure 1-1. Your emotional stages. (*Adapted from Kubler-Ross,* On Death and Dying, *Macmillan, New York, 1969. Used with permission*)

When the reality of your job loss (or the need to seriously start looking) began to sink in, you may have become mad (*anger*). "How dare they do this to me! It's not fair! I'm going to get even!" Once your anger subsided, you might have become even deeply saddened or depressed. It is not uncommon for you to raise questions about your self-worth and technical competence (*depression*). "What do I do now? Perhaps I did deserve this. Obviously, I'm not as good as I thought I was."

While these emotional states are normal and can be pretty intense, most individuals can push through their emotional ups and downs and reach *acceptance,* albeit the healing process may take a while—perhaps even several months. When you are in an accepting state, you can face this personal challenge squarely as a problem to be solved or a hurdle to be overcome. When you accept that your situation is not unusual and that you are not alone (even though you may feel lost right now), you are beginning to get on top of the situation. It sometimes helps to have the perspective that your termination was a business decision, not a personal one, even though that business decision certainly may feel deeply personal.

Our personal experience in dealing with hundreds of clients over the years is that you can move through all these emotional states to acceptance in the blink of an eye—or you may get stuck in denial, anger, or depression for a long time. *Whatever emotional state you happen to find yourself in is ok.* We ask that you work hard at not being concerned if you are in an emotional upset, now or even later in your job search.

Being upset and having emotions is a natural part of life. To deny that you are upset is to deny a large part of who you are, of your uniqueness. Practice getting in touch with your feelings and your "inner voices"—the thoughts that rattle around in your head at night or in stressful times.

Shaping Your Life the Way You Want

Ever wonder why some people have greater control over their lives and why they appear to be happier than others? If you asked them, you would probably discover that their personal control and achievements relate to the kinds of questions they ask, the meaning they attach to things, the extent to which they assume responsibility for how their life and career look, the commitments they make, and their willingness to operate flexibly.

Seem out of reach? Gaining such a life is not at all unreasonable, given that you have been operating like this all your life—getting what you create. To some people, having to change jobs (voluntarily or involuntarily) is incredibly upsetting, yet for others, changing jobs is a time of renewal and hope for something better. Granted, every person's situation is unique, but what makes one person react so differently to a similar event? Simply put, it is the meaning people attach to it.

How you represent some event to yourself—how you believe something to be—will significantly influence how you feel about it. For instance, if you were not happy in your job and you found another position more suited to your personality and skills and you left, it is a pretty good assumption that you felt pleased with your decision and excited about your move. However, if you were terminated from a job that you did not like by a boss you did not respect, you probably experienced both relief and some pain (anger or sadness). Some of the pain may be the anxiety of not knowing what the next step is. If you are like most people in an uncomfortable job, you probably wanted to be rid of the hassles and the upset and just do the work. As the on-the-job hassles increased, so did your frustration and your desire to be rid of the problem. Who knows, you may have created leaving yourself, although you were not aware of it at the time.

To examine where you are on being in control and managing your life, turn to Worksheet 1.

Beliefs: Psychological Traps or Springboards

The quality of your life and how you manage it will depend upon the quality of the questions you ask and the commitment you have to

WORKSHEET 1
You've Created Where You Are!

To help you see that you have been in control of your career all along, please answer the following questions. If you have been involuntarily separated, please consider these questions in the past tense.

Yes	No	
_____	_____	**1.** Are you as happy as you would like to be on the job?
_____	_____	**2.** Are you as productive as you know you could be?
_____	_____	**3.** Are you as creative as you know you have been previously?
_____	_____	**4.** Is your advice sought after as much as it once was?
_____	_____	**5.** Do you get along with your boss as well as you would like?
_____	_____	**6.** Do you trust and respect your boss?
_____	_____	**7.** Have you updated your résumé or thought that perhaps you should?
_____	_____	**8.** Have you ever thought about what it would be like to be employed somewhere else?
_____	_____	**9.** If you could conduct a very discreet search without anyone finding out, would you do so?
_____	_____	**10.** If you had access to a foolproof game plan for successful job changing, would you be interested in it?

Scoring the Worksheet

If you answered no to two or more of questions 1 to 6 or yes to two or more of questions 7 to 10, then chances are very good that you have already left your organization—psychologically and emotionally, that is.

While you may physically be in residence at your company, your heart and and mind are probably somewhere else. Your commitment to turn the situation around, complete the project, reestablish the relationship with your boss—whatever—may seem less important than it once did. If the intensity you once felt *and* the enthusiasm you once exhibited about people, programs, projects, or things is consistently less than before, then we contend that you have made decisions to withdraw or disengage from being 100 percent committed at your workplace, and it may be time to move on.

At some conscious level, you "managed" your job and the people around you the way you wanted—even though you may have felt like your career was sabotaged and as a result you were criticized or even terminated.

change. Rather than have you answer two hundred questions to reveal all the things you need to locate or create the perfect job, we are only going to ask several. Your brain is a remarkable computer that not only has a tremendous capacity to store and retrieve data but also has the capability to provide solutions to your most puzzling conditions, provided you ask good questions. Unfortunately, many of us start off with ideas which hold us back and keep us from operating as fully as we might otherwise. We call these thoughts *disempowering beliefs*.

Disempowering beliefs erode our confidence and inhibit us from fully tapping into our potential, let alone ask good questions. A disempowering belief is any thought or condition you believe to be true which limits you, makes you feel less whole or less powerful. In this next exercise, you will have the opportunity to identify those disempowering or negative beliefs and their cost to you.

Empowering beliefs are invigorating and vibrant; they stimulate us into action and help us expand beyond our immediate situation. Have you ever felt really alive, excited, and in touch with people and the world around you? In that moment, when your confidence was high, be it an instant, a day, or a week, things probably seemed to come together well. At those times, you no doubt believed that you could accomplish just about anything you focused on, if you wanted it badly enough. Those feelings and beliefs that allowed you to stretch and achieve beyond what even you thought possible are *empowering beliefs*. Empowering beliefs help us recontextualize or think about things much more positively. Someone once said: "If you think you can or you can't, you're right!"

Your mind only does what you tell it. If you tell it you can't run a 10K, then you won't. However, if you are a "nonathlete" and you begin to increase your daily runs just a little bit, then you can run a marathon (26.2 miles), if that is your commitment. If you feel you are too old to launch a new business, then you are (even though Harland Sanders didn't launch Kentucky Fried Chicken until he was 65). However, if you approach age as an attribute versus a liability, you will go further. Instead of being too old, recontextualize that disempowering belief to an empowering belief that says, "*I am a seasoned professional with a wealth of experiences any employer would be proud to have!*"

Would you like to see if you have any disempowering beliefs which roadblock your careering success? Turn to Worksheet 2, and circle the responses you feel apply to you.

Recontextualizing My Roadblocks _____

Roadblocks stop you or, at the very best, slow you down from achieving the kinds of gains you are capable of and desire. While your psycholog-

WORSHEET 2
My Perceived Roadblocks

Review and circle those statements which you feel are potential roadblocks to effectively getting a job. On the bottom of this sheet, write down any additional roadblocks you feel you have.

My work is difficult to quantify.

I don't know many people.

I don't earn much money.

My earnings are relatively low.

My former boss may not provide a good reference.

I was terminated.

I am switching industries, and that's difficult.

I worked for an organization which downsized.

I am too old.

I am handicapped.

I don't have a college degree.

I don't have enough education.

I have too much education.

Some career moves have been lateral.

I've only worked for one company.

I am a young person with many accomplishments.

I need to change careers.

My grades were poor.

I have been unemployed before.

I have employment gaps.

I am unemployed now.

I need/want to relocate.

I am reentering the job market after raising a family.

I have changed jobs a lot.

I don't have much business experience.

Other roadblocks: _____

_____

_____

_____

_____

_____

_____

_____

_____

ical and emotional roadblocks are invisible, they are as real as if they were made out of wood and steel.

What we want to help you do is to *recontextualize your roadblocks*. By that we mean, redefine how you think about something. A disempowering belief set in a new context becomes empowering, that is, it is recontextualized! See the examples that follow in Figure 1-2, then identify your top three roadblocks.

ROADBLOCK/ DISEMPOWERING BELIEF	RECONTEXTUALIZED	EMPOWERING BELIEF
Roadblock	**Recontextualized**	**Empowering Belief**
I'm too old . . .	becomes . . .	I'm seasoned!
I'm unemployed . . .	becomes . . .	I'm free to search for the perfect job!
I'm a job hopper . . .	becomes . . .	I'm experienced in many companies!
I'm too young . . .	becomes . . .	I have plenty of energy and years of productive work ahead!
I don't have a college degree . . .	becomes . . .	I have plenty of "hands-on" practical experience, which makes me a well-rounded person.
My Top Three Roadblocks		
1. _____	becomes	_____!
2. _____	becomes	_____!
3. _____	becomes	_____!

Figure 1-2. Recontextualizing your roadblocks.

Operating-Style Shifts That Undermine You _____

Before you are terminated or when you decide to leave a company, you are aware on some level that everything is not well. During this period, without perhaps being consciously aware, you may have modified or stopped certain normal behaviors that have worked well for you in the past. Coincidentally, you may have begun to behave in a manner that does not represent your normal operating style at work.

For example, you may have adopted a cautious style of looking for hidden agendas when your boss talks to you. You may be mistrustful of certain department leaders, and you might be accused of misinterpreting memos sent to you.

You may have started to document everything, or engage in "memo wars," or selectively withhold certain kinds of information. You may have even developed some new convictions or points of view about your abilities, your value, the competency of your boss, etc. It could be that your discussions with your peers or subordinates lately seem more confrontational than "win/win."

It is fair to say that every behavior or point-of-view change you have made during the stressful time just preceding your leaving your company (whether you actually left physically or just emotionally) is potentially flawed. You probably have sent incomplete signals and confusing messages to the people around you which have detracted from your effectiveness. Even worse, unless you identify and correct these "pretermination stress shifts," they can follow you to the next job and detract from your effectiveness there as well.

On Worksheet 3, list the changes in your behavior or points of view which you believe you have made as a result of this pretermination stress. List them, describe them, and tell why you adopted this behavior. Describe what behavior it replaced and how you want to change it to another more effective behavior or perspective. As you reevaluate your behavioral shifts, might there be some clues for you as to why your job is blowing up or has blown up? Then fill out Worksheet 4 to identify some positive actions and attitudes that you can adopt.

I Can't Get Emotional! If I Do, It Will Mean I Have Failed

Talking about setting yourself up for failure! Although well-intended, the above mind-set is neither very realistic nor forgiving.

Recently, we were working with Ned Brown, a very competent strong-willed executive who prided himself on his excellent interpersonal skills and his ability to deal with whatever life threw his way. By all outward appearances he was doing fine. He appeared calm, cool, and collected. He spoke rationally about his concerns, emotions, and disappointments. Ned prided himself on what he said was, "his ability to rise above the debilitating emotions that get in the way of a job search."

WORKSHEET 3
Ineffective Operating-Style Shifts

Behaviors or beliefs I have started up in the last year which are different from how I usually behave or think.

What behavior or belief did I have before this change?

How did these behavioral shifts undermine my effectiveness with my boss, my peers, my subordinates?

What circumstances caused me to make this adaptive shift?

How do I want to handle this issue now and in my next position?

WORKSHEET 4
Discovering What Works and What Doesn't

This exercise will help you break through some of your roadblocks and identify actions which will positively influence your life and help you manage it better.

1. What are the top three things that are **WORKING WELL** in my life, and how can I strengthen them?

2. What are the top three things that are **NOT WORKING WELL** in my life, and what can I do to turn them around *and* enjoy the process?

3. What **THREE ACTIONS** can I take to develop and strengthen a trusting and respectful relationship with the people I work with, especially my boss?

(Continued)

4. What are the top three **DISEMPOWERING** or **NEGATIVE BELIEFS** I have about my ability to really succeed in my job now or in my search for the perfect job and what is the *price I pay* for holding onto these beliefs?

Disempowering Belief	Price Paid for Belief
A.	A.
B.	B.
C.	C.

5. What are the top three **EMPOWERING** or **POSITIVE BELIEFS** I have about my ability to really succeed in my job now or in my search for the perfect job, and *how do I benefit* from holding onto these beliefs?

Empowering Belief	Benefit from Belief
A.	A.
B.	B.
C.	C.

6. What three **BELIEFS** can I hold and what **ACTION** can I take to become more confident, happy, helpful, supportive, and valuable to the people around me *while* enjoying the process?

Beliefs	Action
A.	A.
B.	B.
C.	C.

7. What are **SIX WAYS** I can keep my commitment to positive action and reduce self-sabotage?

A.

B.

C.

D.

E.

F.

Ned's role of business consultant with a *Fortune* 200 firm was going to be eliminated because the company was going through some difficult financial times and felt that Ned's function was an unneeded luxury in the face of cost containment. Ironically, Ned's consulting skills were exactly what the company needed to help itself work through many of the difficult people and business issues confronting it.

Because Ned was so well schooled in the behavioral sciences, he had an excellent grasp of how people and events impacted him and the world around him. In our offices the other day, he acknowledged that he had recently identified the sources of the anger which had most recently surfaced. He also shared with us his technique for identifying them, and we wanted to pass this method on for your use.

Ned found himself a quiet place and allowed his anger to "wash over" him without trying to make any sense out of the people, events, or places which this anger seemed to come from or settle into. He then focused on the people and events associated with his "failure," including himself. He allowed images to form in his mind and take on some form and substance, rather than just a vague sense of disquiet or a feeling of general anxiety. By concentrating on specific people, he was able to identify these people as merely playing out the roles assigned to them and acting out of the values and beliefs that they operated with in life. They were not bad people, rather they happened to intersect with Ned's life and career in a manner that Ned knew did not work for him in the long term. To that end, he was able to disassociate himself from the emotions that were previously "hooking" him when he thought of these people.

Given his newly found peace, Ned related to us that he was not responsible for the upset nor for his termination. Ned considered his pending separation "no fault," as he was still going into the office to work on projects until his separation was made public in two months. He verbalized that he had been harboring some anger because he felt that his position was misrepresented to him and that the company people he interviewed with had either falsely represented or withheld valuable information critical to making an informed decision.

"I feel a lot better after going through this exercise. I'm not angry anymore and feel like I'm on top of the situation. I've learned quite a bit from this process, and I have determined that I am not going to be depressed. For once I become depressed, I know I've given up and have really failed. Being depressed goes against everything I stand for in my life. Being depressed means not being alive, or in control; it means not having any energy nor having any options. I am not going to turn that corner."

"Time out," I cried. "You've just set yourself up for a failure and a big fall, psychologically. By not allowing yourself to feel a particular emotion, you have unconsciously said to yourself that some of your feelings are meant to be suppressed or denied if they show up in your life. Implicit in that position, if you feel a certain way—regardless of the impact it might have on your life—is that you've failed. In addition, your brain doesn't know the difference between an admirable goal and a destructive goal. By setting your mind on the goal of, '*not being depressed*' (versus *being joyous*) you will strive to achieve it.

"It's a well-accepted axiom that what you think about and focus on is what you will become. You have two major problems with setting up this goal, especially because it is you, Ned. First, you are extremely goal-oriented. For you to have accomplished all that you have done in your career you've had to be driven to achieve things important to you.

"Clearly, not being depressed is a very strong goal for you to realize. On the surface, this feels and looks like a great goal to have, but the danger for you is that you will be constantly evaluating how you are doing in the achievement of your goal. You run the risk of constantly assessing the extent to which you are depressed, critically ranking yesterday's depression level against today's depression level. By constantly examining your levels of depression you will find yourself deeply immersed in the emotional state called "depression" because that is what you are choosing to create.

"Second, you are very process-oriented. You delight in your abilities to sort through your emotions, from the specific events around you. You take pride in being able to operate so objectively and being 'on top of it.' It's a confirmation to how you see yourself. Right? Isn't that so, Ned?"

Ned said, "You're absolutely right. Much of my identity is wrapped up in being able to manage my emotions the way I want, not be driven by every external event. You know how people get depressed when it's cold and rainy outside? Not me, my philosophy in life is that you get what you create."

"Bingo! Ned, you clearly get what you create and strive for. You've indicated that your goal is not to get depressed, moody, or be adversely impacted by your recent job loss. You previously revealed to me that you failed in your ability to effectively read the signals in your initial job interview and that you failed to convince your executive team that you should remain on board and help the organization manage through this financial crisis. You've failed before, and you'll fail again. You will benefit greatly if you get off the pedestal you've erected for yourself that says, 'Ned Brown cannot fail.' You are not being realistic. People fail, they make mistakes. Even yourself. You pride yourself in being in control, being objective and 'together.' Those are admirable qualities, and I wish more people had your obvious talent for being able to achieve them. However, this pride is actually well-managed arrogance, driven by the fear that someone is going to see through the defenses you've erected to protect yourself from not being in complete control.

"You need to understand that people know intuitively when you are becoming defensive and when you are congruent. Congruence relates to alignment of your thoughts, feelings, beliefs, values, and behavior. The more aligned you are, the greater your congruence. When you are really congruent, the more 'grounded' you will be, and you will find yourself operating more naturally, confidently, genuinely, and enthusiastically. Ned, people know when you are being defensive and they still find you acceptable and 'together.' Once you get a handle on this you will find that you do not need to spend as much energy on erecting these defenses, and you'll spend this time enjoying being with others and giving of yourself without holding back quite so much."

If you recall, it is OK to have whatever emotion you create and to possess whatever thoughts or beliefs you have—because you created them. It is also critical for you to evaluate your thoughts in light of how they impact your relationship with yourself, with others, and the extent to which they empower or erode your personal power and your career search. To deny these emotions, beliefs, or behavior is to deny that it is OK to be you. So, lighten up. Practice being OK with your emotions, regardless of your expectations.

Mastering Your Emotions and Regaining Control

You may observe that you are creating a lot of negative or critical messages for yourself which, ultimately, get in your way and undermine your ability to deal with this significant change in your life. To master your emotions and regain control in your life, we encourage you to follow a three-step process:

1. Do not suppress or deny these unconscious messages, rather, acknowledge their existence ("Hmmh, I am really angry" or "I'm feeling very unloved right now").

2. Physically recreate the body language you have had in times past in which you were feeling empowered and successful. Move around in your chair or stand remembering when you were successful, confident, bold, and feeling particularly competent. Get in touch with how your body feels and responds to these emotions as problems to solve and challenges to be met.

3. Acknowledge your emotional state, begin to move into action ("Hmmh, I am really angry, and I am going to work on my résumé!"), and reaffirm your ability to generate success ("This is tough, but I've overcome greater obstacles before"). You'll find that forward motion, coupled with this kind of openness and positive reaffirmation, will help create a level of quiet confidence.

Self-Confidence Formula^{SM}

To help you increase your self-esteem and self-confidence, we would like you to consider utilizing what we call the *Self-Confidence Formula.*^{SM} These seven steps are key to helping you become more in control of who you are and how you operate.

1. Develop Superior Credentials and Model Success

During your job search, create a powerful résumé and attention-getting marketing letters which distinguish you from others. If you are currently employed, seek out ways you can strengthen your credentials by enhancing your knowledge, skills, and abilities on the job.

Model success. Identify people that you deem to be successful in that skill area or knowledge area you want to master. Go to them. Ask what specific behavior they engage in or thoughts they hold to be successful. Write it down, verify with them what they do, then model their successful behavior. Do what they do, think the affirming thoughts they think, and feel what they feel. If you are not producing the result you want, you may not be modeling or replicating their "success" behavior or thoughts closely enough. Try again until you produce positive results and can generate powerful affirming feelings anytime you desire.

2. Manage Your Emotions

Strive to create and manage those emotions that you desire—from being energized to being joyful, resourceful, confident, open, dynamic, bold, creative, innovative, and even wise.

Visualize an event or a time in your life which captures that emotion you want to be able to recreate easily, let's say, feeling really confident. Concentrate on a specific scene in which you were confident and zoom in on what you were doing, how you were moving and talking, gesturing, laughing, and smiling. Note who else was with you in this scene. Open your mind up and imagine yourself in the scene, as an observer. Notice how much more bright and more crisp everything looks. While keeping the energy and confidence high, "pop" yourself into the scene and actually experience what you only observed earlier. Feel the excitement and the power of being highly confident, notice how you were standing (if you were, indeed, standing). While remaining at your high confidence level, make a fist and flex your bicep, hold for a moment, then release. Squeeze your fist again and as you do, raise your confidence level higher each time you squeeze your fist. Squeeze your fist again while you allow your confidence to soar. Repeat this process often to recapture these empowered feelings, so you can feel confident, we mean really confident, *any* time you choose—just squeeze your fist.

3. Change How You Think about Things: Recontextualizing

The levels or meanings that you attach to things will significantly influence how you feel about them. If you view something that has happened to you as incredibly unfair, then you will feel victimized and be indignant about it. Conversely, if you feel that the identical event is appropriate and fair, you will probably view this as a normal part of living and move on. For some people, not receiving a promised promotion is a tremendous loss of face, prompting an immediate job search. For others, the promotion loss is a sign that perhaps they did not build the level of endorsement needed for the promotion. So, instead of failure, the lack of promotion is viewed as a learning experience.

If there is something in your life which is not working well, or you have been separated from your company (fired), rather than looking at this even as a major failure, focus your thoughts on what you can gain from this new condition. Certainly, there has been a loss, but there is also the opportunity for significant gain.

4. Learn, Understand, and Apply Models of Success

Models of success (or *behavior models*) help us take a complex topic, such as how humans behave, and simplify it through a representation, or model. Models make real the abstract, not unlike the clay model of a car that is the designer's concept put in physical form so we can see what previously only he saw.

If you incorporate the behavioral models identified in this book, and others that you know to be productive, you have the ability to make significant shifts in the way you think, feel, and act. Obviously, if you make these kinds of changes, you may just significantly alter your life. Who knows, only you can tell.

Throughout the course of this book, a number of behavioral and career search models are identified for your use. They are:

- Managing your emotional roller coaster
- Taking complete responsibility for how your career and life look
- Empowering and disempowering beliefs
- Self-confidence formula[SM]
- Your expectations and the way it really happens
- Operating style shifts
- Networking
- Verbal résumé[SM]
- Stages of the interview

- Success can be stressful
- Improving offers by focusing on needs, not money

5. Identify and Focus on Your Outcome

Determine what you *want* and *need*—in your life and your career—in specific terms, not generalities. Goals such as wanting a better job, more money, less hassles, better relationships, reduced stress are too general. Besides, you may *want* more money, but what you really *need* is better control over your finances. Specific goals enable you to focus on the outcome you desire with greater clarity and determination. The metaphor that comes to mind is taking a picture with a high-quality 35mm camera. In the hands of a bumbling amateur, you might be able to distinguish that the out-of-focus picture is a house but not much beyond that. Conversely, a professional can create an incredibly crisp and powerful photograph of the same subject by precise focusing. Likewise, once finely focused, your goals have the potential to mobilize you into action and achieve your desired outcome.

6. Become Committed to Your Success

The successful achievement of a goal will depend upon two key factors: one, the clarity of the desired outcome and, two, the level of personal commitment to the task. The greater your commitment to your outcome, the greater will be your resolve to let nothing stand in your way. The extent to which you focus your thoughts and actions is the extent to which you will achieve.

It is also important to be aware of when, how, and why you sabotage your commitments so you can make choices and reaffirm your commitment. Like cheating on a diet, failure to be fully committed to your outcome is not final, but it does have its costs.

7. Fine-tune Your Strategy, Remain Flexible, and Pursue Stretch Goals

When you are pursuing a job, not only do you need to know where you presently are and where you are headed, but you also need to be able to quickly adapt your behavior when you are off-track. Every one of us has a built-in adaptive sense so that we are able to make adjustments to how we are responding to our environment. When you sit up, walk, run, gesture, or read, you are making countless adaptive behavioral changes to achieve a result that you might only be subconsciously aware of. Your challenge (and opportunity!) is to heighten your awareness and adaptive skills to keep yourself on track while maintaining a high sense of urgency.

We recommend that you pursue stretch goals worthy of your efforts, goals which will challenge you to be the best you can be while providing a sense of time accomplishment when you achieve them. You will probably find that as you become more experienced in setting and achieving stretch goals, you will have raised your expectations, performance, and outcome. An analogy for you to remember is of mountaineers gazing at a mountain's peak when at its base. As they climb, the mountaineers shift their route as they encounter obstacles until they are finally at the peak they earlier spied. However, that initially visible mountain peak is but an interim stop en route to the mountain's true top. So it should be with you to set new outcomes as you achieve your goals at an ever-increasing rate. Be like the mountaineers standing at one peak en route to another, committed to realizing their dreams, one peak at a time.

You Are Not Alone

The way you deal with losing a job depends on two factors: What kind of an internal support system you have and what kind of external support you get. *Internal support* includes your feelings of self-worth, self-confidence, and the things you believe in. *External support* relates to your family and friends, the kind of support they provide to you.

Often, people are not aware how much their feelings influence how they relate to the world around them. When people are angry, everything in their world is a source of anger and upset. Everything looks and feels upset and out of synch. Ironically, these times when we are most upset and need to be comforted is when we push away from the sources of love, peace, comfort, and harmony. If you are experiencing upset in one part of your life, you probably have upset in *all* parts of your life.

Have you ever experienced a big upset in your life and you know that if you involve others and acknowledge it to them you might find the answer or some measure of peace, but you don't feel like it? It is ironic that

---

> ### The time when you need to reach out to others the most is often the time when you least feel like doing it!

What Will I Tell My Family and Friends?

You may be thinking

I am thinking seriously about changing careers—doing something drastically different from what I am doing now.

Some of my close friends are supportive, while others recommend I take a vacation to get away from it all. What do you think?

I have just lost my job, and I am really embarrassed. If I am embarrassed, my family, friends, and relatives will feel ashamed as well. Maybe the best approach is not to tell anybody.

Your family and friends will want to know how they can help. After all, what are friends and family for if not to assist you when you have a need? If you are having some difficulty knowing what to say, here is an example of some language you may wish to try on for size:

Things at work aren't exactly the best right now. Given the declining sales and the threat of a takeover, I have decided that I better initiate a search for the right job, before I have to involuntarily. Or, if your job has been eliminated . . .

As you may or may not know, my company has recently gone through a reorganization with a number of positions being consolidated or eliminated. Unfortunately, I was impacted. While I am disappointed that my career at my company is over, I am enthused about new career opportunities.

As for your other friends and acquaintances, we recommend that you *delay informing them* of your status or intent until you have a clear career direction in mind. While it is true that the greater percentage of positions are found through personal contacts, it is vital that these valuable leads be informed at the appropriate time and in the appropriate manner.

Your family, your friends—the people who care most about you—want to see you succeed. How you act around them will determine, in large part, how they will behave toward you. In most cases, they will take their cues from you.

Sure, you may feel down or out of step with those around you, but that is when you need to rely on your family and others for support and to help stimulate you into action. In some cases, you will have to help them adjust—it may be a new experience for them too. If your approach is rational, confident, and results-oriented, they will follow suit. Relax; finding the right position for you may be difficult, but it is *not* the end of the world.

In Your World: Two Kinds of People

Mary was devastated. Her husband, Del, was forced out of the company by the president just 12 months after Del was promoted to vice president and just before his tenth anniversary with the company. Mary found this bitterly ironic, because the previous year the president had thrown a big celebration dinner recognizing Del's outstanding contributions and the achievements which led to his promotion.

And now, look what happened—Del got terminated. Mary commented, "Sure, the company lost some major accounts but it was always able to recover before. What was the big deal? Was Del asked to leave to reduce the overhead expenses or did this have anything to do with Del and the president not really getting along? I am positive that Del didn't do anything so terribly wrong that he got fired, or perhaps he wasn't telling me everything."

After his promotion last year, Del was under increasing pressure from all sides to deliver more and perform better. Gone were his mentors and peers that he could open up to and ask advice. In his new role, Del was more isolated and not as happy as he had been previously. He certainly didn't feel he was contributing like he had before. He knew it, and the president knew it, as well. His termination was both shocking and a relief. Even though he had terminated many people in his career, Del had never been terminated before.

Immediately following his termination, many people were stunned and embarrassed, which made Del even more self-conscious. Although Del quickly worked through his emotional upset, Mary was devastated. She took Del's termination as a major slap in the face and was not about to look at this situation positively or optimistically. That would be like "giving in." Mary reasoned that the only way to be vindicated was for Del to be reinstated with a public apology. Short of that, she was going to remain bitterly angry to show others how "wronged" she and Del were.

In the three weeks following Del's termination, only five people called to offer their condolences, and only three couples stopped by to visit. "You really know who your friends are!" seemed to be Mary's refrain. Once a gracious and open woman, Mary became embittered and sour, complaining to anyone who would listen how unfair the company had been to her Del and that all their problems were the direct cause of the president's firing her husband.

Deeply hurt, Mary drove away those who sought the most to provide support and created a lot of excess emotional baggage for Del to handle at a time when he could least afford it. What Mary should have realized is that people took their cues from her. Since she was continually upset and acting out the victim role, her friends eventually withdrew because she was too uncomfortable to be around. However, if Mary was to have helped Del take responsibility for the action, become committed to moving forward, and initiated some supportive calls herself, then her life would have looked decidedly different.

If you have recently been let go, or fear this might happen, you will discover that people seem to fall into two categories: people you expect to support you, and people you do not expect any support from. Since so much of how we relate to the world is done on the unconscious level, it is important to understand how our expectations help get in the way of us being successful. Read through Table 1-1 and analyze your expectations.

You Really Know Who Your Friends Are!

If you discover that the majority of your friends and business acquaintances fall into the category of supporting you—great! However, if you are upset because some of your "former" friends are not supporting you the way you'd like on the job or even acknowledging that you got zapped, it's time for a reality check.

People generally do not know how to handle grief or trauma well. When a significant loss occurs (loss of a marriage, loved one, or job), either to us or someone else, we most often feel awkward or self-conscious. Your friends, neighbors, relatives, and business acquaintances will often seem to ignore your plight because they do not want to make it worse for you. Indeed, some people will pretend your being zapped never happened, trying to help keep your mind off the subject. If you are still at your company, you may need to reexamine the extent to which your recent behavioral shifts have affected your relationships. If they have, then you probably could benefit from apologizing and proceed enthusiastically from that point forward.

Ironically, while your friends may have a strong desire to avoid talking about your termination (or demotion), you probably have an equally strong need to receive support or, at least, acknowledgment that your friends are standing by in case you need help or company.

Table 1-1. Sources of Support and Your Expectations

	YOUR EXPECTATIONS	
THE WAY IT REALLY HAPPENS	People You *Do* Expect Support From	People You Do *Not* Expect Support From
When You *Get* Support, You May Feel . . .	Connected Accepted Complete/Whole Supported	Delighted Surprised Affirmed
When You Do *Not* Get Support, You May Feel . . .	Ashamed Rejected Beat Up Contaminated	Neutral Positive Ambivalent

The Problem and the Cure

When this situation of "avoidance" occurs, be alert to the normal tendency to make others wrong in your relationship ("I guess they aren't my friends, after all!") and yourself miserable ("Perhaps, I wasn't as good as I thought"). Go to those people from whom you need support and acknowledge your situation. Even though you know that they know, this face-saving method will help relieve you from the unnecessary burden of guilt or anger you might be feeling toward another. You might say something along these lines:

> **As you may or may not know, my company has recently reorganized, with a number of positions being consolidated and eliminated. Unfortunately, I was impacted. While I might have been able to remain in the organization in a lessor capacity, I have elected not to put my career on hold for several years. To that end, I am looking for a challenging career opportunity with the company's full knowledge and support. I just wanted you to know that.**

> **While I am disappointed that my career is over at the ABC Company, I am also looking forward to what the future holds. I hope I can count on your support. Thanks. I would like to get back to you later and share my plans for my next step. Would it be alright to call you sometime and to send a résumé to you?**

Eliminating the Fear Your Partner or Spouse Feels

Your spouse or partner occupies a unique place in your career search. Although he or she is not going to be developing your credentials or conducting interviews for you, your partner is directly impacted and involved, nonetheless. This section has been written for you, as well as for your partner. We encourage you to specifically share this section and to discuss it.

Being in the Passenger's Seat

You might feel that the emotional roller coaster you are on is unique to you. Although that is true, your partner experiences similar emotions. One of the spouses we met described this process as similar to sitting in the passenger's seat of a car driving a little too close to the vehicle in front of it and trying to brake with the visor and steer with the rearview mirror. Another partner described his experience as feeling disconnected. "I felt like I was sitting in the back of a long bus driving through a dark tunnel.

I was not only in the dark, but I couldn't even see where we were headed. I had no concept of where we were at any point in time. It was a very scary, fearful, and disorienting time for me." Fear is, indeed, very disorienting and severely limits anyone's ability to operate effectively.

Damage on the Job and off

We are sure it is no surprise to you to hear that when one part of your life seems to be in disarray, other parts may seem to be strained, as well. This holds true for both your partner and yourself. If the job is working great, and you are feeling empowered, your personal life may seem to be richer and more full. Conversely, your personal life has probably taken a beating if for some time you have not had full endorsement from your boss and colleagues, if you have not been contributing to the extent you know you could, or if you have noticed others have been migrating away from you. If you have experienced any of these shifts (or others like them) that have eroded your feelings of self-worth and professional competency, you may have an opportunity to "clean up" some damage with the people in your life you least want to hurt or alarm.

Although you might not feel that you were (or are) the primary author of any upset with your partner, *you* must be committed to resolving it. Whereas the uncertainty of your company's downsizing may have triggered fear in your partner and may have created tremendous financial worries or bitterness or cynicism, *you* need to "own" the cause of the upset. Why? Because you are the one who is or was working there and whose job was in jeopardy. So, if you can objectively consider yourself both the source of the problem as well as the source of the solution, you can effectively take some action.

Emotions and Withholds

Have you ever experienced or witnessed how quickly parents get hooked emotionally when their child is unfairly picked on or taken advantage of at play or at school? If you have, then you can identify with the flood of emotions your spouse or partner may be experiencing.

It is not uncommon for our loved ones to experience emotions in a more pronounced way than we do in a career campaign. Deeper sadness, greater bitterness, more blame, more intense vindictiveness, or more obvious relief. Remember our passenger's seat analogy? Even though you have been directly impacted, at least you can diffuse your emotions by working diligently on your job search. You are, in effect, in the "driver's seat." Your partner, unfortunately, may feel somewhat removed from this process or hampered from working through all the issues.

You may even find yourself withholding many of your emotions or feelings or thoughts because you do not want to disturb others. Some of the feelings are best left unsaid, but many others need to be shared because if you (or your partner) withhold these things from each other, then you run the risk of withdrawing from the very person whose support you need the most. You may find that your partner will not reveal what she or he is feeling to remain strong, protect you from being distracted, or to refrain from generating further upset. Ironically, withholding generally creates the opposite effect. One spouse we knew indicated that she was so upset with her husband for losing his job, she refused to speak to him for two weeks because every time she did, she either yelled at him or cried. In our discussions, she acknowledged that she was tremendously fearful and angry about the family's finances and the jeopardizing of the children's college fund. Conversely, our client felt that sharing all his concerns and deepest fears would set his wife off. However, she already had felt and experienced all the emotions and blackest of thoughts already, so his not sharing *really* reinforced her greatest fears versus eliminating them. Once we were able to vent, laugh, and cry a bit, much of the fear went away because neither of them had to "hide out" any more. Ultimately, our client's campaign seemed to powerfully accelerate after fully communicating and involving his spouse more in the process; the final outcome was a fine opportunity in the person's preferred industry.

Emotional Upsets Your Partner May Be Experiencing

- You, as the employee, are genuinely a nice person, and you have just been emotionally hurt and deeply wounded, and your partner feels both angry and protective.
- Your partner may feel that it's not fair that the person who should leave the company gets to remain.
- Part of your partner's identity, status, and business perks were derived from your title or position, and now they have been threatened or ripped away.
- Both you and your partner want to remain strong for each other, so you may not openly share your concerns or fears as you do not want to alarm each other.
- Your partner may feel ostracized or snubbed by the community and may be cut out from meaningful social or business connections because of the embarrassment or discomfort others feel.
- Your financial plans are in jeopardy.
- Your children may be harassed or shunned in school and, perhaps, even told that you did something wrong.

Dos and Don'ts in Dealing with Your Partner

- Expect the unexpected and don't read too much into emotions. They happen for a number of reasons.

- Recognize that your partner's emotional reactions may be quite different or quite similar to your emotional roller coaster.

- Accept your partner's behavior as being valid (for the emotional state he or she is in), and do not make him or her "wrong" because the feeling is different, uncomfortable, or inappropriate, given your perspective.

- Communicate your own fears or concerns, balancing them out with your knowledge that things will be okay.

- Commit to your partner that you'll do the best you can in your career search and ask for support.

- Express appreciation for the support your partner has given to you, acknowledging that it may have been rough for both of you.

- Assume complete responsibility for the way your career and life looks. Do not blame others, and note when you are choosing to be a "victim." Then choose to reenter a powerful state in which you feel confident, powerful, and in control.

- Involve your partner in this process and demonstrate that you are confident in your abilities and in this proven job search process.

- Plan your work, work your plan, communicate fully and genuinely, and never, never give up.

Now work through Worksheets 5 and 6, using your emotions to plan a positive approach.

The Quest of Self-Discovery: Uncovering Your Hidden Talents

When you are making a career move, the management of your individual God-given talents and resources (your time, energy, creativity, technical skills, job experiences, bank account, and self-motivation) takes on a new meaning. Never before have you had a more important project or work assignment. It is not uncommon to feel out of control if you have been zapped by your organization or if you are feeling uncertain about your long-term future while employed. Instead of feeling burdened, try to think of yourself as an ordinary citizen who has been given an extremely important mission by the most powerful and respected person in the country.

Imagine the scene: Trembling with as much excitement as fear, you walk slowly through a magnificently appointed hall, filled with beautiful

WORKSHEET 5
Venting—a Safety Release

To gain the most value from this exercise, please be totally frank with yourself. Now is the time to vent a bit—let some of those bottled up emotions out. This is your private worksheet. No one else will see your responses, unless you want to share them. Answer the following questions as completely and as thoroughly as you can.

What has happened with my job?

What have I learned?

How do I feel about my boss? My company?

What are all the positive things I can do now?

WORKSHEET 6
Revealing Your Insights to an Employer

Review the responses you created in the previous worksheet and rephrase them as if you are responding to a prospective employer. Notice any differences in how you feel as you shift your language to assume complete responsibility for your exit from your company. (Remember, you do not have to be formally out of a job to feel disconnected to your organization.) Practice reading your responses out loud with conviction—as if you were talking to an employer. Watch for shifts. It's OK to discard "stuff" in your life if it is not working for you.

What happened at your company?

What have you learned?

How do you feel about your company?

What positive things are you doing at this time?

wall hangings, jeweled mirrors, richly carved figurines, and colorful floor tiles. You notice that there are bubbling fountains on either side of the walkway. While you sense the presence of great authority in the hall, you also notice that people are relaxed and moving confidently about. You are puzzled and awed by the electric feeling in this place, its apparent freedom and shared openness. You have never felt anything like it before. Gradually, the walkway slopes upward, and, as you raise your feet, your eyes lift and meet those of your influential and powerful host.

"Welcome, friend. I bid you welcome and give you leave to enjoy all things in this place. My things are your things. You may stay and refresh yourself for a while before you go on your journey. I have chosen for you a mission of great importance that only you can perform. The mission that I personally want you to undertake is to discover your hidden strengths and talents and to then bring back to me a report of how you plan to fully use them.

"These abilities were buried long ago, and now it is time to go on your search of self-discovery. I suspect that your journey will be both easy and exciting as well as long and hard, often filled with seemingly insurmountable trials and tribulations. But I assure you that you have the power and current ability to withstand all trials that come before you and the cunning to defeat all enemies. In addition, you have the heart to push on when you are weary and the physical stamina to climb over the mountains before you.

"To aid you in this quest or to avail yourself of any needed resource, all you have to do is use my name and you will be supported and lifted up. You see, you will be my personal emissary. I give you my signet ring that you should wear on a chain about your neck. You can never overuse this privilege that has been given you, so do not ever feel you have to walk alone or deplete your resources. My aides will assist you when you need it, though they will not alleviate all the discomfort, uncertainty, or obstacles you encounter. For they know that through trials and tribulations, you will grow strong and become mature. Your trip may be frightening and exhausting, but I am confident that you will return victorious and a stronger person for the journey."

Is your own quest to discover and fully utilize your talents and skills in your career search going to be tough? Perhaps. Some individuals experience a sense of tremendous exhilaration, whereas many others approach the task in a much more somber manner. Generally, a well-run career search will be one of the most challenging assignments you have ever undertaken. Why? Because you are never very far away from the source of your frustration and energy. You are the source of the problem and the source of the solution.

Blinded by His Ego, Anger Runs His Life

Rob Small, 47, is married, well-educated and until recently held the position as product development manager in a well-known consumer products company. He had the respect of his fellow employees and seemed to be on the company's "fast track" with one promotion after another. Although he didn't flaunt his successes, Rob felt invincible; Rob felt as if everything he did would work eventually. In fact, he became so successful he forgot what it was to have problems in his life.

Rob had a talent for bringing out new and innovative products for his company. Last year, Rob was responsible for directing a team of six marketing specialists who had laboriously researched, developed, and introduced a startling new product line extension. The new product was expected to generate more than $8 million in first year sales. But lately Rob's performance was off, he hated his job, he snapped at his family, he snarled at his employees, and he became very moody.

What was the problem? How could a once-excellent manager become so ineffective? As it turned out, there was an organizational change in Rob's department, and he did not receive the major promotion he felt he deserved. Rob was so upset he couldn't think straight for several days, even though his boss assured him that the reason for him not getting promoted was because he could not be spared from several critical projects which were currently underway.

Intellectually, Rob understood the reasons, but he was hurt and angry, nonetheless. Unconsciously, Rob was withdrawing from the company, his boss, his team, and, most of all, himself. He felt he lost "face" by not getting the promotion. The more that Rob withdrew (or ran away), the more his performance suffered. Rob found that he no longer liked his work, and he became more angry and depressed as the weeks passed. Within three months of his "missed" promotion, Rob began a discreet job search and within a few more months he left the company with a huge chip on his shoulder, vowing never to be taken advantage of again by a company.

Sound familiar? It should, for it is the same story which is played out in thousands of lives daily. Only the jobs and the names are different. Have you ever experienced a bit of what Rob felt, perhaps in a missed promotion or opportunity for recognition? If you have, welcome to the club. Having your emotions influence your decisions and even "run" your life is all part of the human personality. Although Rob was blinded by his immediate circumstances and feelings of rejections, he still had a choice as to how he lived—to be ruled by his emotions *or* to be ruled by rational thought. Rob's reaction is not all that abnormal. In fact, it is pretty normal for most of us in an employment situation. Our egos get bruised, we become upset, and it is common to feel as if we have separated from our organization.

At that moment, we have "left" the company, even though we still may work there and collect a paycheck. Physically, we are still in our jobs, but psychologically, we have given our 2-week (or 30-day) notice and have split for greener pastures. Sometimes we have so clearly broken off the relationships and have "left" our jobs to such an extent that we feel like strangers in our offices or at our workstations. Work which was quite an important part of our lives may now feel significantly less so. We may even want to walk away from some relationships which we were committed to making work previously.

However, we may be so stuck in our jobs and fearful about leaving that we don't recognize that we have "left." Then usually one of two things occurs: Boredom sets in, *or* our lives are ruled by whatever emotion happens to surface (denial, anger, depression, anxiousness, fear, giddiness, guilt, relief, etc.).

The challenge that faces each one of us is that of understanding more fully the impact the world has on us and the impact we have on our world. Ignorance is not bliss, it is a danger. When we are not aware of the motivations behind our behavior, we are operating blindly in our relationships with our spouse, our kids, our friends, and in our jobs. We clearly run the risk of blowing them up by over-controlling and manipulating others to get what we need. Becoming interpersonally skilled is both an opportunity and an obligation. It is your choice and your responsibility.

Creating the Competitive Distinction: Your Choice, Your Responsibility

Getting to know how to sell yourself to a company as a potentially good employee is simply the best investment you will ever make. But you have to make the choice to put the time and effort into the task. If you are still employed, please be alert to the fact that as you adapt your behavior in preparation to conduct the search for the perfect job, you may find yourself becoming more empowered at work. You may find that as you begin to master your emotions and perspectives, that your relationships become more complete and your interpersonal skills more effective. Who knows? Perhaps as you ready yourself to run in the job-hunting race, you will discover you work in a place which is pretty good, though not perfect, and that you control how your environment looks.

As an employee, you may have been laid off or terminated before, or you know someone who has. Involuntary job loss is increasingly a part of life in today's society. Although you may be very embarrassed, hurt, or angry, try to view your separation as yet another phase in your career—an experience from which to grow. If you are still employed, take this opportunity to learn all you can from this material while still contributing fully to your organization.

Finances and Benefits: Big Factors in Your Search _____

Here are a few things you may wish to consider now about managing your finances during your job search. **LOOK AT ALL YOUR INCOME,** savings, or other sources of money and compare your income with your debts. This is not a good time to make any large installment purchases. Find out where you stand financially. Keep in mind that people often buy things because new items make them feel good, and this is a time when you are trying every way possible to feel good about yourself. So, watch your spending.

Credit cards can generate bills far ahead of when you might get your new job. You may wish to stop buying on credit and start buying on a *cash-only basis* until you are more certain of your income future.

Maintain records of expenses incurred in your job search, because the Internal Revenue Service allows you to itemize some deductions. Check with an accountant to verify the limits of coverage and how you might save yourself some taxes.

Your Severance Agreement

If you have been involuntarily terminated, make certain that you fully understand your severance agreement, including salary continuation, medical and life insurance benefits, employment constraints (noncompete or behavior clauses), bonuses, stock options, and any other benefits which you may normally be eligible for at your organizational level. Ask questions if you do not understand any salary continuation or benefit coverage to which you may be entitled.

Regardless of how you came out (or are coming out) of your company and how it feels, no one wants you to be financially or emotionally damaged. Do not feel rushed in this process. You have too much at stake not to understand your benefits. Granted, you may not fully understood all the legal language contained in the severance letter or agreement outlining your entitlement. If you cannot completely explain the entire "package" to someone else, such as your spouse, for example, then see the human resources representatives again for an in-depth explanation. They would be happy to define things for you.

Be Advised: Remain professional in this meeting with human resources. Be calm, cool, and collected. No outbursts of anger or blame. Remember the old adage, "Don't burn any bridges." The more you are in control, the greater the "bridge building." You will greatly enhance your image in the company as a direct result of this behavior. Regardless of how you feel right now, at this moment, it is critical for your references and personal networking that you appear in control and supportive of the organization, even in these tough times in which you lost your job through no fault of your own.

The following is a list of severance issues you should know about:

- How long will my salary continue?
- What deductions will be made?
- How long will my medical and life insurance last?
- When and for how long can I extend my medical, dental, and HMO insurance coverage after I leave my company?
- Can I collect unemployment compensation?
- What should I do with the lump sum of money from my retirement plan?
- To what extent is my performance incentive bonus at risk?
- Are there any "noncompete" or other restrictive clauses in my severance agreement which may limit my ability to find meaningful employment, and what legal rights does the company have?

Unemployment Benefits

If you involuntarily left your organization, regardless of any documents you signed indicating that you resigned, **you may be eligible to receive unemployment insurance benefits now. Do not stand on false pride thinking that unemployment benefits are welfare.** Think of this money as your search fund, helping you underwrite miscellaneous expenses you incur for postage, stationery, gas, parking, and so on.

Some localities consider certain monies you receive from severance benefits to be separate and distinct from unemployment compensation, that is, you can receive both. Ask if your employer will allow you to collect unemployment compensation. When in doubt, make arrangements to register immediately for unemployment with the state job service people, because waiting may impact your total wage base upon which your unemployment compensation is based.

Strengthening Relationships and Completing Commitments at Work

When we are interrupted suddenly during a project or activity, particularly one to which we have dedicated considerable effort, planning, and energy, we are often somewhat unbalanced until we get back and finish that work activity. We like to complete what we start.

Our normal desire to complete assignments often creates several weeks of anxiety following a job loss (or the decision to voluntarily leave the company). This anxiety may appear as a recurring concern about a responsibility and what may have happened to it or who took over the task to which you were so dedicated. (Could anyone care for your project the way you did?) Even more sobering is the thought that your efforts will not be picked up by anyone, that your work will be ignored, that your work may not have mattered to anyone.

You and your work mattered. However, things obviously changed and priorities shifted. Projects which were previously important to the company in financially stable times often become categorized as nonessential to the business survival when profits have slipped. Although intellectually you may know all that, emotionally you may still be frustrated because you may want to manage the effective transition of your project rather than just abandoning it. Or you just want to "move forward and put this behind you." To that extent, it is important that these recurring concerns be put to rest so they do not interfere with your progress in a well-managed career transition.

Worksheet 7 is designed to help you complete any ongoing concerns which you may still have about projects, responsibilities, assignments, or worries which you were handling at the time of your voluntary or involuntary departure. Complete the worksheet for yourself, not for your current or former company. There is no need to show this exercise to anyone unless you want to. Follow these instructions:

1. Write down a brief description of each project, assignment, responsibility, problem, or activity which you will leave or have left incomplete upon your departure. Include anything you may be worrying about now or may be concerned about its outcome later.

2. Describe the item, indicate what you have done so far, list the steps that you planned to take to complete the item, and mention the people you would suggest as the most logical to handle things so that the item can be satisfactorily concluded.

3. Picture yourself telling your current (or former boss) all this relevant information in the most confident and convincing manner. Imagine your boss thanking you for your concern and promising to handle your suggestions well in light of the organization's changing needs.

A note of caution: If you actually do decide to communicate this information to your former boss or current boss upon leaving, do it for your own sense of completion only. You may wish to send the information versus presenting it face-to-face, as the initial reaction may not be

WORKSHEET 7
Completing My Prior Work Assignments

The following is a list of actions, projects, assignments, or responsibilities which I was handling at the time of my departure from the company. These items are prepared primarily to complete my thinking about assignments I was handling. If this information is also helpful to the company, then I am pleased.

ITEM: _____

Describe the action, project, assignment, or responsibility:

This item is important because:

Current status (what's finished):

What still must be done:

Individuals who may help in finishing the item:

(Continued)

ITEM: _____

Describe the action, project, assignment, or responsibility:

This item is important because:

Current status (what's finished):

What still must be done:

Individuals who may help in finishing the item:

what you expect, and both you and your boss may need to "save face." If you send the information expecting gratitude, and you do not get it, you may just add to your frustration and upset.

If you do share this information, and there is no need to do so, send it just to finish your responsibility for any loose ends so you do not continue to carry these concerns with you, like extra baggage, into your search for that perfect job.

Summary: Don't Take Time Off!

So what are you going to do? If you are out, you could take it easy. Maybe you wanted some time to paint the house, or spend time outdoors to work on your tan, or perhaps do some work on the car. Being unemployed may look like the best time to do these things. If you are still employed and toying with the idea, begin to put your credentials in order. Through this process, you might realize how valuable you are and rekindle relationships in such a way that you will want to stay.

However, the clock has already started ticking for you. Whether or not you are fully aware of it, you are in a very competitive situation; there are always a lot of people out looking for jobs. Because there are generally more people than jobs, companies are taking the time to hire only the best people available for each position.

But the fact is, **YOU DO NOT HAVE THE TIME.** Look at it this way: This may really be the first time in a while that you have had a chance to take a long look at your professional life. This is a wonderful chance to take control of your future and find an opportunity that makes the best possible use of your skills and abilities—not just a job for a job's sake.

Right now, if you are unemployed, your full-time job is to find a job. And if you *are* employed, finding a job is your new part-time job. You will need to discover and effectively utilize your talents, skills, and abilities in search of the kind of career opportunity you want and need.

If you delay your search until your benefits run out or until you are thrown out, you may be passing on a priceless opportunity to get a running start at the rest of your working life. The alternative could well be a long period of unemployment after your benefits have run out or remaining dissatisfied where you are.

SOME EXCEPTIONS: Just so you don't think we are unfeeling in your time of need, we recognize that you may be living in a particular circumstance which prevents you from aggressively committing to a full-blown career search right now. We understand that.

If you are still employed, keep the pressure on yourself to do something for your search every single day. Again, this can be answering an advertisement or gaining additional skills in your workplace. You may be working in an office setting in which you have no privacy and where personal calls are not permitted. Obviously, it's tough to actively conduct a phone campaign with these kinds of restrictions.

We've worked with people who were zapped who had prepaid vacation plans, who were on funeral leave, or who were recovering from varying forms of physical or emotional trauma. Indeed, being zapped is extremely stressful, and you may need a bit of a breather. However, it has been our experience that one of the quickest ways to regain your confidence is to leap right into the search. If, after you get your résumé together, a process which reaffirms your accomplishments and value to a company, you want to take some time off, great! At that point, you probably deserve a breather.

> # It is your choice. . . . Invest wisely in your future.

IN SEARCH OF WHO YOU ARE

Uncovering Your Talents, Skills, and Career Options

The Entrepreneur—Fact or Fantasy?

Roberta James was the human resources manager for a medium-sized manufacturer in Chicago, reporting to a director of administration. When she was most recently zapped she was really shocked. Bobbi, as her friends called her, did not believe that she would ever be dismissed, for no one had ever told her that she was doing a poor job; or, at least that's what Bobbi led herself to believe.

Among some of Bobbi's peculiar quirks was her inability to maintain eye contact for more than about 5 seconds at a time. In our counseling with her we indicated that her lack of credibility with people was in direct relationship to this issue. "No, no. That's never been the problem!" protested Bobbi as she stared out the window. "Riiiightttt," was our response, as we rolled our eyes heavenward. The fact that Bobbi didn't see this as a problem was no surprise to us, as she constantly missed cues obvious to everyone but herself. Clearly, Bobbi was not aware that she always averted her eyes when she was under some stress and when she was trying to make a statement. With her consent, we pointed this problem out every time we saw it with a little buzzer noise, "Buzz!" In addition, we levied a fine of a quarter every time she turned her eyes away without good cause. When the pool of monies got over $10, Bobbi began to catch herself and modify her behavior.

Bobbi came out of her company during the summer and, although she had full outplacement support from her company, which included unlimited administrative support and office usage, Bobbi elected to work at home to be closer to her family. Bobbi wanted to make up for lost time, as she felt she had neglected her family while she was working.

Bobbi spent quite a bit of quality time with her kids that summer, swimming, playing ball, working on her tan, and losing the extra 20 pounds she had been carrying. Although she was successful as a parent, she did not make much headway with her job campaign. After much coaxing on our part and depleted savings on hers, Bobbi reemerged declaring that, "I've decided to start my own business because when I was working I didn't have enough time for my family."

While we help many would-be entrepreneurs launch their businesses by codeveloping business plans and marketing strategies, we also encourage people to fully assess the viability of this option. In our opinion, Bobbi did not have what it took to be an entrepreneur, for several reasons. First and foremost, Bobbi did not demonstrate a high sense of urgency; she did not push herself to produce excellent work. Further, she avoided risk at almost any cost, could not stay focused on a project long enough to complete it, and was unable to work without a fair amount of structure. Additionally, she did not have a clear picture of what was involved in launching your own business. Bobbi thought that all entrepreneurs (since they were not with any big organization) could take summers off regularly.

Needless to say, we helped Bobbi regain a realistic career focus and relaunch her search for the perfect job for her within a somewhat structured, yet nurturing company. Several months later, she successfully landed a position in a company as the number-two human resources manager. Regarding her family, Bobbi learned to more effectively prioritize her work so she now gets more done in less time. Her extra time? She now spends it with her family in a less pressured environment.

What Do You Want to Do with the Rest of Your Life? _____

This Step will help you review your experiences, capabilities, interests, and motivations and focus your objectives for your next career move. In essence, you need to answer the question, "What do you want to do with the rest of your life?"

Your self-assessment will help identify those dimensions, both on and off the job, which tend to motivate you and those employment environments in which you are able to optimally contribute. Through this process of self-discovery, you will have the opportunity to examine, evaluate, and discuss the many parts that comprise the total "you."

Have fun with these exercises and look to learn, not resist. All these exercises have been developed and field tested by thousands of candidates before you, so we know they help quickly "ground" you and help you to have some keen insights. The interesting fact about careering is that virtually everyone has a job at some point in their lives, and every person has some definite opinions about this topic. Clearly, this is your search—not ours. We recognize this but are asking you to fully participate in these exercises, putting your ideas about careering aside until you have completed the work. If you already know exactly what you want to do and are clearly in pursuit of your career goals, then you may wish to complete these exercises as a solid confirmation.

Career Assumptions

At this stage in your career you may be (check one or more):

_____ **1.** Questioning the validity of your career direction.

_____ **2.** Interested in staying in your chosen area of expertise.

_____ **3.** Intent on exploring other options that now may be open to you.

No matter which of the options you checked above, there are probably some assumptions under which you have been operating:

Assumption A: You got into your profession or field of study because you liked it better than something else.

Assumption B: For a wide variety of reasons, you chose the place you are now because it attracted you or it was the "lesser of two evils."

Assumption C: You have stayed there this long because some of your needs were being met—at least minimally.

Assumption D: You are not somewhere else because you have not been lured away or you have not overcome your resistance to moving.

Assumption E: (Identify any other assumptions or ideas that are relevant to you.)

Focusing on Career Factors:
Liked Best—Liked Least

The four main components of your relationships and roles within any organization are:

1. **Position and Duties.** The actual duties and responsibilities which you perform.

2. **Supervisors and Bosses.** The people you work directly for, as well as your boss's supervisor.

3. **Peers and Subordinates.** Your coworkers, subordinates, and individuals evaluated as occupying lower positions in the organization.

4. Organization and Culture. The style and personality of the overall organization as well as the personality of the department in which you worked. Organization culture deals with the organization's values, policies, and operating style.

Worksheets 8, 9, 10, and 11 are designed to provide you several things:

- Identify those dimensions (factors) you want to have in your next job as well as what you want to avoid.

- Establishes a values checklist so you can evaluate potential job offers against each other.

- Helps you zero in on specific areas in the interview that are of particular interest.

In each worksheet, list as many things as you can that you *liked best* and *liked least* in your most recent position. After you have completed this, go back through the exercise again, listing what you *liked best* and *liked least* for your next previous jobs until you have covered all the significant jobs you have held. For example, in Worksheet 9, Supervisors and Bosses, you will identify those things you liked best and liked least about your most recent boss, your next previous boss, and so on, until all your relevant bosses have been covered. Follow the same procedure for Worksheets 10 and 11.

When complete, you will have a comprehensive list of the kinds of actual duties and responsibilities within jobs, relationships, and organizational environments which you enjoy and which cause you to grow and be nurtured, and those which you don't like and probably want to avoid in the future.

Your Personal Self-Description

"Can Do" Overplayed Meant "Good-bye"

Robert Kohn was an extremely successful sales and marketing executive whose aggressive "Can Do!" style was credited for his rapid promotion to vice president at an age where most of his peers were at least 15 years his senior.

Bob was described as bright, personable, with a quick and analytical mind, practical, ambitious, and driven. Bob was noted for his ability to cut through the extraneous issues and activities and get to the heart of a matter. He always seemed to be able to recommend practical solutions to even the most complex problems.

Although Bob had the ability to relentlessly pursue a sale or seek to solve the unsolvable, he also seemed to go through more than his share

WORKSHEET 8
Position and Duties

What I Liked Best	What I Liked Least

What are the most important attractions and considerations for you now with regard to the kinds of duties and responsibilities you would like in your next position?

_____

_____

_____

_____

WORKSHEET 9
Supervisors and Bosses

Qualities I Liked Best	Qualities I Liked Least

What are the most important attractions and considerations for you now with regard to the kind of supervisors or bosses you most want to have in your next assignment?

_____

_____

_____

_____

WORKSHEET 10
Peers and Subordinates

Characteristics I Liked Best	Characteristics I Liked Least

What are the most important attractions and considerations for you now with regard to the characteristics of peers and subordinates you want to see in your next position?

_____

_____

_____

_____

WORKSHEET 11
Organization and Culture

Characteristics I Liked Best	Characteristics I Liked Least

What are the most important attractions and considerations for you now with regard to the corporate culture, organizational characteristics, and values in your next assignment?

_____

_____

_____

_____

of promising and talented managers. It got so bad that a number of Bob's subordinate managers paid confidential visits to the president, to whom Bob reported. To his team, Bob was one of the best bosses many of them had had, though he always tried to remake people in his own image. The result was that many of the company's emerging star performers got run over and damaged in the process.

After repeated conversations and confrontations with Bob, the president lost his patience and optimism that this issue was correctable. Bob's unwillingness to change and to see how he impacted others got in his way of fully relating to his team and to key customers. When the company's sales plunged and significant contributors left in droves, the president reluctantly fired his star performer before the organization blew itself up.

Although Bob was an emotional basket case for a few days, he also knew that much of his anger was ego-driven. He just couldn't imagine people not wanting to keep him. He quickly realized, however, that he was responsible for his departure, as he was clearly operating against the corporate culture and interpersonal style of his boss and many peers. Bob had forgotten one of the fundamental reasons for any exit, be it voluntary or involuntary, and that is "fit." In his search, Bob's first requirement was to learn more about himself and how he functioned with other people. Why? He wanted to prevent his experience from happening again, and he needed this awareness so he could "package" himself better in a career search.

Packaging Your Strengths and Weaknesses _____

Preparation for a job search requires that you develop a clear understanding of those behavioral traits which influence how you think, feel, and operate. The goal of Step 2 is two-fold: (1) to provide insight into you, as a person, and the kind of job or environment in which you best operate and contribute and (2) to enable you to talk about yourself appropriately, confidently, candidly, and convincingly without embarrassment, awkwardness, or hesitation.

Strengths are those behavioral traits which seem to work for you and get your needs met. **Weaknesses** are those behavior traits you deem to be your strengths carried to an extreme or used inappropriately, or that behavior seen by a person with whom you have a poor relationship.

In Worksheets 12 through 15 you will be asked to identify:

Personal strengths

Examples of applied strengths

Personal weaknesses

Written self-description

WORKSHEET 12
My Personal Strengths

Review the following list and *circle* the words that you would use, or your business associates might select when describing your strengths. After you have circled a number of strengths, please go back through the list and highlight your top-10 strengths.

accomplished	consultative	extroverted	liberal	positive
adaptable	constructive	fair	logical	pragmatic
alive	cool	firm	loyal	precise
ambitious	cost-effective	flexible	mentor	probing
analytical	courageous	focused	methodical	productive
anticipative	courteous	forceful	modest	proud
approachable	creative	frank	motivator	provocative
argumentative	daring	friendly	mover	purposeful
articulate	decisive	generous	objective	questioning
artistic	demanding	genuine	observant	quick
assertive	democratic	global	open-minded	realistic
astute	dependable	good-natured	opinionated	reflective
attentive	detailed	gregarious	optimistic	reliable
bright	determined	happy	orderly	resourceful
calm	diplomatic	helpful	organized	respected
carefree	disciplined	honest	outrageous	respectful
caring	discreet	human	outspoken	results-oriented
charismatic	discerning	humorous	partner	
coach	distant	imaginative	patient	scientific
compatible	driving	independent	people-oriented	self-reliant
competitive	easy	individualist		shrewd
conceptual	effective	initiator	perceptive	sincere
confident	efficient	innovative	perfectionist	smart
confrontive	eloquent	inspiring	persistent	smooth
conscientious	energetic	intense	personable	sociable
conservative	enthusiastic	introverted	persuasive	sophisticated
considerate	exacting	intuitive	pleasant	straight-forward
consistent	expansive	kind	polished	

(*Continued*)

strategic	systematic	thinker	tough-minded	visionary
supportive	tactful	thoughtful	verbally skilled	winner
sympathetic	talented	tolerant		

Other strengths:

_____

_____

_____

_____

_____

_____

_____

_____

_____

WORKSHEET 13
Examples of Applied Strengths

Please transfer your top 10 strengths from the previous worksheet and provide an example which would illustrate how you applied your strengths on the job.

MY TOP STRENGTHS (Begin with your strongest characteristic)	**A SUPPORTING EXAMPLE FROM** **MY WORK EXPERIENCE**
1. _____	1. _____
2. _____	2. _____
3. _____	3. _____
4. _____	4. _____
5. _____	5. _____
6. _____	6. _____
7. _____	7. _____
8. _____	8. _____
9. _____	9. _____
10. _____	10. _____

Personal Weaknesses

Employers are interested in how well you can do the job, how well you might fit in to their organization, how well you know yourself, and to what extent might you be "damaged" by this experience. Worksheet 14 uses this "formula" for describing your weaknesses as overplayed or overextended strengths as follows:

1. State your strength

2. State the excess of the strength

3. Tell how it shows up

4. Tell how you manage it, so it's not a problem

Example

Strength: "As I mentioned, I set high performance goals for myself and others."

Excess: "I'm aware that sometimes I can become impatient if things aren't moving as fast as I'd like or if it seems that people aren't pulling their own weight."

Examples of Weaknesses as Overplayed Strengths

STRENGTHS	WEAKNESSES AS OVERPLAYED STRENGTHS "SOMETIMES I CAN BE SEEN AS . . ."
"Bright"	"Having all the answers"
"Ambitious"	"Driven to succeed"
"People-oriented"	"Not moving quickly enough on tough people issues"
"Task-oriented"	"Not considerate enough of others' feelings"
"Detail-minded"	"A bit of a perfectionist"
"Decisive"	"Somewhat impulsive"
"Hard working"	"A workaholic who overcommits"
"Setting high performance standards"	"Demanding of myself and others to succeed"
"Practical"	"Conservative, using tried and true approaches"
"Innovative"	"Using nontraditional methods"
"Sensitive"	"Emotional . . . I become deeply committed"

Shows up by:	"When I feel pressure around performance goals or deadlines, I can become a bit intense and focused on results and have a tendency to push my people to perform."
Managed by:	"So, I have learned to communicate my expectations and timetables more fully and look to have people keep me posted on a project's status on a regular and ongoing basis. When I use this approach, my weakness is not a problem— it's a safeguard."

After you complete Worksheet 14, fill out Worksheets 15 and 16. The more completely and honestly you fill out these worksheets, the more insights you have about yourself and the world around you. In addition, by preparing for these difficult issues you will significantly enhance your confidence and your ability to answer tough interview questions.

Deciding What You Want in a Job: Position Selection Criteria

As you completed each of the preceding exercises, you, no doubt, began to decide (or remember) those aspects of your job and company that you *really want to have* in a new job or company. Refer to those things that you "liked best."

For those elements that you *really want to avoid,* refer to those things you identified as "liked least" and rephrase them in a positive manner. The following is an example of how to turn negatives into positives or to state what you want to see in the new job.

Turning Negatives into Positives

LIKED LEAST	POSITION SELECTION CRITERIA (I WANT . . .)
No latitude to develop own work schedule	Freedom to plan work
Boss always played favorites	Everyone treated fairly and uniformly
Stuck in dead-end job	Promotional opportunities are present
Work load is a back breaker	Work load is balanced and evenly paced
Underpaid	Equitable pay with the opportunity to expand responsibilities and compensation

---

WORKSHEET 14
My Personal Weaknesses

Transfer your top 10 strengths from Worksheet 13 onto this worksheet. Review the examples below, then complete the formula for your top overplayed strength or weakness.

Personal Strengths	Weaknesses as Overplayed Strengths
Bright	"Having all the answers"
Ambitious	"Driven to succeed"
People-oriented	"Not tough enough"
Task-oriented	"Not considerate enough of others"
Detail-minded	"A bit of a perfectionist"
1.	
2.	
3.	
4.	
5.	
6.	
7.	
8.	
9.	
10.	

Strength: _____

_____

Excess: _____

_____

Shows up by: _____

_____

Managed by: _____

_____

WORKSHEET 15
My Personal Self-Description

Write a one- to three-paragraph description of yourself in short phrases and sentences. List as many characteristics as you can, including your behavior; values; likes; dislikes; principles; beliefs; attitudes; convictions; points of view; philosophy about life and business; styles of being a manager, spouse, parent; strengths, and weaknesses. Remember to use short words and phrases; this is not intended to be a writing exercise or your autobiography. Uncomfortable? Here is your chance to become confident as you prepare this response, as every interviewer will ask you to describe yourself, one way or another.

_____

_____

_____

_____

_____

_____

_____

_____

_____

_____

_____

_____

_____

_____

_____

_____

_____

_____

_____

_____

_____

WORSHEET 16
Reasons for Leaving Your Job

This exercise is designed to help you identify those factors which led to you leaving your job. These factors can be used to isolate those things you want to avoid in the future, if at all possible. Regardless of the circumstances and how it happened, you are leaving or have left your current job. Critically evaluate that job. What factors below are most likely to apply to you?

Place a *1* by those factors that apply to your most recent job. Then go through the list again with your next most recent job and place a *2* by the applicable items. Repeat for all the significant jobs you have held, numbering them appropriately. Place an *x* by those factors which would cause you to seriously consider leaving your future job.

_____	Takeover possible	_____	Not confident
_____	Situation unstable	_____	Unchallenged
_____	Reorganization possible	_____	Dislike boss
_____	Industry in tough times	_____	Dislike peers
_____	Lost promotion	_____	No work friends
_____	Burned out	_____	Poor political environment
_____	Unable to contribute	_____	Feel left out
_____	Lower income than I need	_____	Wrong field or industry
_____	Wrong location; wrong job	_____	Physical work too little or too great
_____	Commute too long	_____	People contact too little or too great
_____	Travel too much	_____	Little freedom
_____	Bored and dissatisfied	_____	Not enough time with family
_____	Little recognition	_____	Difficult hours
_____	Little responsibility	_____	Stressed
_____	Low self-esteem	_____	Want to expand job

Other reasons I have had or would have for leaving jobs:

_____

_____

_____

_____

_____

_____

Hopefully, you will be faced with the difficult task of deciding among several fine job offers. Worksheets 17 and 18, which focus on position selection criteria, are an attempt to help you objectively evaluate job offers and quantify their value. In addition, these criteria identify those areas or topics in the interview about which you want to get detailed information.

This approach will enable you to more effectively distance yourself from the many emotions that influence career decisions. For instance, if you are an enthusiastic person, you run the risk of being unduly influenced by your potential boss's contagious enthusiasm, even though the position may not be your best career move. To the extent that your criteria for the ideal job are present, the greater you will be favorably impressed by this right opportunity, not only emotionally but also intellectually.

The list of position selection criteria is a guide and should not completely displace your gut instincts. Your ratings for a given company may say "Go," but your feelings about the job or the relationships in the company may say "Whoa." You may find that some criteria are so important for you that if they are not present, the company (or offer) is considered to be knocked-out of consideration. The potential for career growth and advancement is certainly an issue worth considering. Through the use of the position selection criteria, you have the opportunity to more objectively evaluate those things which are important to you in your career.

Instructions

1. Using the following format list those things (criteria) you want in a position. This process will help you sort through the many issues which influence making a career decision.

2. Review Worksheet 17, filled out for our fictitious job seeker, Mike Commons, for ideas or a format. Please do not merely copy Mike's list, though some of Mike's criteria and concerns may fit exactly with your own. Your goal is to develop your own list in Worksheet 18, personalizing those things that you want in a job. If Mike's criteria seem to fit your own, please feel free to use any of them.

3. **Absolute Scale** Reread all your position selection criteria and assign a rank to them, according to what you want and need. Do not worry too much about being completely accurate; this is not a test, and these priorities can shift as you gain more experience with this exercise.

4. **Company Evaluation** Since the evaluation of positions in companies only occurs after interviewing, you may put this section aside for now. Please feel free to add to this list throughout the course of your job search. This criteria list will be used later in Step 11. To objectively

WORKSHEET 17
Position Selection Criteria

COMPANIES INTERVIEWED

EXAMPLES OF MIKE COMMONS'S CRITERIA:	My Absolute Scale	Company 1	Company 2	Company 3	Company 4
Positions and duties					
Freedom to plan work available.	1	3			
Pay is equitable.					
Duties are challenging.					
Duties vary.					
Supervisors and bosses					
Boss communicates and shares knowledge.					
Confident with good sense of humor.					
Peers/subordinates					
Staff is educated, trained, and motivated.					
Mentors are present.					
Organization					
Everyone challenged to be their best.					

EVALUATION KEY

My Absolute Scale
1. Essential for me in the job.
2. Important for me in the job.
3. It would be nice to have.
4. Not of major significance.

Company Evaluation
1. Clearly available in this job.
2. Probably available in this job.
3. May be there occasionally.
4. Clearly not available in this job.

WORKSHEET 18
Position Selection Criteria

	My Absolute Scale	COMPANIES INTERVIEWED			
		Company 1	Company 2	Company 3	Company 4

Note: You may reproduce this sheet for added criteria with our compliments. Copyright © 1992 Robertson Lowstuter, Inc. (708) 940-4400

evaluate a company before or after receiving an offer, read each of your selection criteria and assess its availability. Decide on a ranking and write it down for every single item on your list.

5. After you have assessed every single criterion, evaluate any "opposites" or significant shifts in your absolute score and your company score. By way of explanation, turn to Mike Commons's list and note that his first criterion, "Freedom to plan work" was rated a *1*. Obviously, Mike considers this dimension pretty important.

Accordingly, Mike's interviewing strategy with his first company was to determine the extent to which the "freedom to plan work" was present. Mike scored company 1 a *3*, as he perceived this criteria to be present only occasionally. Given that Mike deemed this dimension to be essential and it only showed up occasionally, this is what we would call a significant difference. Based on this difference, Mike would circle *3*, as he needs to seriously evaluate why that is the case and to see if other significant negatives exist. The reason for the lower rating may simply have been that Mike failed to ask penetrating questions which would have revealed this critical data. No matter the reason, to be satisfied that he fully explored this dimension, Mike gets to zero in on this issue and ask more probing questions.

Probing Questions Mike Can Ask

1. "What are the company's and the department's annual operating plans?"

2. "Describe how the planning process works and who is involved on corporate strategies and department plans."

3. "Who determines what programs and projects get worked on and receive funding?"

4. "Once given an assignment, what latitude will I have with regard to time or dollar spending, as well as the direction of the project?"

5. "How often and in what form do you like to be kept informed?"

6. "To what extent will I be able to plan my work?"

7. "Can you give me an example of when someone else in your department was able to plan their work in a similar manner you described?"

8. "How do you feel about giving this much freedom to your team?"

We recommend against multiplying or adding your absolute scores with the company scores. Although this quantification may make you feel better, it is statistically worthless. Why? For two reasons. First, you probably have not gone through the laborious process of "weighing" and validating each item. Second, it is virtually impossible for you to be completely objective in the scoring process because you, like others before you, will react more favorably to one company (and criteria) over another.

The goal of Worksheet 19 is to give you an opportunity to capture some of the parameters of your ideal job that you have been working on in all the previous worksheets. Presumably, you have identified various ideal elements of the position, relationships, organization environments, industries, and geographic locations in which you operate most effectively, distinct from those which do not work for you. As a general rule of thumb, the more restrictive you are, the longer and more difficult your search. Fill out Worksheet 19.

WORKSHEET 19
My Ideal Job

DESCRIBE YOUR NEXT IDEAL JOB. (Job title, duties, location, kind of company, kind of industry)

_____

_____

_____

_____

_____

_____

_____

_____

_____

_____

_____

_____

_____

_____

_____

_____

_____

_____

_____

_____

_____

_____

_____

(Continued)

26 Questions to Ask as You Explore Chosen Career Paths

If you have ever considered a radical departure from your current type of position, company, or industry, you should consider answering some practical questions.

1. What is your career path? Describe title, function, industry.

2. Who do you know who might be an expert in this area, someone from whom you can learn and someone whose behavior and career path you can model?

3. What skills are required to effectively perform in this role or industry?

4. What appeals to you when you see yourself in this role?

(Continued)

5. What motivates you to want to do this?

6. What are the *POSITIVE* aspects of this job?

7. What are the *NEGATIVE* aspects of this job?

8. What skills, abilities, and contacts do you *HAVE* to succeed in this role?

9. What skills, abilities, or contacts do you *LACK?*

(Continued)

10. To be fully equipped to function in this role, what is required?

11. Who do you know who is already successful in your ideal role?

12. What specific actions have these successful people taken to be successful?

13. How would you establish credibility?

14. What are you willing to do to be successful? By when?

(Continued)

15. How will you know when you've acquired the necessary skills for this job?

16. What do you *GAIN* by pursuing this dream?

17. What do you *LOSE* by pursuing this dream?

18. What do you *GAIN* by *not* pursuing this dream?

19. What do you *LOSE* by *not* pursuing this dream?

(Continued)

20. How can you support yourself financially?

21. If you were someone else, would you invest in you? Why? Why not?

22. Are you truly enough of an expert to be successful?

23. How will you create a sufficient distinction for you to succeed?

24. How much of a market is there for your services, how is your competition, and to what extent will you be able to capture business?

(Continued)

25. How will you earn enough to support yourself in both the short term and long term?

26. How extensively are you prepared to risk your worldly possessions on this career move?

WRITING A KNOCK-OUT RÉSUMÉ AND MARKETING LETTERS THAT GET READ

From Ad Nauseam to Value-Added

Jim Roland's résumé was an 8-page narrative which was a combination of a curriculum vitae and a functional résumé. It listed everything that Jim felt was relevant to his background since earning his Ph.D. in electrical engineering. In addition to his production experience, his earlier work history included university teaching. Jim thought his 8-page résumé was reasonable, given that his favorite college professor and mentor had a 20-page curriculum vitae crammed with numerous patents, publications, consulting engagements, and his many academic posts.

As Jim switched career paths from academia to industrial R&D he saw no reason to change his résumé, and no one advised him differently. However, over the course of 20 years his original company had been acquired twice and merged with a third corporation which considerably changed Jim's R&D mandate and organizational dynamics.

New management demanded a more aggressive results-oriented approach from Jim and his group which, heretofore, had enjoyed a more leisurely paced work environment. Granted, his group produced results, but not at the pace now demanded. After much discussion with the new director, Jim decided to negotiate an arrangement to consult on a full-time basis while he looked for the right job while still on the payroll. In this capacity, Jim held two jobs: researcher for his company and career searcher for himself.

When we started working with Jim, he clearly indicated that he wanted to remain in some form of an industrial R&D capacity. To that end, we jointly developed credentials to more appropriately reflect his academic orientation while highlighting his accomplishments. The result was a hard-hitting 2-page résumé which got rave reviews within

Jim's target marketplace. In fact, his résumé so powerfully distinguished him from his competition that two search firms sent representatives from Toronto to meet and interview him during an international symposium in Scottsdale, where he was speaking. Even ol' "unflappable Jim" was impressed.

Our World As It Really Is

We live in a world of people and tasks. If we are able to get along well with people, our chances for success increase significantly, in both work and personal situations. Knowing who we are is important in achieving success as it helps in understanding what we are doing well and what we can improve.

Our self-perception—who we are and what we have done—is built upon bits and pieces of information received from others, as well as ourselves. From this irregular and limited flow of communication we tend to accept some bits of information and reject others. We tend to selectively determine that some results in our career are important while other accomplishments are forgotten.

What Do Employers Really Want? Results!

Employers want to hire, develop, promote, and reward people who can contribute to the achievement of the company's goals, including its growth and profitability. (Even nonprofit associations need to make money to fund their programs.) Accordingly, you need to quickly demonstrate that you are the kind of person who can make things happen and achieve results. A well-constructed résumé will help you do that.

Packaging Your Talents and Abilities: The Résumé—an Advanced Marketing Tool

Résumés—the topic almost always creates an uproar, as people have such divergent views on the subject. The controversy is not surprising, given the extremely personal nature of the document and the times in which it is utilized, namely job hunting. Looking for that ideal job can be a bit taxing on the nerves and the pocketbook. It's no wonder that we rise to the defense when someone criticizes our résumé—after all, it does represent us, doesn't it? A résumé represents us only partially, much like a photograph captures only a portion of who we really are.

A well-developed résumé is a powerful marketing tool which will sell you in advance of your being able to personally tell your story in an interview. A résumé is not meant to be a "tell-all" document which identifies all the things in your background that you alone find fascinating. If you effectively put yourself in the role of the hiring authority and evaluate your résumé in light of this person's busy schedule, you may find yourself pruning out many of the extraneous pieces of your old or current résumé.

Do you really need a résumé? Yes, without a doubt. Even if you get connected through a well-known networking source and a résumé was not asked for, you definitely need it so you can:

- Be intimately familiar with the span of your accountability, the scope of your responsibility, and the accuracy of your accomplishments.
- Provide one to someone if they ask for it. If you do not have one, you will throw one together that may not represent you in the most powerful manner.

A résumé provides a context for who you are, what you say you are, and how you can contribute. It is no longer appropriate to have a résumé filled with self-serving superlatives such as "dynamic, hard-hitting, dedicated, charismatic leader who thrives on challenges, hard work, and little pay." This kind of language tends to turn people off, not on. Let your activities, programs, or projects reflect those traits you want highlighted without a lot of "puffing" on about them.

Eight Key Résumé Guidelines

Please utilize these guidelines and considerations as suggestions, not mandates. If you find that you have difficulty adapting these ideas to your unique set of circumstances, that's OK. Your résumé is your résumé; it's not ours. Your résumé has to represent you in an accurate and powerful manner for you to be proud of it.

If you find yourself rejecting any or all of these guidelines without some deliberation, we encourage you to ask yourself why? Is it that we are clearly off base (given your situation) or is it that the material contradicts what you have been doing? Instead of rejecting some of these ideas out of hand, we recommend that you determine where you could apply this material for your own gain.

1. **A résumé is a marketing tool.** The tool is designed to prompt the "résumé scanner" into contacting you for a preliminary screen, then a face-to-face interview. A résumé never obtained a job for anyone by itself.

2. **A résumé is not a "tell-all" document.** Your résumé should not be longer than 2 pages. If you have a tremendously rich background, you can always include some of that information on what we call the "addendum." The addendum is helpful in capturing some of the older or less pertinent data, so they do not get lost on the "cutting room floor." Experienced individuals (10+ years of experience) probably will require 2 pages. Two pages provide an opportunity to identify a number of your accomplishments and create a sense of substance, depth, and capability. If you have fewer than 10 years of experience you may be able to fully capture what you have done on 1 page, provided your extracurricular activities and work aren't too extensive. **There is no advantage to a 1-page résumé that cuts out too much of your background and accomplishments which may be full and rich with relevant experiences.**

3. **A résumé portrays what you can do by revealing what you have done.** A well-written résumé is a must. If your writing skills are not as well developed as the decision maker, you run the risk of being seen as a poor communicator. When in doubt, give your résumé to a person whose judgment you trust and whose writing abilities you respect. If your résumé is easily understood by a stranger or friend who is not an expert in your field, then chances are you are beginning to be understood.

4. **A résumé should have broad appeal.** The language and the examples used should not be written to a particular function, industry, or geography, to avoid precluding the possibility of an opportunity outside of your previous industry. For example, a skilled industrial engineer should be able to effectively cross over from the chemical industry to assembly-line manufacturing of components for fire extinguishers.

5. **A résumé should be results oriented. A results-oriented résumé is generally more powerful and impressive than one which highlights only responsibilities.** Obviously, the more impressive the résumé, the greater the likelihood that you will be called for a telephone screen.

6. **A résumé needs to avoid the obvious.** Presumably, the hiring manager will be knowledgeable about your field or your type of experience so you do not need to belabor how you did something if it's clear to a seasoned professional. Keep explanations simple and straightforward.

7. **A résumé cannot engage in puffery.** Do not, under any circumstances, lie or deliberately use misleading statements in your résumé. It will invariably "catch you" and your credibility will be completely suspect. Then, where are you? Your résumé has to be accurate, accu-

rate, accurate! If you were part of a team effort, don't indicate that you "led" the project if you didn't. Say instead that you "co-led." There is a distinct difference between honest, creative wording and false elaboration. Puffery is easily spotted by seasoned managers and skilled interviewers. If you get caught with your data down, your credibility may be irreparably damaged, and everything on your résumé is now suspect. Do not risk a golden opportunity for the sake of portraying something you are not or in possession of degrees or training you do not have. Employers will check you out if they are interested, so do not lie or cheat on your résumé. Besides, what you did will come out in the reference check anyway. When in doubt about a statistic, leave it off or verify it with someone in your former company.

8. **A résumé should be visually attractive and easy to read.** The vast majority of individuals handling résumés are scanning for quick first impressions. In our research, you have only 5 to 8 seconds to hook the résumé scanner with your cover letter and only 8 to 10 seconds to hook the scanner with your résumé. In fewer than 20 seconds, your résumé will be unceremoniously tossed into one of three stacks to be read in a more leisurely manner later. Clearly, it is to your advantage to have your résumé land in the high-priority stack first, since there are no guarantees that résumés in the other piles will ever be read.

We Take Our Accomplishments for Granted

Almost every one of us takes for granted the results we have achieved in our jobs throughout our careers. Whatever the jobs might have been. There is dignity in all work, no matter how menial. If you look hard enough you will find some way in which you contributed to your organization. Some of our accomplishments are recognized as being important, others are not. Therefore, it is important that you recall from memory, identify, and prepare an extensive list of at least 10 to 25 accomplishments or areas of significant responsibility and involvement. Why 10 to 25 accomplishments or key responsibilities? Why not only 2 or 3? You may be thinking, "I cannot possibly come up with 25 accomplishments, let alone list all of them on my résumé." You are right, such a list would be awkward and cumbersome. However, developing a lengthy list will do a number of things for you:

1. Build up the confidence that you have indeed accomplished a tremendous amount in your lifetime

2. Sharpen your awareness of the areas in which you possess abilities

3. Provide you with an in-depth base of information about your accomplishments and skills to talk about in interviews

4. Provide the necessary focus you need to be credible and enthusiastic in interviews

5. Aid you in seeing the results of your efforts in terms of contributions, rather than in job titles, job descriptions, or responsibility statements

6. Be the basis upon which your résumé will be built

7. Will allow you to respond effectively to the penetrating questions posed by a tough interviewer

Now do the exercise in Worksheet 20.

Highlighting Your Responsibilities and Results

Now that you have completed Worksheet 20, follow these steps to sort through your responsibilities and results:

1. Identify all your jobs and your relevant job duties. Please indicate the years involved. Keep in mind, the most recent or last 10 years of employment are generally the most relevant.

2. Use the brainstorming technique of jotting down these accomplishments, or major areas of responsibility, as fast as they come to mind. Do not worry about how well they are written, go for a long list. If you prefer, use a 3-x-5 card for each accomplishment.

3. After you have exhausted all possibilities, go back and identify time, location, and company for each result mentioned. This is the start of your fine-tuning process.

4. Next, assign an A, B, or C priority to every contribution. "A" priorities are those which have contributed a great deal to the company, perhaps required a lot of people, or were very difficult to achieve. "B" priorities are important but did not contribute quite as much monetarily. "C" priorities represent those activities which were necessary but not critical.

5. Fine-tune your accomplishments according to the following guidelines:

   • Describe your accomplishment in brief, crisp, and specific terms, highlighting the financial impact in terms of dollars, numbers, or percentage contribution ($, #, or %) whenever possible.

   • Your accomplishments should indicate to the reader how they made life easier, saved money, improved productivity, resolved problems, or attained something for the first time.

   • Begin your accomplishment statements with action verbs (Here are two examples: "**Saved** $85,000 by . . . ; **reduced** operating expenses $150,000 through . . .")

WORKSHEET 20
Accomplishment Triggers

Below is a list of common *action* verbs which may be helpful in triggering your memory about the jobs you held, the accomplishments you achieved, and the way you see yourself. You can even use them in writing your accomplishment statements. **CIRCLE** those that relate to what you have done. After you have circled all those that are relevant, go back and **HIGHLIGHT YOUR TOP-10 ACTION VERBS** to help you develop your accomplishment statements.

Accomplished	Enlarged	Performed	Strengthened
Administered	Established	Planned	Stressed
Achieved	Examined	Presented	Stretched
Analyzed	Expanded	Presided	Structured
Approved	Founded	Processed	Succeeded
Arranged	Generated	Produced	Superseded
Built	Governed	Promoted	Supervised
Catalogued	Grouped	Proposed	Systematized
Completed	Guided	Provided	Terminated
Conceived	Headed	Purchased	Traced
Conducted	Implemented	Recommended	Tracked
Consolidated	Improved	Recruited	Traded
Contracted	Improvised	Redesigned	Trained
Controlled	Increased	Reduced	Transferred
Converted	Indexed	Reorganized	Transformed
Coordinated	Installed	Researched	Translated
Created	Innovated	Reshaped	Trimmed
Cut	Introduced	Revised	Tripled
Delivered	Instituted	Scheduled	Uncovered
Demonstrated	Invented	Serviced	Unified
Designed	Investigated	Set-up	Unraveled
Developed	Launched	Simplified	Utilized
Devised	Led	Sold	Vacated
Distributed	Maintained	Solved	Verified
Directed	Managed	Sorted	Widened
Disapproved	Moderated	Sparked	Won
Doubled	Negotiated	Staffed	Withdrew
Earned	Operated	Started	Worked
Edited	Organized	Straightened	Wrote
Eliminated	Originated	Streamlined	

6. Describe any opportunities you saw and the recommendations you made that would have made this effort or your organization more successful or effective had one of them been implemented. Do not be concerned if you were *not* able to execute the program, for great projects get put on hold for a wide variety of reasons. What does matter is that you recognized some problems and acted to solve them. Companies are looking for problem solvers and people who are committed to being the best they can be.

To make your data collection easier and your credentials more reflective of what you have done, please consider *results* falling into three categories:

Actual results: Bona fide achievements based on your efforts.

Estimated results: Those results which are in the process of becoming. We refer to a new product in its first year of introduction that is expected to yield significant returns in its third year. So, perhaps the third year sales should be highlighted since it better reflects your true accomplishments.

Potential results: Those results which have not *yet* been even partially realized as a perfectly viable program, project, or system but might have been except for a valid reason. To that end, what would have the result been if the program had been fully executed? That is the potential result.

Do not overstate—or understate—what you did. Be honest, straightforward and aboveboard.

Accomplishments: What? So What?

Virtually everything you do or have done in your career has a bottom-line impact in some form or another, whether you realize it or not. Your responsibilities, tasks, projects, and duties represent the *What* of your job. The following guidelines and Worksheet 21 can assist you in identifying your career results:

1. **What.** Identify all the *responsibilities, duties, activities, tasks,* and *projects* for each job you held.

2. Assign a priority to each entry (*A, B,* or *C*) and begin to work on the *A* priorities first.

3. **So what?** After you have fleshed out your accomplishment statements as much as you can, ask yourself the question, *"So what? So what difference did I make?"*

WORKSHEET 21
What + So What? = "Result" ($, #, %)

Read the example below and complete the blanks for practice. You will probably find this exercise both very rewarding and somewhat frustrating; however, it will start you moving in the right direction. Remember, any new skill or effort employed at first seems awkward until you master it. Then it becomes easy—like driving a car or riding a bike.

Introduced new MIS system which *increased* productivity 17% gaining $173,000.

_____	increased	_____
_____	reduced	_____
_____	eliminated	_____
_____	avoided	_____
_____	led to	_____
_____	protected	_____
_____	enabled	_____
_____	built	_____
_____	consolidated	_____
_____	created	_____
_____	generated	_____
_____	improved	_____
_____	redesigned	_____
_____	_____	_____
_____	_____	_____
_____	_____	_____
_____	_____	_____
_____	_____	_____
_____	_____	_____

Ten Parts of a Résumé

Although your résumé needs to reflect the unique aspects of your background, some elements are common to most résumés:

1. Contact information
2. Objective
3. Career summary
4. Business experience and employment history
5. Accomplishments and responsibilities
6. Professional affiliations
7. Education
8. Patents, publications, awards, recognition
9. Military
10. Personal data

1. Contact Information

Name, address, telephone number—this section is all pretty straightforward. Center all the information with your name in all capital letters and all other contact data in upper- and lower-case type. Include your office telephone only if you are in private quarters and your repeated closing of the office door will not raise suspicions. If your residence phone is not covered during the day make some arrangements to have coverage through an answering service (more expensive) or a telephone answering machine. The only people hung up about telephone answering machines these days are people not looking for a job. Do not risk losing a call or an opportunity for an interview because you don't have telephone coverage. And don't assume that the persistent interviewer will track you down at home during evening hours. Who is looking for the job—you or someone else? Never, ever, assume someone is going to be as committed to your success as you are. Take responsibility for being easy to contact.

2. Objective

In most cases, we recommend against having an objective statement; these statements are either too limiting and restrictive or too broad and general to have any meaning. You run the risk of eliminating the possibility of being considered for several career options because the résumé scanner "pigeon-holed" you.

Protests aside, objective statements generally identify the type of position, the organizational level, and sometimes industry. For example:

Objective: To obtain a challenging Plant Manager position in the chemical coatings industry. Prefer nonunion plant environment.

Objective statements provide a helpful sense of direction for the reader if done well, but they are not for everyone:

- If your career objective is clear and you have no desire to consider other possibilities, then *include an objective statement.*
- If you have multiple career objectives or options, and the identification of them would be confusing for a prospective employer, then *exclude an objective statement.* Instead, plan on using your cover letters to isolate career options and use a career summary on your résumé.

3. Career Summary

Composed of 60 to 100 words, the career summary allows the résumé scanner to quickly determine if the résumé represents enough of a fit to continue scanning. Its goal is to boldly telegraph the quality and strength of the person behind the résumé—you! A career summary or background summary is a snapshot of:

- Functional areas of expertise
- Significant technical strengths or skills
- Relevant personal qualities
- Industries served
- Results realized

The following is an example of a good career summary:

CAREER SUMMARY

Demonstrated record of business turnarounds and launching new products in competitive categories. Broad background in general management, business development, strategic planning, and asset management. Known for quickly developing creative solutions to complex problems and for building and leading teams which produce results, increase sales, and enhance profits.

4. Business Experience

Identify organizations starting with the most recent employer first. If you are unemployed, indicate "start" date to present. Do not reveal a "left" date because some companies are still negative about interviewing people who have been terminated. Again, do not mislead, rather wait for the right time to indicate your status of "looking with the full knowledge and support of the company." If your career spans more than 25 years, you may wish to consider collapsing all the work (and the names of your employers) longer than 15 years ago under the title "Previous Business Experience," located just before the education section. If you use this summary listing of previous employers, be sure to write a solid summary paragraph (no more than 8 lines) which reflects the work which you have had or the titles and the type of companies. Significant gaps of employment should be identified, but minor gaps can be minimized by using only "years" of employment, instead of "months and years." Clarify any such gaps in the interview so you do not get "caught with your data down"! (Look at the second page of Bill Robbins's résumé at the end of this section; note the "innocent gap" of employment from 1986 to 1987, where he was actually unemployed from September 15, 1986 to February 2, 1987.)

Do not falsify any information. Obviously, you need to volunteer information which clarifies the situation, both past and present. If you have some significant issues concerning how to portray this on your résumé or how to verbalize it, you may wish to ask a respected senior business executive for his or her opinion.

When you are employed at a division or strategic business unit of a much larger, well-known organization, identify the major corporation first (in capital letters) followed by the division's name (in upper and lower case): ALCOA The Stolle Corporation

5. Responsibilities and Accomplishments

As previously indicated, organizations hire individuals who demonstrate they can both handle the responsibilities of the assigned job as well as produce results. To that end, a results-oriented résumé is highly advantageous. However, a résumé can be so skewed toward accomplishments that it becomes too busy with facts and figures. That's distracting and not effective. Ironically, rather than illustrating the ability to get things done, your résumé may indicate a preoccupation with "things" or that you are trying too hard to prove yourself.

6. Professional Associations and Affiliations

List only those technical or managerial associations that are appropriate to your organizational level or functions area. Do not include groups which you have long outgrown or societies which may limit your professional flexibility. Some associations may infer that your expertise (or how you view yourself) is much lower than it really is.

Avoid listing those affiliations that isolate your age, race, sex, marital status, or religion. Although community organizations are very worthwhile, for the most part they are usually inappropriate to list on the résumé. Exceptions to this are when your involvement is part of your company role (public relations, for example) or if it reflects a significant leadership capacity. Nonetheless, please be careful here; you don't want to create the impression that you spend a lot of your employer's time on your personal organizations.

7. Education

List the highest degree first. Identify the degree, field of study (or major), college or university, and year of graduation. If you have a graduate degree, as well as an undergraduate degree, list them both. Do not list your high school diploma or an associate degree if you have a higher degree. If you have a high school diploma only, list it with any additional post–high school education, such as vocational education or company seminars. If you are a recent college graduate or are returning to the workplace after some absence, you may wish to include your college or university grade point average (GPA), provided it is at least a B average. Any GPA less than a B average may mistakenly highlight that you feel a C grade is something to be proud of, whereas an employer may see you as only an average performer. Although this might be true, don't inadvertently raise a red flag advertising that fact.

8. Patents, Publications, Awards, Recognition

If you have a limited number of these, it is probably best to highlight them in the résumé. However, if you have a significant number of patents, publications, or awards, you might want to develop an extra sheet labeled "Addendum." This information is more important for people with technical, scientific, medical, research, or academic backgrounds and goals than for administrative or general management people.

9. Military

Identifying military experience is certainly appropriate, provided you do not indicate dates which would reveal your age, particularly if you are in your late fifties. However, if you are marketing yourself as a leader and your highest rank was private first class, you may wish to reconsider telling people you were in the military.

10. Personal

This section is strictly optional. Most people exclude it on the grounds it is not "legally" necessary to provide personal, non-job-related data. Personal information gets in the way more than it helps. By excluding personal information no one is going to assume that you are hiding something, like you are really 75, or wanted by the police in three states, or so severely handicapped that you are unable to perform the job.

On the positive side, having some interesting facts about yourself provides the opportunity for some ice-breaking conversation. Many people have fascinating hobbies and interests and are rightfully proud of their skill in these areas. The greatest danger in listing hobbies, though, is that you and the interviewer could develop great rapport and be completely off the point of the interview. The goal of your résumé is to get you the interview. Your goal in the interview is twofold: highlight how you can contribute to the company and "peel back the layers" of the company so you know what you are getting into. Tragically, we have seen individuals build tremendous relationships with prospective employers yet did not get the chance to emphasize their credentials because they got caught up in their personal stories.

If you still want to highlight your personal interests and hobbies, just be careful. Keep things conservative. You may feel that you are reflecting your community involvement and personal commitment to your fellow man, but the résumé scanner may see it differently.

Hobbies, such as scuba diving, flying, sailing, sky diving, race car driving, sword swallowing, and tightrope walking may all reflect your courage and independence but they also highlight an unnecessary hospitalization liability for the employer. Soooo—when in doubt, leave it out.

Searching for the Best Résumé

One can create numerous "looks" for a résumé, but there are fundamentally four types:

- Chronological
- Functional
- Combination (chronological and functional)
- Narrative

1. Chronological Résumé

A chronological résumé is the most common type seen and displays your business career in reverse chronological order, beginning with the latest job first. This format quickly allows the reader to know what you are doing now and where you are most recently experienced. The assumption is that the most recent experience is also the most significant and revealing as to your responsibilities, accomplishments, skills, and abilities.

2. Functional Résumé

You should probably consider a functional résumé if your previous experience is clearly more significant than your recent experience or if you have worked in quite a number of different companies and you are interested in concealing your job hopping. A functional résumé would highlight disciplines and results achieved first, so the résumé scanner would, hopefully, focus on your results rather than the number of positions you've held.

A major concern that most employers have is that the functional résumé could be hiding something like advanced age, severe handicap, felony conviction, unstable work record, history of hospitalization, or major periods of unacceptable unemployment. (Raising a family is seen as completely acceptable, and many companies look very favorably upon women who interrupt their careers for this significant and tremendously challenging responsibility.)

3. Combination (Chronological and Functional) Résumé

The combination résumé is most often used to identify a number of promotions within the same company (perhaps even within the same function). The format lists the titles in reverse chronological order (with years only), followed by the major responsibilities of the most recent position(s) which are most representative of the breadth of the job and the talents of the person.

4. Narrative Résumé

Occasionally, situations call for a letter format of your credentials. This is particularly true if you are highlighting something from your background, skills, or abilities that is not readily obvious upon reading your résumé. A narrative résumé, by necessity, needs to be highly telegraphic and easily understood—almost at a glance. A "letter" résumé that is more than 1 page is clearly at a disadvantage in the stack of typeset and printed résumés.

Which résumé format is best for you? Because of the number of factors involved, there is no one right format. Your decision will be based on your credentials, career goals, and personal considerations. However, we prefer a chronological résumé, since it seems to be easier to read and appears to be the most straightforward. (See "The Résumé Format Preferred by Employers.")

Accordingly, the majority of the résumé samples included in the back of this section are chronological. However, Bill Robbins has a functional résumé and Mike Commons, George Pratt, Donna Samuels, and Sam Donovan all have combination résumés which have more than one job or job title combined because of similar job activities. *Whatever your choice, keep the layout crisp and highly telegraphic.*

The Résumé Format Preferred by Employers

FULL NAME
Street Address
City, State Zip Code
(XXX) XXX-XXXX

CAREER SUMMARY

This is a summary of your experience, knowledge, and abilities. The summary highlights for the reader who you are and what you are capable of doing.

PROFESSIONAL EXPERIENCE

CURRENT EMPLOYER   Year Started–Present

Describe your current employer, including the size of the business, number of employees, and the type of product or service provided.

Job Title   Year Started–Present

In two or three sentences, briefly describe your job responsibilities. Be sure to use the present tense and incorporate action verbs.

- Starting with an action word, describe in one or two sentences an accomplishment from your present job.
- When listing your accomplishments, you can describe problems you have solved, money you have saved, or new procedures you have developed.
- You can also highlight frequently performed tasks, special skills, or list projects you have completed.

Job Title   Year Started–Year Ended

In two or three sentences, briefly describe your job responsibilities in your previous position. Be sure to incorporate action verbs and use the past tense.

- List accomplishments from this position using those same action words you used above.
- You will use three to five accomplishments for each position you describe.

PREVIOUS EMPLOYER   Year Started–Year Ended

Describe your previous employer, include the size of the business, number of employees, and type of product or service provided.

Job Title   Year Started–Year Ended

In two or three sentences, briefly describe your job responsibilities in your previous position. Be sure to incorporate action verbs and use the past tense.

- List accomplishments from this position using those same action verbs you used above.
- You will use three to five accomplishments for each position you describe.

PREVIOUS PROFESSIONAL EXPERIENCE

After you have listed job titles and accomplishments for approximately 8 to 10 years of your most recent experiences, summarize your remaining work experience in a short paragraph.

EDUCATION

Degree	Major	College or University	Date Graduated
Graduate	Major	High School	Date Graduated

PROFESSIONAL AFFILIATIONS

List professional organizations you belong to. Include any offices you have held.

SPECIAL SKILLS

Skills   Equipment Operated   Software/Programs

Résumé Preparation Hints

- **STOP** working in this book.

- Begin to pull together all the relevant data on your background—the companies you've worked for, their size, their exact names, your titles, areas of accountability, and accomplishments. Complete all sections thoroughly. How well you complete the exercises here will have a direct influence on the quality and clarity of your résumé.

- The more details you provide, the more powerful a résumé you will create. Obviously, however, there is a balance to be struck in developing the details in your résumé. Too many facts and figures can be as distracting as too few data are disappointing.

- Reread the "Résumé Format Preferred by Employers" carefully and review the résumé samples which follow this section. Fill in all the information requested in each section. Missing information should be looked up. You may ask a friend or former colleague for details to complete this section. Missing information will weaken your résumé and, ultimately, your ability to interview convincingly.

- Have your résumé typeset and printed on heavy linen paper. We recommend number-24 bond. Check all data, company names, and spellings for accuracy. Errors of this nature are your responsibility, not your typist's or your printer's. Errors send a strong message that you may not be very disciplined and accurate in your work. Have others read your résumé for both clarity and typos. You should reread your résumé *backward—one word at a time*—to catch spelling errors.

- If you are interested in developing powerful, attention-producing cover letters that help you market your credentials, you will find the section which follows the résumé samples to be of help. (We have mentioned that here so you won't get lost in the number of résumé samples.)

Twelve Résumé Samples

J. Michael Commons	(Combination)	Sales and Marketing
William J. Robbins	(Functional)	Manufacturing
Roberta W. James	(Chronological)	Human Resources
Robert R. Kohn	(Chronological)	Marketing/General Management
James H. Roland	(Chronological)	Research & Development
Jennifer M. Heinz	(Chronological)	Administrative Professional
Frank L. Wade	(Chronological)	Product Development
Donna H. Samuels	(Combination)	Finance
Roger M. Dalton	(Chronological)	Operations
George C. Pratt	(Combination)	Materials Management
Kate M. Kendall	(Chronological)	Product Manager
Samuel M. Donovan	(Combination)	General Management

J. MICHAEL COMMONS
2312 Jefferson Street
Chicago, Illinois 60607
(312) 555-1212

CAREER SUMMARY

Experienced sales and marketing manager skilled in new-product introduction, field sales, account penetration, and dealer service. Develops effective promotional campaigns, training programs, and customer approaches that produce results and increase sales and profits.

BUSINESS EXPERIENCE

TCA CORPORATION   1967–Present

A leading international manufacturer and marketer of diverse food products.

Midwest Regional Sales & Marketing Manager   1984–Present

Manage, develop, and direct $300 million in annual sales nationally for specialty cereal markets. Establish and manage the performance of the marketing plan and $80 million operating budget. Build and strengthen 500 dealer/distributor network with 16 district managers.

- Comanaged the consolidation of two major divisions which eliminated $3.5 million in duplicate services and streamlined the sales forces, enabling greater market penetration.

- Increased sales $80 million by launching a $1 million product line through a national promotional campaign, including pricing, dealer presentations, and dealer incentives.

- Personally managed $15 million highly demanding "house accounts" from product design and prototype manufacturing to full production and product acceptance.

- Realigned territories nationally which increased dealer coverage 25% while eliminating $215,000 in excess travel expenses.

- Created and conducted product and sales meetings and training programs for company and dealer personnel, significantly increasing sales within multiline dealers.

Sales Manager: Eastern Region   1980–1984
Product Manager   1977–1980

Responsible for building and directing a $190 million region with 10 district managers covering 26 states. Operated as product manager, introducing products from concept through manufacturing, packaging, advertising, promotion, and dealer purchase.

- Achieved 120% of annual sales goal, contributing $30 million in additional annual sales.

- Designed and conducted highly impactful annual distributor award and training conferences which revitalized the company's image and support with distributors and was credited for sales increasing 18% in less than two years.

- Created and produced an innovative four-color catalog for new product lines which simplified ordering process and increased sales 5% during its first year.

- Recruited, trained, and directed 11 field sales professionals who currently manage $20 million in annual territory sales.

District Sales Manager: Southwest   1967–1977

Developed and managed one of the company's largest sales territories (Houston), selling to this rapidly growing market. Implemented the marketing plans and expanded customer support.

- Increased annual sales 26% through target marketing, creative selling, dealer presentations, and quality customer service.

- Received Special Achievement Award in 1978 and Salesman of the Year in 1979.

PROFESSIONAL AFFILIATION

Sales and Marketing Executives International (SMEI)

EDUCATION

MBA	Marketing	Northern Illinois University	1967
BBA	Marketing	University of Notre Dame	1965

Graduate School   Sales/and Marketing Program   Syracuse University   1985

PERSONAL

Married, three children.   Excellent health.
U.S. Army, E-4.   Honorable Discharge, 1961.

WILLIAM J. ROBBINS
Three Wilkshire Court
Cincinnati, Ohio 80045
(513) 555-1212

Experienced general manager with a demonstrated track record in manufacturing, maintenance, engineering, and facilities requirements. Skilled in production enhancements, operational troubleshooting, preventive maintenance systems, and team building. Able to contribute equally well in turnaround situations with mature products or with emerging technologies and new products.

RESPONSIBILITIES AND RESULTS

Manufacturing and Operations

- Increased profits over $600,000 annually through the development and implementation of a highly effective QC effort which reduced the number of defective parts by 95%.

- Established a reliable order processing and follow-up system which accelerated replacement parts sales $900,000 annually. The time to deliver parts dropped from an average of over 75 days to under 30 days.

- Initiated an on-line MRP system for inventory control and purchased parts based on min-max manufacturing requirements. Eliminated stock shortages, reduced special production runs, and secured favorable price concessions from raw material suppliers. Total annual savings exceeded $230,000.

- Negotiated the interest-free use of a special milling machine for a year which will save $912,000 in annual labor and outside machining costs. Productivity is expected to increase 75% annually.

Engineering and Maintenance

- Developed and installed a fully integrated, on-line preventive maintenance program which reduced operational downtime 23% and improved productivity 12%. Annual profits increased $3 million.

- Generated $1.7 million in annual savings by consolidating functions and by implementing management controls, cross-training, and innovative productivity improvements.

- Redesigned manufacturing process equipment which eliminated the need for $2.5 million in capital expenditures while improving overall productivity 15%.

- Added $250,000 in annual profits by manufacturing parts in-house, which reduced the dependency on third-party manufacturers. Purchased molds and dies and negotiated favorable raw material purchases with foundries, finishers, and suppliers.

BUSINESS EXPERIENCE

THERMOFORMER, INC.   1987–Present

Director of Manufacturing and Operations

Responsible for the turnaround and development of manufacturing, production, purchasing, shipping and receiving, material handling, and maintenance. Reporting to the president, develop annual and strategic plans and manage an operating budget of $6.5 million.

POPULAR PRODUCTS, INC.   1981–1986

Manager of Engineering and Maintenance

Provided the strategic direction to maintenance, facilities, and engineering. Managed process and productivity improvements, safety and health, operator training, and vendor selection. Directed a work force of 150 and a $9 million capital budget.

THE MONTBERRY COMPANY   1978–1981

Associate Director of Engineering and Technical Services

Built and directed a highly skilled technical group providing hands-on consulting support to plants throughout the United States in operational troubleshooting, maintenance, equipment development, engineering, and process improvements.

PREVIOUS BUSINESS EXPERIENCE

Held increasingly responsible maintenance and engineering management positions with ABC, Inc. and General Corporation, directing production supervisors, industrial engineers, mechanics, machinists, and general laborers for diverse operations, buildings and grounds, and security.

Developed the annual and strategic plans, set policy, and directed programs which achieved manufacturing efficiencies and material savings.

PROFESSIONAL AFFILIATIONS

American Institute of Plant Engineers
The Packaging Institute

EDUCATION/PERSONAL

Lake Forest Graduate School of Management   Managers Program
Moraine Valley Community College   Industrial Supervision

Married, three children. Health excellent. United States Navy, NCO.

ROBERTA W. JAMES
One Bridge Lane
Lake Forest, Illinois 60045
(708) 555-1212

CAREER SUMMARY

Experienced employee relations manager and attorney-consultant skilled in labor relations and EEO. Demonstrated hands-on record of cost reductions, productivity improvements, contract negotiations, arbitration, grievance management, union decertification, and directing union-free environments.

BUSINESS EXPERIENCE

HEALTH CARE CORPORATION   1976–Present

Corporate Manager Employee Relations   1986–Present

Provide hands-on employee relations direction to $4.2 billion manufacturing group and major information services business unit. As lawyer-consultant, responsible for merger/acquisition issues, union avoidance, union relations, EEO/AAP, labor cost reduction, productivity improvements, employee training, and organizational restructuring.

- Successfully defeated major union organizing campaign by the Teamsters in a 2700 employee facility. Protected core business, generating $500 million in product sales annually, by maintaining its nonunion status.

- As merger transition team member, completely revised corporate human resource policies and procedures and provided strategic direction to 200 offices and facilities, domestically and within Puerto Rico, encompassing 40,000 employees.

- Established and directed a Review and Appeal Board that evaluated and justified all 450 merger-related corporate staff terminations, representing more than $30 million in annual payroll savings. No discrimination claims or lawsuits resulted.

- As chief spokesperson, effectively negotiated the collective bargaining agreement with a 120-person union which enabled the sale of a $20 million stainless steel subsidiary.

- Developed proactive union prevention videos and supervisory development programs which oriented more than 2400 employees to the company's commitment to remain union-free.

- Managed legal consulting budget of $100,000, directing contingent of outside lawyers handling diverse labor and EEO issues.

Divisional Human Resource Manager   1983–1986

Directed human resources for six autonomous divisions employing 1600 people, generating $320 million in annual sales. Managed compensation and benefits, safety, EEO, organizational planning, training and development, employee relations, and union relations.

- Originated and directed the human resource department which supported and kept pace with the 45% sales growth of an acquisition to $37 million annually. Business unit achieved "Best-Managed Company," based on its performance.

- Comanaged the turnaround of a hostile employee relations climate by introducing operating and management practices which ultimately led to the decertification of a recently organized OCAW union. Operating cost savings exceeded $6 million annually.

- Comanaged the sale of a small, specialized $2 million health care business unit, including handling of international Teamsters Union representative, turnover of all personnel files and records, and complete technology transfer.

- Increased profits $1.5 million annually by introducing and directing a comprehensive Employee Participation and Involvement Program in three facilities encompassing 800 employees. Product quality increased, manufacturing costs decreased, and labor relations improved.

Manager Labor Relations   1980–1983

Provided strategic labor and employee relations direction to 23 diverse manufacturing and distribution facilities throughout the United States and Puerto Rico. Maintained nonunion environments and managed NLRB activity, union-organizing campaigns, contract negotiations, and the grievance process.

- Successfully defeated aggressive union organizing campaigns conducted by the Teamsters, Rubber Workers, International Association of Machinists (IAM), and Bandero Roja (Puerto Rico).

- Created and introduced a proactive "how-to" union avoidance guide and trained 30 employee relations managers in its use. Topics included signs of organizing, card signatures, management rights, employee communications, distribution of materials, and handling work slowdowns/stoppages, violence, or sabotage.

- Saved $2.5 million in annual labor and campaign costs for three major domestic facilities by eliminating all union-organizing activity. Developed, refined, and implemented progressive labor relations and employee relations policies, for both unionized and nonunionized settings.

- Directed a corporatewide organizational climate/employee opinion survey which encompassed 20,000 employees, identifying operational and employee relations problems and opportunities. Productivity and process improvements saved $5 million annually.

PREVIOUS BUSINESS EXPERIENCE   1967–1980

Held increasingly responsible management positions in labor relations, EEO, and personnel relations for the Health Care Corporation and The W.C. Johns Company.

- Directly responsible for handling EEO charge activity, OFCCP audits, and for coordinating employment-related litigation. Protected $250 million in government contract business and avoided EEO payouts totaling $1.5 million.

- Responsible for labor relations in a management trade association of 120 companies, employing 5500. Handled arbitrations and NLRB activity.

- Negotiated and administered eight union contracts including: Carpenters, Cement Masons, Ironworkers, Millwrights, Operating Engineers, and Teamsters.

EDUCATION

JD	College of Law	University of Denver	1972
BA	Psychology	American University	1966

Licensed Attorney

ROBERT R. KOHN

(616) 555-1212   1101 Campau Drive, Holland, Michigan 49423

CAREER SUMMARY

Accomplished general management executive with P&L experience in marketing, distribution, and operations. Direct and manage businesses, new products and strategies to achieve sound operating earning results.

Highly participative, team-building management style establishes high personal performance standards with strong loyalty to company goals.

BUSINESS EXPERIENCE

MIDWEST SUPPLY CORPORATION   1976–Present

A leading international $3.5 billion supplier of industrial products.

Vice President: Midwest Area   1979–Present

P&L general management responsibility for $91 million region with 235 employees in four operating locations. Develop and direct operating earnings plan and market share strategies. Manage assets, manufacturing, sales, inventory, financial, distribution, and employee motivation and development.

- Achieved consistent 28% annual earnings improvement and grew the business 22% annually for five years.

- Centralized the order-processing function, reducing operating costs $500,000, and improved order turnaround and customer relations.

- Restructured and refocused the sales organization, achieving 21% decrease in staffing while increasing sales $2 million annually.

- Spokesman for the *Compensation Task Force* established by the corporate president. Defined key compensation and recognition policies adopted by the corporation.

- Installed participative training and operating efficiencies in a $5 million manufacturing plant. Decreased labor costs 20% and increased operating profits 6%.

- Recognized as top performer in 1983 and received president's *Business Excellence* award for exceptional management of earnings, sales, profit margin, and expense ratios.

Director of Marketing   1978–1979

Directed all marketing, advertising, product introduction, technical liaison, and market research for this $750 million division. Managed six product managers.

- Negotiated agreement with a new manufacturer for a state-of-the-art product. Increased market share from 15% to 65% in one year.

- Conducted supplier business analysis which led to strong supplier relationship and to acquisition of two companies valued at over $100 million with $35 million sales.

- Formed a product introduction team to promote a highly competitive prime vendor program. Signed up an additional 5% of all customers in the United States with a year-to-date sales increase of $10 million.

- Highly goal-oriented management approach has led to over 50% of product managers being promoted to vice president positions.

Regional Manager   1976–1978

Complete P&L responsibility for a $12 million regional distribution center with a $1.2 million operating budget and 22 people. Managed operating plan, customer service, quality, inventory, and transportation.

- Increased sales 38% in one year, achieving 110% of earning plan and recognition as the top sales increase region in 1978.

- Increased sales $4 million and improved a weak customer service situation through selective product selling and increased quality standards.

Product Manager: Hospital Supply Division   1976–1977

Nationally responsible for sales of $125 million surgical and anesthesia product lines. Negotiated with manufacturers and directed product quality, cost, pricing, delivery, sales, and customer service.

- Introduced the respiratory products line, quickly generating 30% market share valued at over $20 million annually.

PRIOR BUSINESS EXPERIENCE

Operated as sales representative for Conglomerate Industries (1971–1976), directing up to ten sales representatives in do-it-yourself flooring covering business. Increased sales 45% annually and added 40 new retailers per year.

EDUCATION

BS	Business Administration	University of Delaware	1971
	Finance for Non-Financial Managers	Wharton Business School	1981
	Executive Marketing Program	Columbia University	1982

JAMES H. ROLAND, PhD
203 West Old Plum Grove Road
South Bend, Indiana 46619
(219) 555-1212

CAREER SUMMARY

Experienced technical manager skilled in scientific program development and management. Demonstrated abilities in R&D, marketing, business development, consumer affairs, and public relations.

Known for building teams which produce results, creating innovative solutions to complex problems, and for high-profile technical association contributions.

BUSINESS EXPERIENCE

THE CONGLOMERATE COMPANY   Specialty Products   1981–Present

Senior Manager Technical Center   1986–Present

Manage R&D, product evaluation, staff development, and industry association contacts. Provide professional/technical support to international operations, regulatory affairs, legal, sales and marketing, public relations, and customer service.

- Provide the Center's strategic direction and corporate input regarding product specifications and product claims validation for 110 product labels representing $650 million in revenues.

- Through effective product specification development, testing, and reporting, repositioned a major product line into a premium category greatly expanding its potential for distribution. Third-year sales are expected to increase three-fold to $300 million.

- Protected a $150 million product line by identifying a significant flaw in it and by developing a test program which resolved the problem.

- Improved the testing output of the R&D facility 25% while holding staff constant, resulting in $100,000 annual profit gain.

Manager Technical and Consumer Information Centers   1984–1986

Directed technical and preference testing, consumer response, claims validation, regulatory affairs, and marketing interface for major products. Had complete product development responsibility for $100 million worth of product lines.

- Eliminated $3 million in annual product costs by utilizing raw material substitutes with no loss of quality.

- Reduced operating expenses $250,000 by consolidating activities, streamlining priorities, and reducing departmental headcount 25%. Overall productivity increased two-fold.

- Developed an effective consumer information function for a $400 million business unit, cutting the customer response time 50% with existing staff through solid leadership and management controls.

R&D Manager: Technical Products Division   1981–1984

Provided the strategic direction for R&D, clinical quality assurance, technical staff development, and product and preference testing. Managed new products from concept, test designs, data collection, summarization, reporting, and technical support.

- Effectively managed application R&D through the sale of this $300 million division to a major competitor.

- Coordinated and assessed the company's cooperative testing program, evaluating two new products expected to yield $25 million in sales annually.

- Developed an interdisciplinary program which upgraded the department's involvement with and influence throughout the division.

THE HOMAN COMPANY   1965–1981

Product Manager   1978–1981

Responsible for P&L, marketing, and strategic planning for $5 million in specialty and generic products. Had extensive public relations exposure in TV, radio, and print media.

- Conceived a new product which generated $3 million in annualized sales. Directed the research, developed the literature, and marketed the product throughout the United States.

- Enhanced gross profits $200,000 by developing a product-tracking system which balanced manufacturing and sales demands. This approach greatly improved production scheduling and finished goods inventory availability.

- Responsible for the strategic product development and multilevel marketing for a unique product which generated $14 million in 1989 worldwide sales.

PREVIOUS BUSINESS EXPERIENCE

Operated as **Research Head: Application Research** (1970–1978) and as **Scientist and Project Leader** (1965–1970) for Homan, managing research for health-related products.

EDUCATION

UNIVERSITY OF MINNESOTA   Minneapolis, Minnesota

Doctor of Philosophy	Technical Research	1965
Masters of Science	Chemistry	1962

Complete listing of patents, publications, honors, awards, associations, and professional activities available.

JENNIFER M. HEINZ
56585 Quince Road
Portland, Oregon 91664
(503) 555-1212

CAREER SUMMARY

Experienced administrative manager, skilled in providing complete administrative support to sales, customer service, and general manager. Excellent interpersonal and organizational skills with the ability to quickly resolve conflicts and generate solutions.

Effective in:

- Unisys CPC, Professional Write and Professional File
- Typing and filing
- Toshiba Printer (P351SX)
- Mailing machine, and diversified office machines and telephone systems

BUSINESS EXPERIENCE

FORERUN   A Simpson Company   1983–Present

A leading $200 million philanthropic organization supporting the arts, free enterprise, and start-up ventures.

Senior Administrator

Responsible for administrative and secretarial support to the executive director, managing partner, and 26 associates serving more than 300 accounts and benefactors.

- Access recipients needs, quote prices for projects as large as $250,000, and interface with philanthropy, marketing, distribution, benefactors, and the public.

- Regularly create and maintain records and reports on giving activity and volume, including daily order and shipment totals by region, by territory, by customer, and by product line.

- Develop own correspondence, handle the entire staffs' correspondence, draft letters, and maintain numerous confidential files.

- Provide giving information to benefactors and distributors and direct dealer/ architect inquiries to the appropriate parties.

- Initiate customer credit requests for special pricing allowances, promotions, display material, co-op merchandising support.

- Make complete travel and meeting arrangements, handling all logistics for ground and air transportation, overnight accommodations, and scheduled meetings.

- Keep the operations running smoothly, on a day-to-day basis as the philanthropy team travels a significant part of the time.

TECHNICS ENGINEERS GROUP, INC.   1980–1983

Executive Assistant

Provided comprehensive administrative and secretarial support in accounts payable, accounts receivable, sales, and general accounting. Developed and generated numerous reports for management's use in directing the business.

- Had full responsibility for accounts payable for all four company locations. Maintained vendor files, prepared vouchers for computer checks, and prepared manual checks, as needed.
- Edited and formatted monthly project reports on clients, including the preparation of statistical tables, charts, graphs, and cover layouts.
- Assisted the project manager in developing proposals detailing services, costs, and personnel requirements to complete the work, on time and within budget.

THE BAND-AID CORPORATION   1974–1980

Executive Assistant: The Housing Assistance Supply Experiment (H.A.S.E.)

Coordinated and organized meetings of the Board of Trustees of the Housing Allowance Office (H.A.O.), as well as H.A.S.E. Prepared the agenda, took official minutes, and performed wide-ranging secretarial functions in support of the chairman and the board.

- Prepared and submitted monthly reports to Band-Aid's corporate group in Washington, D.C., which enabled a detailed report to be developed for HUD.
- Participated in Band-Aid/H.A.O. meetings regarding operational matters and on productivity teams working to improve managerial and operational effectiveness.
- Performed administrative and secretarial duties for site office staff and visiting Band-Aid and HUD personnel.

PREVIOUS BUSINESS EXPERIENCE

Held responsible secretarial positions for **Technical Management Business Group** (1973–1974) and **Columbia University** (1970–1973). Responsible for daily office operation, including purchasing, collection of student payments, and limited leasing duties.

EDUCATION

Columbia University   New York City   Business   1970–1973
Graduate   Business   Washington High School   1968

Ongoing education includes various secretarial and administrative courses.

FRANK L. WADE
1215 Maremont Circle
Cleveland, Ohio 12498
(216) 555-1212

Experienced general management executive, responsible for corporate P&L in high-technology businesses. Profitably operate existing businesses and expand market growth by developing new products and market strategies while ensuring cost-effective, quality manufacturing operations.

BUSINESS EXPERIENCE

HOSPITAL PRODUCTS COMPANY   1978–Present

A $100 million manufacturer of disposable health care products to institutional and retail markets.

Group Vice President   1982–Present

Responsible for achieving the corporate profitability goal. Direct sales, marketing, advertising, quality assurance, research and technical development. Coordinate financial, manufacturing and engineering areas.

- Increased corporate book value 400% in four years by introducing 100 new products, which increased overall company sales 75%.

- Successfully started three new business units, using new technologies, which generated first-year sales of $4.5 million.

- Captured 40% share of a $15 million market in 18 months by initiating and implementing a focused new-product marketing strategy against a major competitor.

- Restructured the $40 million domestic retail distribution network and established controls in each segment. Defined service, facility, and merchandising standards, replaced underperformers and achieved $2 million in additional sales annually.

- Identified, coordinated and implemented manufacturing and engineering cost reductions exceeding $6 million in two years.

- Developed and introduced a comprehensive, quarterly P&L statement by product line for each business unit. In a major product line, efficiency improvements increased gross profit 5% in six months.

Vice President, Director: Research and Development   1978–1982

Built a productive, business-oriented technical group to firmly position Hospital Products Company as an industry leader in new products and technology. Restructured and turned around an unproductive technical organization which generated new products achieving 40% of the retail sales.

- Increased sales $4.5 million annually by creating and introducing more than one new product per month for five years.

- Created and launched three proprietary product features in an $8 million business expansion, establishing product-line leadership in the industry.

PLACE LABORATORIES   Hospital Products Division   1975–1978

A $300 million division manufacturer of high technology medical products for the hospital industry.

Manager: Biomedical Concepts and Material Research

Developed medical products from concept through pilot plant and market introduction.

- Generated a $50 million business through developing, manufacturing and successfully introducing a highly sophisticated, precision I.V. pump line.

- Rescued a $50 million product line from total loss when a supplier's factory burned, by quickly developing and successfully launching a new PVC film for flexible I.V. containers. New PVC products provided line expansion with six new I.V. solutions and allowed entry to a new $30 million marketplace.

- Conducted state-of-the-art research in areas of artificial kidney and pancreas research, cell culture development, and burn care products.

MEDICAL INSTRUMENTS COMPANY   1967–1975

A $1.1 billion producer of medical care instruments and products.

Manager: Extracorporeal Devices

Developed medical products, processes, and formulas. Primary products were in areas of biomedical engineering, biochemistry, and pharmacology.

- Developed and commercialized several, major state-of-the-art products involving complex technical field interdisciplines, manufacturing, and quality management. These resulted in first-year new-product sales of $6 million in hemodialysis and blood detoxification.

EDUCATION

Ph.D.	Material Science	University of Illinois	1967
MS	Physics	Case Western Reserve	1965
BS	Physics	Reed College	1963

DONNA H. SAMUELS

127 Jefferson
Winfield, Texas 90601
(214) 555-1212

CAREER SUMMARY

Experienced controller skilled in financial reporting, systems development, and cost accounting/analysis. Proven track record of effectively managing company assets, auditing, taxes, accounts payable, and accounts receivable. Build and direct teams of professionals which produce results and increased profits. Certified public accountant.

BUSINESS EXPERIENCE

SERVICES AMERICA, INC.   1986–Present

Assistant Controller   1987–Present
Audit Director   1986–1987

Responsible for corporate accounting and $250 million in assets. Manage financial reporting, cost accounting and analysis, pricing analysis, accounts payable, accounts receivable, billing, tax/payroll administration, and banking relations. Routinely interface with the parent company's finance and operations groups in England.

- Developed, staffed, and managed the performance of a proactive accounting staff which kept pace with the company's phenomenal growth in three years from $75 million to $375 million in annual sales.

- Increased cash flow $24 million annually while trimming bad debts $400,000 per year by creating and implementing effective financial controls and a computer-aided billing system.

- Eliminated the loss of $3 million in finished goods annually by conducting an in-depth operational and financial audit that generated comprehensive reforms, management controls, and security measures.

- As a due diligence management team member, participated in the acquisition and divestiture of four operating companies valued at $141 million.

- Provided the financial strategic analysis, direction, and support to the complete turnkey design, construction, and start-up of a $35 million, highly automated, state-of-the-art manufacturing facility.

WARD & COMPANY, INCORPORATED   1984–1986

Audit Supervisor

Directed operational and financial audits for up to 260 stores, merchandising centers, purchasing and corporate functions, nationally. Managed a staff of 10 professionals and a $1 million budget.

- Increased net revenues $40 million by recommending and implementing changes in accounting methods for service contracts.

- Reduced capital expenditures $30 million for "Specialty Stores," the company's new strategic marketing thrust for the 1990s. Established broad-based financial controls, management processes, performance measures, and capital expenditure guidelines.

- As an expert witness and consultant in real estate litigation, successfully defended the company, thus avoiding more than $300 million in escalated lease payments. Additionally, recovered $8.5 million in lease overcharges.

ABC INTERNATIONAL, INC.   1980–1984

Audit Manager

Comanaged the staffing, development, and training of a proactive start-up audit team, supporting six business units, worldwide. Operated as hands-on manager, conducting/directing audits and performing special projects.

- Materially aided in the divestiture of a $10 million subsidiary by compiling its financials for the buyer's due diligence team and its external auditors.

- Avoided $100,000 in annual external auditor fees through enhanced competencies of internal audit team.

- Codesigned and executed fully integrated computer systems which significantly enhanced management decision making, asset utilization, and financial reporting.

PREVIOUS BUSINESS EXPERIENCE   1978–1980

As **Staff Auditor** for **Big Eight CPA Firm**, performed audits of client financial statements and prepared tax returns for diverse partnerships, corporations, and individuals. Experienced in consolidations, LIFO inventories, FASB pronouncements, and SEC reporting requirements.

EDUCATION/PROFESSIONAL AFFILIATIONS

BA   Accounting   Texas College   1978

Ongoing management and technical education includes courses in general financial management, materials management, inventory management, MRP, and systems development.

AICPA (American Institute of Certified Public Accountants)
IIA (Institute of Internal Auditors)

ROGER M. DALTON
1241 Grove Court
Garden Grove, California 54004
(714) 555-1212

Experienced general manager with significant P&L responsibility. Accomplished in sales, marketing, and operations management. Successfully develop and execute short- and long-range profit and strategic plans within fast-paced organizations. Build and lead highly motivated, results-oriented teams which create and manage business growth.

BUSINESS EXPERIENCE

ADAMS LABORATORIES   1974–Present

Director of Operations

Total P&L responsibility for the operations of $1.4 billion distribution and marketing division with $110 million in expenses and 1800 employees. Direct new-product introductions, MIS, customer service, purchasing, assembly, distribution, and materials management. Serve on President's Advisory Council setting policies and establishing business direction.

- Directed operations team of 125, managing 60 profit centers with inventories exceeding $130 million.

- Consolidated and streamlined three major operating units which effectively responded to a dramatically changing marketplace, generating $25 million in additional earnings.

- Achieved $18 million in expense reductions by improving productivity 38% and eliminating redundancies. Reduced operating expenses as a percent of net sales, from 14.0% to 11.5% over a four-year span.

- Reduced on-hand inventory $30 million and eliminated $8 million annually in cost of capital.

- Directed $30 million annual construction plan which upgraded 35 distribution centers and expanded aggregate space utilization 45%.

Held increasingly responsible line and staff management positions in Boston, Minneapolis, Houston, and Chicago with Adams Laboratories from 1974 to 1980. Managed $30 million distribution operation of 145 employees and 5000 products based in Boston with profit centers in Buffalo and Hartford.

EDUCATION

MM	Management	Northwestern University	1986
BA	Economics	University of Notre Dame	1974
	Executive Marketing	Columbia University	1983
	Financial Management	Wharton Business School	1980

GEORGE C. PRATT

(317) 555-1212   40 Circle Drive, Indianapolis, Indiana 46236

CAREER SUMMARY

Experienced material management executive skilled in vendor selection, contract negotiation, inventory control, production planning and scheduling, and customer service. Effectively develops strategies, programs, and systems which enhance customer satisfaction, profits, and sales.

BUSINESS EXPERIENCE

FOODS CORPORATION Commercial Products   1970–Present

Commercial Products is a $2 billion broad line food service manufacturer and distributor of consumable and durable products.

Procurement Manager: Indianapolis District	1988–Present
Procurement Manager: Chicago District	1982–1988

Responsible for materials management and purchasing of $95 million worth of finished goods, supplies, and services for a $110 million sales district. Source and evaluate vendor manufacturing capabilities and negotiate national contracts. Manage a $7 million inventory and direct a proactive team of 15 results-oriented professionals.

- Eliminated $1.3 million in cost of capital and inventory expenses annually by increasing inventory turns and eliminating slow moving products.

- Generated new sales of $863,000 annually by codeveloping and launching the VIP Vendor Program for key suppliers. Program developed partnership relationships and yielded $180,000 in "sign-up" revenues.

- Increased annual profits $3 million by effectively negotiating and utilizing rebate programs with manufacturers, vendors, and brokers.

- Increased annualized product sales $700,000 through product-line expansion, long-range "buy-in" efforts, target marketing, the development of promotional pieces, and product training.

- In the $60 million Chicago sales district, created, developed, and directed a purchasing group responsible for "least landed cost" procurement of 2700 line items for more than 287 suppliers and brokers, nationally.

- Codeveloped the strategies for the upgrading and redo of all private label packaging for $512 million worth of branded product sales.

- Achieved customer service levels of 99% (next-day delivery) through strategic purchasing, highly motivated staff, and efficient storage, retrieval, and expediting.

Manager of Administration   1981–1982

Directed sales, marketing, and operational administrative support functions for the rapidly expanding key accounts/national accounts department. Worked closely with major chains, supervising private label production requirements and special needs.

- Set up procedures which guaranteed close to 100% service level for 18 major accounts generating $200 million in sales annually.

- Developed and presented the operating and strategic business plans and prepared material for significant presentations to senior management and client principals.

- Provided comprehensive marketing research, production planning, order entry, proposal bid preparation, and general administrative support to the regional sales force and major customers.

Manager of Inventory Control   1979–1981

Had corporatewide inventory management responsibilities. Provided consulting support to general managers and established and managed food service inventory ordering and control systems in 32 districts throughout the United States.

- Provided the strategic direction to inventory management, personnel training, product handling and distribution corporatewide for this $2 billion business unit.

- Assisted in the start-up for four new district warehouses (317,000 sq. ft.), including training of personnel, ordering products, and setting up purchasing and material-handling systems.

PREVIOUS EXPERIENCE 1970–1979

Held progressively responsible procurement planning and inventory control management positions in numerous locations. Worked extensively with frozen foods, meat, poultry, seafood, and nonfood products and comanaged production planning and scheduling for the Wilkes Barre, Pennsylvania plant.

EDUCATION

MBA	Business Administration	Magnesium University	1989
BA	Industrial Engineering	Technological University	1970
	United States Air Force	E-4/Inventory Specialist	1966–1970

KATE M. KENDALL
1716 North Wells Street
San Francisco, California 97345
(815) 555-1212

CAREER SUMMARY

Accomplished marketing manager with exceptional creative abilities, project management, and analytical skills. Proven expertise in the development of marketing and sales strategies, advertising, and promotional programs. Strong leader able to build and direct interdisciplinary task force teams.

BUSINESS EXPERIENCE

TARO DESSERTS   1988–Present

Senior Product Manager: Retail Division   1989–Present

Manage marketing for the $88 million retail dessert business with four major product lines. Responsible for business analysis, developing marketing plans, and implementing programs.

- Maximized profit on major product line, reducing trade spending from 17% of net sales to 7% by initiating price rollback and returning to a traditional promotional plan.

- Developed a turnaround strategy projected to halt sales decline in a key product by shifting promotional spending.

- Averted a proposed $1.2 million capital expenditure for packaging changes through targeted consumer market research.

Business Manager: Deli Division   1988–1989

Responsible for planning, analysis, and implementation for a new business venture including development of promotions and new products.

- Reduced product development and introduction time frame over 50% to successfully introduce a major new product to the marketplace.

- Developed comprehensive selling and merchandising strategy for highly profitable, underdeveloped business segment projected to increase sales 100%.

- Gained an 18% sales increase on focus items by obtaining full-line placement authorizations from retailers and reducing out-of-stock situations.

FAST FOODS, INC.   1986–1988

Product Manager: New Products   1987–1988
Associate Product Manager   1986–1987

Managed the development and introduction of new poultry products including analysis of business trends, new-product concept research, promotional events, advertising, and packaging.

- Created and implemented roll-out and expansion strategies for five major new product lines.

- Revised positioning strategy on a unique product line to increase consumer interest.

- Created a successful new advertising campaign which exceeded standards for purchase intent and recall supporting a $60 million product line.

DRESSING, INC.   1985–1986

Brand Assistant

Responsible for specialty products segment, test marketing of a new product, coordinating multibrand promotions, and business analysis.

- Developed new product promotion coordinating activities and acted as liaison across brands and with outside agencies.

PREVIOUS BUSINESS EXPERIENCE

Held a position as a summer intern in marketing for Major Consumer Company. Worked as a sales representative for A & A, Inc. building sales in the Chicago metropolitan area for the full line of confectionery products.

EDUCATION

MBA	J.L. Kellogg Graduate School of Management Northwestern University	1985
BB	Western Illinois University	1979

SAMUEL M. DONOVAN
1121 Furlong Drive
Wilkes Barre, Pennsylvania 18705
(717) 555-1212

Experienced general manager with significant P&L responsibility. Demonstrated abilities in sales, marketing, manufacturing, operations, distribution, asset management, and strategic planning. Builds and manages highly motivated, results-oriented teams that increase sales, enhance profits, and manage rapid business growth.

BUSINESS EXPERIENCE

COWITT COMMUNICATIONS CORPORATION 1985–Present

Vice President, Sales and Marketing	1986–Present
Director of Operations and Administration	1985–1986

Provide the strategic direction for sales, marketing, distribution, operations, human resources, capital spending, and administration for a $1.2 billion division encompassing five states and 21 branch offices. Develop and manage a $30 million expense budget and 450 employees.

- Restructured and revitalized the selling effort which will increase sales $120 million in 1990. Eliminated one of the four layers of management, which achieved significant efficiencies, improved communications, and saved $480,000 in operating costs.

- Increased field productivity 44% through effective management controls and reporting, focused accountability, enhanced recognition, and training.

- Generated $85 million in new revenue by turning around a troubled telemarketing operation and improving performance from no growth to 35% growth with the unit becoming the company leader in quality and output.

- Avoided the loss of $30 million in existing base revenue through restructuring the account maintenance organization.

- As director of Operations and Administration, managed profitability, human resources (1600 employees), distribution ($40 million in assets), construction ($32 million in capital), and real estate (55 sites).

MAGEE SUPPLY CORPORATION 1973–1985

Vice President and General Manager 1980–1985

Had complete P&L responsibility for $150 million manufacturing and assembly operation with 26 locations and 385 employees. Directed marketing and sales, production, quality assurance, product development, engineering, purchasing, and safety.

- Increased revenues from $48 million at a 34% annual compounded growth rate by developing and implementing comprehensive manufacturing, operations, sales, capital expansion, and human resource strategies.

- Managed the turnkey start-up and staffing of two new businesses generating $40 million in annual revenues. Company became the market leader within two years, while tripling assembly capacities with a $10 million capital expansion effort.

- Improved productivity 38% and achieved $2.5 million in manufacturing cost reductions through quality circles, "production scoreboarding," plant automation, and new employee performance standards.

- Established cost accounting and computer support systems that eliminated more than $200,000 in manufacturing variances annually and reduced on-hand inventory $900,000.

- Reduced raw material costs $1.5 million annually through an aggressive OEM purchasing and vendor performance program.

PREVIOUS BUSINESS EXPERIENCE

As **Vice President, Packaging** for Magee Supply Corporation (1976–1980), responsible for profitability and general management of a $48 million assembly business, turning it around, and growing it from $10 million.

- Through a highly dedicated team, attained 20% annual compounded sales growth, four consecutive years.

- Built, staffed, and launched seven new operations and significantly modernized eight plants with productivity gains exceeding 30% and the direct labor/sales ratio dropping from 8.5% to 6.0%.

- Reduced turnover from 54% to under 18%, within three years, saving $110,000 in annual recruitment, training, and productivity costs.

- Increased market share from 31% to 52% in a highly competitive commodity marketplace by elevating service, productivity, finished goods quality, aggressive marketing, and product bracketing.

Held increasingly responsible positions in operations, distribution, and customer service for Magee Supply Corporation (1973–1976).

EDUCATION

| MBA | Marketing | University of Illinois | 1973 |
| BS | Business | University of Illinois | 1970 |

Executive Marketing Program   Columbia University   1980

Writing Powerful Marketing Letters

Target Company
Target Company: Follow-Up after Rejection
Search Firm/Employment Agency
Search Firm/Target Organization: Follow-Up
Personal Contact
Advertisement: First Mailing
Advertisement: Second Mailing
Interview "Thank-You"
Interview: Needs/Capabilities
Follow-Up: Rejected after Interviewing
Offer-Too-Low Follow-Up
New Position Accepted

Each time you mail a résumé, send it with a cover letter which reinforces your credentials and accomplishments, indicating the value you can add to the organization.

A well-written letter is a key ingredient in securing an interview. Directed at decision makers, letters connect you with the people most likely to grant you interviews.

Keep in mind that you are dealing with résumé scanners, and you have only 5 to 8 seconds to hook the scanner with your letter and 8 to 10 seconds with your résumé. Eighteen seconds or so is not a tremendous amount of time to get your point across.

Effective letters exhibit the following attributes:

1. Are brief, crisp, succinct, and punchy.
2. Are directed to a specific individual, not merely an office holder.
3. Contain specific information about your credentials, responsibilities, accomplishments, and potential benefits to the reader's organization.
4. Request specific action to be taken by the organization.
5. State the action you plan to take with the individual in the organization.
6. Are professional, yet warm and inviting.
7. Mention your commitment to follow up with a telephone call.

Cover Letter Format

The following format outlines the key points to be made in a cover letter:

1. Introduction
2. Objective
3. Qualifications and Accomplishments
4. Request for interview

Advertisement Letters

Advertisement letters may begin as follows:

> **Your recent advertisement indicated you were seeking an experienced (position title). Since your requirements and my background appear to be a match, you may find my credentials of interest.**

Search Firm Letters

Letters to search firms could start with:

If you are conducting a search for a (position title), you may find my credentials of interest. Enclosed is a résumé for your consideration.

Following are several sample cover letters.

Letter to:
TARGET COMPANY
(Managerial)

Dear:

As an experienced sales and marketing manager, I am skilled in new-product introduction, field sales, account penetration, and dealer service. My strengths lie in developing distinctive promotional campaigns and training approaches which quickly produce results, improving sales and profits.

I am actively pursuing challenging sales management and marketing management opportunities in which I can significantly contribute to a growing organization. I work equally well in companies with mature product lines or in companies with emerging technologies.

Highlights of my accomplishments include:

- Developing and managing a 500 dealer-distributor network, selling diverse product lines.
- Reorganizing two major divisions and streamlining territories, nationally, which enabled greater account penetration and increased sales.
- Creating and managing impactful promotional campaigns, dealer meetings, and sales training programs for the field sales force.

I would sincerely appreciate the opportunity to discuss with you how I could contribute to the growth and profitability of your organization.

Thank you for your consideration. I look forward to hearing from you soon.

Sincerely,

J. Michael Commons

Enclosure: Résumé

Letter to:
TARGET COMPANY
(Administrative)

Dear:

An experienced administrative support professional can be a valuable asset to an organization. As a creative problem solver, I have the ability to exercise sound business judgment, evaluate priorities, and direct special projects.

Highlights of my background in facilities management, customer service, training, and meeting planning include:

- Protecting a $200,000 project for a major client by locating misdirected product and expediting its delivery to meet a critical installation deadline.
- Coordinating five major renovations of a 5000-sq.-ft. showroom involving a total capital budget of $900,000.
- Directing administration and project support for regional manager, area sales operation manager, and sales representative of a leading furniture manufacturer.

I would like to talk with you personally to discuss how my excellent interpersonal, communication, and management skills could contribute to your team.

You can reach me at the number listed above. Thank you for your consideration. I look forward to hearing from you.

Sincerely,

Jennifer M. Heinz
Enclosure: Résumé

Follow-Up Letter to:
TARGET COMPANY—AFTER REJECTION
(Managerial)

Dear:

Thank you for the consideration which you gave my credentials. Your company is one of the top five companies that I have selected as an ideal place to work. I sincerely appreciate your indicating that you will keep my résumé on file and your commitment to contact me as an appropriate fit develops.

I am sorry that there were no opportunities for me at this time. However, I feel my marketing and sales background can significantly contribute to your company's long-range plans, at some point.

Thank you for maintaining my candidacy as a priority. I hope that you will keep my résumé in your top desk drawer as your growth plans materialize. I would like to be considered in your core group of good people that will "make it happen."

I will keep you posted on the progress of my job search, from time to time, and to see if we can keep in touch about future possibilities at your organization. I will call you within the next few days for the purpose of introduction.

Sincerely,

J. Michael Commons

Enclosure: Résumé

Letter to:

SEARCH FIRM/EMPLOYMENT AGENCY

(Managerial)

Dear:

As an experienced sales and marketing manager, I am skilled in new product introduction, field sales, account penetration, and dealer service. My strengths lie in developing distinctive promotional campaigns and training approaches which quickly produce results, improving sales and profits.

I am actively pursuing challenging sales management and marketing management opportunities in which I can significantly contribute to a growing organization. I work equally well in companies with mature product lines or in companies with emerging technologies.

Highlights of my accomplishments include:

- Developing and managing a 500 dealer-distributor network, selling diverse product lines.
- Reorganizing two major divisions and streamlining territories, nationally, which enabled greater account penetration and increased sales.
- Creating and managing impactful promotional campaigns, dealer meetings, and sales training programs for the field sales force.

I would sincerely appreciate the opportunity to discuss with you how I could contribute to the growth and profitability of your client's organization.

Thank you for your consideration. I look forward to hearing from you soon.

Sincerely,

J. Michael Commons

Enclosure: Résumé

SEARCH FIRM/TARGET ORGANIZATION
When your credentials appear to be too strong
for available opportunities.*
(Managerial)

Dear:

I wonder if you could help me? I need feedback on my enclosed résumé. Several firms have commented that my credentials appear to be too strong, given the opportunities I am seeking, namely, a senior marketing role at the managerial or director level.

I am pleased that these people feel my record reflects steady growth and significant contribution. My team and I accomplished quite a bit over the years, and the enclosed résumé reflects this. However, I am open to the possibility of making a lateral move for an opportunity to significantly influence and contribute to an organization's growth and profitability.

Would you please consider critiquing the enclosed? Given my career goals (sales manager or director of sales), do you feel my résumé is: fine (make no changes), too strong (power down), or too weak (power up)?

I would sincerely appreciate your candid response. Please feel free to mark right on my résumé and send it back to me. Thank you for your consideration.

Sincerely,

J. Michael Commons

Enclosure: Résumé

  * *Note:* It is recommended that this type of letter be used sparingly and with some caution. You don't want to communicate that you don't know how to put your résumé together or that you're desperate. However, the result you desire is that your credentials will stand out and be seen as powerful and appropriate.

Letter to:
SEARCH FIRM/EMPLOYMENT AGENCY
(Administrative)

Dear:

If you have a current search for an **administrative support professional,** the enclosed résumé may be of interest to you.

Highlights of my background in facilities management, customer service, training, and meeting planning include:

- Protecting a $200,000 project for a major client by locating misdirected product and expediting its delivery to meet a critical installation deadline.
- Coordinating five major renovations of a 5000-sq.-ft. showroom involving a total capital budget of $900,000.
- Directing administration and project support for regional manager, area sales operation manager, and sales representative of a leading furniture manufacturer.

I would like to talk with you personally to discuss how my excellent interpersonal, communication, and management skills could contribute to your client's team.

You can reach me at the number listed above. Thank you for your consideration. I look forward to hearing from you.

Sincerely,

Jennifer M. Heinz

Enclosure: Résumé

Follow-Up Letter to:
SEARCH FIRM/EMPLOYMENT AGENCY
(Managerial)

Dear:

I appreciate your continuing interest and support of me, even though we haven't yet connected with an active search assignment. As promised, I am keeping you updated on my situation, as it might be useful to you as things develop on your end.

If you recall, it has been a few weeks since I first wrote to you concerning my intentions for a senior marketing position. Since launching my search, I have had initial exploratory interviews with eight companies and have been slated three times by search firms for additional discussions. While I am pleased and flattered with the level of activity, it is still early in my campaign, and I am intent on making the best possible career match.

If you have an active or pending search for which I might fit, it may be mutually advantageous for us to meet within the next several weeks.

My primary objective remains a responsible sales and marketing position. My secondary targets are senior management positions in business development or consulting. I remain flexible regarding location and employment terms.

Your help and support are sincerely appreciated and remembered.

Sincerely,

J. Michael Commons

Enclosure: Résumé

Letter to:
PERSONAL CONTACT
(Managerial)

Dear:

It was a pleasure to touch base with you recently concerning my career search. Thank you for your care, concern, and support. As we discussed, personal networking is certainly the most effective means of creating the level of visibility that ultimately leads to interviews and later offers. Thanks for the help.

To recap our discussion, I am an experienced sales and marketing manager skilled in new-product introduction, field sales, account penetration, and dealer service. My strengths lie in developing distinctive promotional campaigns and training approaches which quickly produce results, improving sales and profits.

Highlights of my accomplishments include:

- Developing and managing a 500 dealer-distributor network, selling diverse product lines.
- Reorganizing two major divisions and streamlining territories, nationally, which enabled greater account penetration and increased sales.
- Creating and managing impactful promotional campaigns, dealer meetings, and sales training programs for the sales force.

After reviewing my credentials, I would appreciate hearing about names of individuals and/or companies you feel it would be appropriate for me to contact.

I look forward to hearing from you soon. Thanks again for your help.

Personal regards,

J. Michael Commons

Enclosure: Résumé

Letter to:
PERSONAL CONTACT
(Administrative)

Dear:

It was great to talk with you recently. I really appreciate your support and welcome any leads that you might have. As promised, I am enclosing my résumé for your review; perhaps, it will trigger some additional ideas.

To recap my background, I am an experienced administrative support professional with a strong background in facilities management, customer service, training, and meeting planning.

Highlights of my background include:

- Protecting a $200,000 project for a major client by locating misdirected product and expediting its delivery to meet a critical installation deadline.
- Coordinating five major renovations of a 5000-sq.-ft. showroom involving a total capital budget of $900,000.
- Directing administration and project support for regional manager, areas sales operation manager, and sales representative of a leading furniture manufacturer.

As a creative problem solver, I have the ability to exercise sound business judgment, evaluate priorities, and direct special projects. I would like to hear about any leads or opportunities which may be appropriate.

You can reach me at the number listed above. Thanks again for your help, care, and support. I look forward to hearing from you soon.

Personal regards,

Jennifer M. Heinz

Enclosure: Résumé

Letter to:
ADVERTISEMENT
(Managerial)

Dear:

In response to your recent advertisement for (title) in the (paper's name), please find enclosed my résumé for your consideration.

As an experienced sales and marketing manager, I am skilled in new product introduction, field sales, account penetration, and dealer service. My strengths lie in developing distinctive promotional campaigns and training approaches which quickly produce results, improving sales and profits.

Highlights of my accomplishments include:

- Developing and managing a 500 dealer-distributor network, selling diverse product lines.
- Reorganizing two major divisions and streamlining territories, nationally, enabling greater account penetration and increased sales.
- Creating and managing impactful promotional campaigns, dealer meetings, and sales training programs for the field sales force.

I would sincerely appreciate the opportunity to discuss with you how I could contribute to the growth and profitability of your organization.

Thank you for your consideration. I look forward to hearing from you soon.

Sincerely,

J. Michael Commons
Enclosure: Résumé

> *Note: Dear Sir* is an acceptable and preferred salutation to a blind ad rather than *Sir or Madam.*

Letter to:
ADVERTISEMENT
(Administrative)

Dear:

In response to your advertisement for (position) in the (newspaper), I am enclosing my résumé for your review.

My experience as an administrative support professional can be a valuable asset to your organization. As a creative problem solver, I have the ability to exercise sound business judgment, evaluate priorities, and direct special projects.

Highlights of my background in facilities management, customer service, training, and meeting planning include:

- Protecting a $200,000 project for a major client by locating misdirected product and expediting its delivery to meet a critical installation deadline.
- Coordinating five major renovations of a 5000-sq.-ft. showroom involving a total capital budget of $900,000.
- Directing administration and project support for regional manager, area sales operation manager, and sales representative of a leading furniture manufacturer.

I would like to discuss how my interpersonal, communication, and management skills could contribute to your team. You can reach me at the number listed above. Thank you for your consideration. I look forward to hearing from you.

Sincerely,

Jennifer M. Heinz
Enclosure: Résumé

> *Note: Dear Sir* is an acceptable and preferred salutation when responding to a blind ad rather than *Sir or Madam.*

ADVERTISEMENT (SECOND RESPONSE WITHIN THREE WEEKS)
(Managerial)

Dear:

Several weeks ago I responded to your ad for a sales and marketing manager in the (paper). I can well appreciate that you have been inundated with responses and have not been able to get back to every person. Nonetheless, I would like to indicate my continued interest.

To recap, I am an experienced sales and marketing manager skilled in new product introduction, field sales, account penetration, and dealer service. My strengths lie in developing distinctive promotional campaigns and training approaches which quickly produce results, improving sales and profits.

Highlights of my accomplishments include:

- Developing and managing a 500 dealer-distributor network, selling diverse product lines.
- Reorganizing two major divisions and streamlining territories, nationally, which enabled greater account penetration and increased sales.
- Creating and managing impactful promotional campaigns, dealer meetings, and sales training programs for the field sales force.

I would sincerely appreciate the opportunity to discuss with you how I could contribute to the growth and profitability of your organization.

Thank you for your consideration.

Sincerely,

J. Michael Commons

Enclosure: Résumé

ADVERTISEMENT (SECOND RESPONSE WITHIN THREE WEEKS)
(Administrative)

Dear:

I responded to your ad for a Customer Service Coordinator in the *Sunday Herald* on February 12th. As I have not yet received a response from you, I am taking the liberty of writing to you again.

You requested an individual who had excellent customer service and administrative skills, one who could work alone with little supervision. With my background in furnishing administrative support to an outside sales force, I know I can make a valuable contribution to your team.

I have usually worked very independently, handling routine correspondence, typing, and telephone work while the sales force was out of the office. I have often received calls from upset customers, listened to their concerns, soothed their "ruffled feathers," and then followed the problem through to a cost-effective solution.

I am enclosing a second copy of my résumé for your review. I hope you will contact me to discuss how my experience could add to the growth and profitability of your company.

Sincerely,

Jennifer M. Heinz

Enclosure: Résumé

Letter to:
INTERVIEW "THANK-YOU"
(Managerial)

Dear:

Thank you for the recent interview. It was a pleasure to discuss employment opportunities with you at _____ for the position of _____ . As I indicated, I am interested in pursuing matters further and welcome the opportunity to do so. My proven track record fits what you are looking for at _____ , and I am confident that we could be of mutual benefit.

I was particularly intrigued with the way your business was structured. Your commitment to generating a sound return for investors, while not losing the standards of quality manufacturing or effective people management, impressed me.

As agreed, I will call you in several days to see how we can proceed. Thank you again for your consideration.

Sincerely,

J. Michael Commons

Enclosure: Résumé

INTERVIEW "THANK-YOU"
NEEDS/CAPABILITIES
(Administrative)

Dear:

I would like to thank you for the opportunity to interview at XYZ Corporation last Friday. Everyone I met made me feel quite welcome. I understand what you meant when you explained that XYZ was a large company with a "family feeling."

After hearing about your plans for the future and your current departmental needs, I feel that I am ideally suited to help your team achieve its goals. I am pleased that you feel the same.

Highlights of my background and your requirements match well.

YOUR NEEDS	MY CAPABILITIES
Establish product-tracking system	Protecting $200,000 for a major client by locating misdirected product and expediting its delivery to meet a critical installation deadline.
Manage HQ design and renovation	Coordinating five major renovations of a 5000-sq.-ft. showroom involving a total capital budget of $900,000.
Provide field administrative support	Directing administration and project support for regional manager, area sales operation manager, and sales representatives.

I am eager to join the "XYZ family" and look forward to speaking with you soon to discuss how we can take "the next step."

Sincerely,

Jennifer M. Heinz

Letter for:
FOLLOW-UP: REJECTED AFTER INTERVIEWING
(Managerial)

Dear:

Thank you for the favorable and positive consideration which you provided me during my interviews at _____. I felt truly welcome and everyone I met was extremely gracious and professional.

I am sorry that this was not the opportunity for me, however, I feel my marketing and sales background can significantly contribute to _____ long-range plans, at some point.

Thank you for committing to maintain my candidacy as a priority. I look forward to your keeping my résumé in your top desk drawer as the new growth plans of _____ materialize. I would like to be considered in your core group of good people that will "make it happen."

As promised, I will keep you posted on the progress of my job search from time to time and periodically review my future possibilities at _____.

Best regards,

J. Michael Commons

Letter for:
FOLLOW-UP: REJECTED AFTER INTERVIEWING
(Administrative)

Dear:

I was, of course, disappointed to hear that I came in second in your selection of an administrative assistant for the Training Department of ABC Company. You are known as a premier employer in this area and are on my list of the top five companies I would like to work for in my next job.

If you should have any future needs, either in Training or another department, I would like to be considered for the position. I have extensive experience in providing secretarial support to large staffs, planning meetings, and coordinating the work of outside contractors. I can work equally well as a sole contributor or as a member of a team.

Once again, I was very impressed with what I saw in my visits to ABC Company. Your enthusiasm for your products is contagious. I will touch base with you periodically to update you on the progress of my search. I look forward to pursuing new opportunities in the future at ABC Company.

Sincerely,

Jennifer M. Heinz

Letter That:
FOLLOWS AN OFFER WHICH IS TOO LOW
(Managerial)

Dear:

Thank you for the opportunity to meet and revisit the specifics of _____ offer and the advantages in joining your company. I appreciated your observations concerning the dynamics of a smaller manufacturing organization and how it might support some of my longer-range goals. The possibilities are exciting, and I am even more interested in joining your team.

As we discussed, there are several distinct benefits to bringing a more senior manager, like myself, on board. I offer an experienced marketing management approach, balanced with a keen sense of cost-effective innovation.

I am confident that you can see how the breadth and depth of my background can contribute to your immediate needs as well as represent a sound investment for your future growth.

_____, I am enthusiastic about the opportunity to join _____ and would like to creatively explore how we can reach a mutually agreeable compensation arrangement.

While money is important, it is not the only career consideration, as we both acknowledged. My interest is in remaining whole, salarywise, over a year's time. I would like you to consider some "wrinkles" which might include a hiring bonus and/or a guaranteed 6-month and 12-month salary increase.

Let's discuss how we might come to a mutually satisfactory and rewarding employment decision. Thank you for your consideration.

Personal regards,

J. Michael Commons

Letter That Announces:
NEW POSITION ACCEPTED
(Managerial)

Dear:

I wanted to get back to you and say thank you for all your help, care, and support over these last few months. As you know, I have conducted a selective campaign of existing job opportunities, during which time I explored not only the private sector but consulting and equity situations as well. I felt this was a critical time in my career, especially in terms of future growth and job satisfaction.

With these priorities in mind, I have recently accepted a position with Acme Corporation as its National Sales Manager. I will be responsible for

_____

_____

_____

_____

My new contact information is:

J. Michael Commons
National Sales Manager
Acme Corporation
1216 Any Street
Plainview, PA 55500
(713) 555-1212

I genuinely appreciate your consideration and response to my initial contact and look forward to a continuing professional relationship in the future. Thanks again.

Personal regards,

J. Michael Commons

Letter That Announces:
NEW POSITION ACCEPTED
(Administrative)

Dear:

I would like to thank you for the help and support you offered me during my recent job search campaign. Your concern and ideas were very much appreciated.

I have recently accepted a position with XYZ Company as the Customer Service Coordinator. As you may know, XYZ Company is a $150 million company which designs, manufactures, and sells widgets internationally.

In my position as Customer Service Coordinator, I will answer incoming customer calls, furnish information, solve problems, and forward calls when necessary. In addition, I will be furnishing secretarial support to the director of Customer Support Services.

I am excited about my new position. XYZ Company is a growing concern and I hope to be able to grow with it. You can reach me at:

Jennifer M. Heinz
Customer Service Coordinator
XYZ Company
1587 Success Lane
Anytown, USA
(312) 555-1212

Thank you again for your support. I look forward to talking with you again soon.

Personal regards,

Jennifer M. Heinz

BUILDING AND MANAGING YOUR REFERENCES

A Painful Lesson Learned

Jennifer Heinz was born and raised in New York City. She attended a local community college and met her husband, Tom, while he was in the master's program at Columbia University in New York. Jennifer and Tom would be described by friends as "bright and highly assertive." Their acquaintances would describe them as "pushy and relentless." After college, Jennifer enjoyed 10 years of an increasingly successful administrative secretarial career with a major Wall Street conglomerate with worldwide operations.

Tom had an opportunity to be promoted into a senior management role in another firm out of New York City. After much negotiation, Tom was swayed, and the family moved to a medium-sized city in the midwest. Soon after relocating, Jennifer landed a senior administrator's role in a well-funded, conservative philanthropic organization, a truly plum job.

Jennifer and Tom immediately felt the cultural change from the East Coast. Both of them were used to being highly confrontational and straightforward in their dealings with business colleagues and neighbors. Unfortunately, they didn't catch on until all the social invitations dried up and Jennifer's peers stopped asking her for advice: Being isolated didn't stop Jennifer; she just did what she knew worked— she became all the more aggressive. After all, it had worked for her in the past. Her peers described her as extremely competent . . . for a bulldozer, for they felt "run over" by Jennifer more than once. Jennifer was in a classic "mismatch" between her personality and the conservative corporate culture of her firm. She knew intuitively that she was beginning to wreak havoc on her career, and now was the time for her to be in a more challenging role in a more assertive company environment. To that end, Jennifer put together and sent out a very strong résumé, followed up with networking calls.

As Jennifer picked through the rubble of her business and social relationships in building a personal network of leads for a new job, she was horrified to discover that many "golden opportunities" in town evaporated because of the way she was perceived by others in positions of influence. Only after being confronted by her old mentor and best reference, did Jennifer become painfully aware of how she impacted others. Once she cleaned up these damaged relationships and improved her interpersonal skills, Jennifer was able to successfully land an entry-level management role utilizing her strong administrative and organizational skills.

References Are Valuable and Should Be Used with Care

Your references are people who can speak enthusiastically and effectively about your career focus, performance, abilities, personal traits, and character. You will need to select five to seven business references with approximately four to five additional "back-up" business references, if requested. You will also need three personal references (for application forms that sometimes request them). Your business references, in all probability, will be called. You must select them carefully, prepare them well, and use care in giving out their names.

How to Present Your References

Do not put references on your résumé. List them on a separate page of paper with your name, address, and phone number at the top. If you would like to include a personal reference—someone who knows you outside of your job—make sure that person knows how to answer questions well, will say good things about you, and will make sense in your business context.

Before selecting a reference to submit to prospective employers, follow several important steps. Do not ever take for granted that your references are fully prepared to support you in your targeted job. Your references may view you from only a narrow perspective. It's your job to broaden their view of you through discussions of your career goals and by reminding them of your accomplishments.

Give out your references in the following situations:

1. When asked.
2. At the close of an interview in which you have a strong interest in the position, volunteer to provide a list of references.
3. As a follow-up technique to remain highly visible during a competitive interviewing period.

Do not mail references with your résumé, and do not "wear out" your references by having them answer questions about a job you do not want. If you are feeling coerced into providing a list of references, and you need to do so to "save face," identify only one to three people or indicate your reluctance to provide references at this time. If you do reveal references, you need to get back to these people and indicate your strategy and ask for their support on this "back-up" opportunity.

Do Letters of Reference Really Work?

You may not find letters of reference as helpful as they were 10 years ago. Employers don't trust them as they may omit data that might be unfavorable. While clerical, secretarial, and administrative employees often use reference letters, managers infrequently use them and executives rarely, if ever, use them.

Never let a letter of reference take the place of talking with your references personally. They will be contacted anyway. Most employers don't ask for or use letters of reference, so don't push your references for a letter of support. They will support you more readily over the phone than putting something down on paper.

Selecting, Interviewing, and Managing Your References

Before selecting people who will be your references, determine the key positive points you want presented. For example, if you are a chemist and you are ready for advancement to senior scientist, you will need people to say that you are both technically sound as well as an effective project leader. Identify the four major things you want most to be said in support of your job objective. Then, select those who are knowledgeable about these elements.

> ## STOP! Complete Worksheet 22 before proceeding further.

Who Should Provide A Reference?

Anyone who can speak knowledgeably and positively about your responsibilities, contributions, work skills, abilities, attendance, accomplishments, or effectiveness could be a *business reference*. Anyone who

WORKSHEET 22
Four Things You Want from Your References

Identify the four major dimensions or traits you want your references to highlight. They should be general enough to portray the breadth and depth of your strengths, abilities, and experience.

1.

2.

3.

4.

can speak positively about your personal background, reliability, personal habits, and character can be a *personal reference*. These may be neighbors, friends, pastors or rabbis, or even employees in your targeted company. Some companies will request only business references, so clarify the kinds of references they are seeking.

You may wish to consider the following as business references:

- Current or former bosses
- Other current or former supervisors in your company or previous companies
- Department supervisors
- Fellow employees or friends with whom you have worked
- Major clients, vendors, or consultants with whom you have worked
- Subordinates who can describe your managerial style

It is now time to select your references. From among the categories just mentioned, who are the ten people who will give you the best reference on your four key items you have just written? Select ten names (see Worksheet 23). Then narrow the list to your strongest six references. Now it's time to prepare people to be your references.

Ten Ways to Prepare Your References _____

Do not assume that you know what your references will say. Speak to them face-to-face (if possible) and ascertain how they will respond to questions before you give out their name. Companies do check references. They can be of great help to you, and they can also hurt your chances if they give a poor or lukewarm reference.

Keep in mind that, although you provide some references, prospective employers will interview previous bosses and/or coworkers. You have some control over the references you provide and very little control over your "automatic" references unless you take the initiative and meet with them to prepare and qualify them to answer questions about your past performance.

The following are 10 guidelines for preparing references:

1. Arrange for a meeting at which you ask if your possible reference would be willing to speak for you. Review with each reference the "Common Questions Your Reference May Be Asked" (see Worksheet 24).

2. Tell your references about the kind of job you are seeking. Ask if they are comfortable in recommending you for such a position. Give

WORKSHEET 23
My Potential References

1. Name: _____ Title: _____

Company: _____ Phone: _____

2. Name: _____ Title: _____

Company: _____ Phone: _____

3. Name: _____ Title: _____

Company: _____ Phone: _____

4. Name: _____ Title: _____

Company: _____ Phone: _____

5. Name: _____ Title: _____

Company: _____ Phone: _____

6. Name: _____ Title: _____

Company: _____ Phone: _____

7. Name: _____ Title: _____

Company: _____ Phone: _____

8. Name: _____ Title: _____

Company: _____ Phone: _____

9. Name: _____ Title: _____

Company: _____ Phone: _____

10. Name: _____ Title: _____

Company: _____ Phone: _____

WORKSHEET 24
Common Questions Your References May Be Asked

1. How long was the employee with your company?

2. What position or job did he/she hold?

3. What responsibilities did he/she have?

4. What were the employee's most significant accomplishments?

5. How long did he/she work in that position? (Mos/Yrs)

6. How long was he/she under your supervision? (Mos/Yrs)

7. Describe the employee's strengths.

8. Describe the employee's weaknesses.

9. How would you describe the employee's performance?

10. Provide an example of the employee's self-initiative.

11. Describe his/her attitude toward the job.

12. How would you evaluate his/her relationship with peers?

13. What was his/her last salary?

14. Would you consider him/her for rehire?

15. If you would not consider for rehire, give reasons:

them a copy of your résumé and familiarize them with the data. This review provides an opportunity for you to clarify your accomplishments.

3. Suggest that you would appreciate their especially strong recommendation in three or four key areas (review Worksheet 22). Ask, "If I outline those areas, would you be willing to try to work them into your recommendation?" Then, outline several specific areas of strengths or areas in which your competence is a key to success in gaining job offers.

4. Ask about weaknesses. "One of the questions I keep getting is one in which they ask about my strengths and weaknesses. I'm sure that you will get that weakness question. May I ask if there is anything that I should be aware of that might come up in response to a weakness question like that—so you and I, at least, are consistent?" See "Examples of Weaknesses as Overplayed Strengths" in Step 2.

5. With former bosses, clarify reasons for leaving. Tell them what you are saying, and ask if they are comfortable saying that as well.

In steps 4 and 5, if you disagree with your references:

- Listen carefully.
- Don't argue.
- Offer more favorable wording. Turn to "Examples of Weaknesses as Overplayed Strengths" in Step 2.
- Ask if they would be comfortable using more favorable wording.
- Thank the person.
- If you feel the reference they would provide would be negative, you may ask another close, former business associate to check this out.

6. Ask if it would be OK if you sent your reference a copy of your notes which you will jot down later, summarizing all the subjects you have covered. Suggest that it might be helpful as a reminder. Then, write up a *reference summary* using the format in Worksheet 25 and send it to your references with your thank-you note. Prepare an original, separate summary for each reference. Don't worry, the reference summaries will look very similar, so don't feel that you are creating a lot of extra work for yourself; you're not.

7. Thank your references for agreeing to support you. After your meeting, send a thank-you letter and your reference summary in which you confirm the points discussed.

8. Tell your references that you will let them know to whom you give their names so they will not be surprised when they are called.

WORKSHEET 25
My Reference Summary

Career Focus

_____

_____

Summary of strengths

_____

_____

_____

_____

_____

Developmental needs

_____

_____

_____

_____

_____

Reason for leaving

_____

_____

_____

_____

_____

9. Gain their commitment to call you if they are contacted. This enables you to more fully manage both the referencing process (because it keeps everyone in the communications loop), and it allows you to legitimately keep the pressure on prospective employers to press for reference checking. Presumably, this will be to your advantage: If a company checks you out early, given the strength of your references, you might very well "knock out" the other candidates under consideration for the job you're interviewing.

10. Ask if it would be okay to recontact your references to keep them posted of your career search, then do so periodically.

STOP!

Review the sample reference summary on page 148 written to a reference after a meeting.

Now turn to Worksheet 25 and write out a one-page summary using these ideas for each of your references to refresh their memories of your conversation when they are called. Forward a summary to each of your references.

Note: **Your reference summary is to be given *only* to your references—*not* to a prospective employer. Your reference summary is a written endorsement to be presented verbally by your references.**

Preparing Your Reference Sheet

Now that you have selected your references and spoken to them, you are now ready to prepare a handout of your references to be used in your campaign. This will, of course, be neatly typed as our example on page 150 illustrates.

You need to include each of your reference's name, title, company, and phone number with area code.

- You do not need addresses. Your references will be called by search firms or prospective employers.

- Use business or home phone as your reference wishes. If your references are OK with calls in the evening, then include the residence number.

- If one of your references is retired, put *formerly* before his or her title. If one of your references is unemployed, you may wish to consider the emotional state in which he or she is in before using as a reference. If

J. MICHAEL COMMONS
2312 Jefferson Street
Chicago, Illinois 60607
(312) 555-1212

REFERENCE SUMMARY

CAREER FOCUS

Mike is looking for an upper-level sales and marketing management position within a manufacturing or service environment.

SUMMARY OF STRENGTHS

Sales and marketing specialties include: Sales and profit improvement, market share increases, target-marketing strategies and programs, budgeting and planning.

Dealer development specialties include: Selection, development, performance management, and business growth. Provide ongoing strategic business planning support and guidance to dealer management.

Mike is qualified as a broadly experienced generalist with practical strengths in product development, customer relations, pricing, service, and national accounts. He is a team player who works well with shop floor people, financial staff, and cross-divisional people.

DEVELOPMENTAL NEEDS

Mike is a quick decision maker, and sometimes his pace gets ahead of his team and they see him as too demanding and impatient. He understands this and has learned to be more patient with slower moving staff to make sure that they fully understand his ideas. This has given him very good results. Sometimes Mike loses the "big-picture" on projects. He has learned to set up full project schedules to manage his detailed approach. He now is strong in accuracy and is also a good planner.

REASON FOR LEAVING

Michael has been moving well within the corporation since he joined it in 1967. Recently the company has found that it needed to consolidate the operations, due to slipping profitability. Upon the consolidation, there was no need for two senior sales and marketing managers, and Mike was the less seasoned manager. As there is no current line or staff position available, Mike has decided to pursue his career outside of the company with our full knowledge and support.

your potential reference is likely to be upset because of being unemployed and may damage you, you may wish to reconsider including him or her as a reference at this stage of your interviewing. If pressed by an employer to include your unemployed reference, then you may wish to do two things. First, qualify or alert the company to the fact your reference may still be a little upset about having been recently terminated, and, second, help your friend to get emotionally settled down and prepared for the reference call.

To help manage the reference-checking process, it is recommended that you identify several key points for each reference. Write a brief, crisp sentence or two that tells (1) how the person knows you, and (2) those things about you that this person is able to best describe about you. These brief descriptions help to condition the reference checker to focus on those areas which you and your references have already agreed are your strong points.

STOP!

1. **Study the sample page of business and personal references on page 150 to spark some ideas for your own reference list.**

2. **Complete Worksheet 26 incorporating your own language.**

Remember, list five to seven people who can speak with specific knowledge of your job performance abilities. State how they know you and the key characteristics they are best qualified to describe.

How to Offset Poor or Damaging References

First, don't *assume* the reference is poor. Find out by asking about the sensitive area. Most references don't really want to hurt you. They may just be hesitant about saying something negative and, as such, a comment may sound like lack of real support.

During your face-to-face meeting with your reference, offset a potentially damaging referral by rephrasing some of the comments. Negative comments like, "He is too impatient" could be worded, "He has a high sense of urgency." Before any reference meeting, prepare a list of your strengths and weaknesses (as overplayed strengths). Anticipate your reference's most typical comments, and be prepared to volunteer some weaknesses or developmental areas if there is any hesitation on the reference's part. Refer to "Weaknesses as Overplayed Strengths" in Step 2.

J. MICHAEL COMMONS
2312 Jefferson Street
Chicago, Illinois 60607
(312) 555-1212

BUSINESS AND PERSONAL REFERENCES

Mr. Fred C. Shefield
Vice President, Sales and Marketing
Backwater Corporation
(312) 555-1212

I reported to Mr. Shefield for 4 years as sales and marketing manager. Mr. Shefield can talk about my problem-solving skills, ability to create innovative marketing campaigns, and my track record of generating product sales and profits.

Mr. Bradley N. Ruben
Vice President and Treasurer
The Maxter Group
(312) 888-1111

When I was at Maxter, Mr. Ruben was the director, Product Management Group, for the USA, Canada, and Europe. He can effectively provide some insight into the ways I developed and managed people and my program development/planning skills.

Mr. Frederick P. Hudson
Director, Creative Design
Corporate Marketing Services
(217) 555-1212

Mr. Hudson is an advertising and marketing professional whose firm I have hired and directed on numerous occasions. He and others have seen me effectively balance a results-oriented approach with a distinctive flair for the creative.

Ms. Susan P. Watney
Manager, Human Resources
Raiters Corporation
(404) 123-5555

Susan is both a business and personal reference. She has known me for 15 years in positions of increasing responsibility. Susan has been reporting to me for three years.

WORKSHEET 26
My References

Name: _____ Title: _____

Company: _____ Phone: _____

Job characteristics this person would best support:

Name: _____ Title: _____

Company: _____ Phone: _____

Job characteristics this person would best support:

Name: _____ Title: _____

Company: _____ Phone: _____

Job characteristics this person would best support:

Name: _____ Title: _____

Company: _____ Phone: _____

Job characteristics this person would best support:

Name: _____ Title: _____

Company: _____ Phone: _____

Job characteristics this person would best support:

Name: _____ Title: _____

Company: _____ Phone: _____

Job characteristics this person would best support:

When references are clearly "bad news," follow these steps:

1. Work out a nondamaging way of talking about the problem.
2. Raise the issue yourself with a potential employer, telling it "your way."
3. Provide another reference with a different point of view on the subject.

Minimizing Potentially Weak References

If you are fairly certain that your boss will provide only a moderately strong reference, you may purposefully exclude him or her from your reference list . . . hoping that your prospective employer will not call.

We consider that your references fall into two categories: provided and automatic. *Provided references* are those people whom you've identified as knowing your talent, skills, and abilities. Those people are on your list, you've contacted them, they've agreed to support you, and you feel comfortable with what will be said as you have provided them with a reference summary. Your *automatic references* are those people to whom you reported, who provided you direction, or who were responsible for training you, either in school or on the job. It's logical to include your automatic references, unless there is something to hide or the relationship wasn't as strong as you'd like to portray.

Excluding your automatic references represents a potential "red flag" to an astute interviewer. Expect the question, "Why didn't you include your immediate manager as a reference, given that you are looking with his full knowledge and support?" (Good question, indeed. Keep reading.) While in the interview, you can minimize a potentially weak reference by a former colleague or boss by indicating something like the following:

> **I excluded my boss because given her heavy travel schedule and the way we worked independently from one another, she does not have as much knowledge of my results as the people I served. You are certainly welcome to call her, as long as you keep in mind that she doesn't know me as well as the references on my list.**

USING APPLICATION FORMS TO YOUR ADVANTAGE

A Minor Inconvenience with a Major Impact

Peter Adelman was ready. In fact, he felt more prepared for this interview than for all his other interviews combined. He had painstakingly developed a powerful results-oriented résumé that really highlighted his public relations and corporate communications credentials in the best possible manner. He had done his homework— both on the Acme Corporation, as well as on Acme's major competition, and the industry in general. He had utilized the on-line periodical listing services of the local and regional libraries for recent articles. He had tapped into his personal network for the "inside skinny" on Acme, and he had contacted two product buyers who had purchased both from Pete's company as well as Acme. In addition, Pete also had the most recent annual report, three of the last employee newsletters, and some product literature all supplied by his interviewer, Max Jordan— Acme's president.

Not only was Pete prepared mentally, physically he was set also. Those 15 extra pounds he carried on the job were a thing of the past, and his new Armani suit made him feel like a million bucks! He looked sharp, he was talented, he knew what the company needed from his research, and his background made him ideal for the top corporate public relations role.

Arriving at Acme's corporate headquarters, he pushed his way through the smoked glass revolving doors and strode across the polished marble flooring to the receptionist station. Despite all his preparation, Pete noticed a slight fluttering sensation in his stomach as he announced his appointment with Max Jordan. The receptionist coolly yet efficiently had Pete sign in and processed the over-sized visitor's badge for him to clip onto his new suit. Along with the plastic badge, she also set in front of him a green application form with the command, "Fill this out and bring it back to me. Then I'll let Mr. Jordan's secretary know you are here." Pete was taken back by her crisp, almost abrupt tone that seemed to imply that he had done something wrong and was being punished. He found this process somewhat intimidating and demeaning and his treatment not at all in keeping with his warm conversations with Max previously.

"Thank you for the application form. I would like to complete this later after Mr. Jordan and I meet and not before. We have a 1:00 meeting. Would you please let his secretary know that I am in the lobby now." The receptionist's retort: "They know you are here. It is standard procedure for all job applicants to fill out the application form. Have a seat and fill this out. I'm to buzz them when you are finished."

With his anger on the rise and his confidence crumbling, Peter settled into a lobby chair next to three other people well into their application forms.

Application Forms May Be Hazardous to Your Search

Why Do Companies Use Applications?

Companies use application forms to collect employment and personal data on job candidates in a standardized format. The argument for having an application form completed ahead of the interview is that it enables company personnel to quickly zero in on areas of interest or concern, including salary, reasons for leaving, immediate supervisors, references, health, any criminal record or physical handicap, titles, responsibilities, and accomplishments.

Peter Adelman's experience is not that uncommon. If you are being considered for a management role, do not be shocked if you are handed an application form and asked to complete it before being allowed into the "inner sanctum." And the unannounced screen by the personnel—what a surprise! While you may find this kind of treatment an affront, many companies use this process to screen out marginal candidates, thereby saving valuable executive time. Time is money, and, as the competition for good jobs is often fierce, people in staffing feel justified in collecting data in a standardized format which eliminates their having to search out information which candidates might otherwise conceal.

Who Completes Application Forms?

Nonmanagerial salaried exempt and nonexempt employees are almost always given applications to complete; middle-level managers are asked less often. Surprisingly, even executives are asked to complete a company's application form or an executive search firm's personal history form. Why? Given the potential financial impact of a good hire (or a mishire) at the senior executive ranks, companies and search firms are verifying professional and personal data. Detailed background checks of your credentials (education, work history, and, perhaps, even salary history) are increasingly commonplace. Nonetheless, senior executives are rarely asked to complete applications. If an application form is extended, it generally is done in conjunction with the processing of an offer and is seen more as a formality than a screening device.

How to Avoid Applications

Many times you can't avoid applications. If it is company policy or a well-entrenched practice, you're stuck and you have to complete it. However, we do recommend that you manage this process better than our friend, Peter Adelman. Consider following these steps, in the order in which they appear, with the first one most preferred:

1. Prior to the Interview, During Your Data Collection Phase.
Before the interview, try the following:

> **I am looking forward to our meeting and discussing further your plans for the company and how I might fit in. In order to fully prepare for our meeting, can you have your secretary pull together the latest annual report, articles, in-house newsletters, and any other literature you might have which would help me understand the company better? While I am going over this material, is there anything you would like me to complete and bring to our meeting, like an application form or a nondisclosure form, if you need these? If these are required documents, I would rather not cut into our valuable time together by filling out forms on site.**

2. At the Company, When Handed an Application Form.
One approach that works is:

> **Thank you for the application form. But that will not be necessary. Please tell Mr. Jordan I am here for our 1:00 business meeting.**

If this approach doesn't work, try:

Thank you for the application form. Mr. Jordan and I have already talked about the need to complete one for the files but we have agreed that I should take this with me and send it back to him directly after our discussion. Would you please ring Mr. Jordan's secretary for me now?

If you didn't verify the delaying tactic ahead of time, this approach might work:

Thank you for the application form. I am looking forward to completing it. However, since I don't have all the information with me that I need to complete it accurately, what I would prefer to do is take it with me and mail it back or drop it off later. Which would you prefer? Oh, you want me to complete it now? I would really prefer not to do that. Applications are only used if I get hired; this one would become part of your permanent record, and inaccuracies would not reflect well on my candidacy and how I do things. I'm sure you understand how important it is to put my 'best foot forward.' Thank you for being so gracious. I promise to complete this if Mr. Jordan and I proceed further in our discussions.

3. If Forced to Complete the Application Form on Site Prior to the Interview.

If you're stuck, be gracious and do not sulk or give the receptionist a hard time. It's a common practice to ask the receptionist for feedback on the way candidates interacted with her prior to their formal interviews. Always have your "interviewing mode" engaged, even when driving into the parking lot or riding up the elevator. You never know who might be watching or standing next to you.

Carry your completed application with you at all times. You do not want to have to recreate important and highly detailed information from memory. Why risk making errors when filling the #*%&!@ form out? You want to avoid this extra hassle by having the majority of this information already captured on the standardized application form shown in Worksheet 27. Or, if you prefer to use your own application form, that's fine, as long as the information is accurate and reflects your current status.

What to Bring

In addition to at least three clean résumés, bring two identical pens (fine point pens give you a better shot at the small lines and boxes), a fine lead pencil with an eraser, and a paper clip to attach your résumé to the application.

WORKSHEET 27
Application for Employment

We consider applicants for all positions without regard to race, color, religion, sex, national origin, age, marital or veteran status, the presence of a non-job-related medical condition or handicap, or any other legally protected status.

(PLEASE PRINT)

Position(s) Applied For	Date of Application

How Did You Learn About Us?
☐ Advertisement ☐ Friend ☐ Walk-In
☐ Employment Agency ☐ Relative ☐ Other _____

Last Name	First Name	Middle Name

Address	Number	Street	City	State	Zip Code

Telephone Number(s)	Social Security Number

If you are under 18 years of age, can you provide required proof of your eligibility to work? ☐ Yes ☐ No

Have you ever filed an application with us before? ☐ Yes ☐ No

If Yes, give date _____

Have you ever been employed with us before? ☐ Yes ☐ No

If Yes, give date _____

Are you currently employed? ☐ Yes ☐ No

May we contact your present employer? ☐ Yes ☐ No

Are you prevented from lawfully becoming employed in this country because of Visa or Immigration Status?
Proof of citizenship or immigration status will be required upon employment. ☐ Yes ☐ No

On what date would you be available for work? _____

Are you available to work: ☐ Full Time ☐ Part Time ☐ Shift Work ☐ Temporary

Are you currently on "lay-off" status and subject to recall? ☐ Yes ☐ No

Can you travel if a job requires it? ☐ Yes ☐ No

Have you been convicted of a felony within the last 7 years? ☐ Yes ☐ No
Conviction will not necessarily disqualify an applicant from employment.

If Yes, please explain _____

WE ARE AN EQUAL OPPORTUNITY EMPLOYER

(Continued)

Education

	Elementary School				High School				Undergraduate College / University				Graduate / Professional			
School Name and Location																
Years Completed	4	5	6	7	8	9	10	11	12	1	2	3	4	1	2	3	4
Diploma / Degree																	
Describe Course of Study																	
Describe any specialized training, apprenticeship, skills and extra-curricular activities																	
Describe any honors you have received																	
State any additional information you feel may be helpful to us in considering your application																	

Indicate any foreign languages you can speak, read and / or write			
	FLUENT	GOOD	FAIR
SPEAK			
READ			
WRITE			

List professional, trade, business or civic activities and offices held.
You may exclude memberships which would reveal sex, race, religion, national origin, age, ancestry, or handicap or other protected status:

_____

_____

_____

_____

References

Give name, address and telephone number of three references who are not related to you and are not previous employers.

1. _____

2. _____

3. _____

Have you ever had any job-related training in the United States military?

☐ Yes   ☐ No

If Yes, please describe _____

Are you physically or otherwise unable to perform the duties of the job for which you are applying?

☐ Yes   ☐ No

(Continued)

Employment Experience

Start with your present or last job. Include any job-related military service assignments and volunteer activities. You may exclude organizations which indicate race, color, religion, gender, national origin, handicap or other protected status.

1.

Employer	Dates Employed		Work Performed
	From	To	
Address			
Telephone Number(s)	Hourly Rate/Salary		
	Starting	Final	
Job Title	Supervisor		
Reason for Leaving			

2.

Employer	Dates Employed		Work Performed
	From	To	
Address			
Telephone Number(s)	Hourly Rate/Salary		
	Starting	Final	
Job Title	Supervisor		
Reason for Leaving			

3.

Employer	Dates Employed		Work Performed
	From	To	
Address			
Telephone Number(s)	Hourly Rate/Salary		
	Starting	Final	
Job Title	Supervisor		
Reason for Leaving			

4.

Employer	Dates Employed		Work Performed
	From	To	
Address			
Telephone Number(s)	Hourly Rate/Salary		
	Starting	Final	
Job Title	Supervisor		
Reason for Leaving			

If you need additional space, please continue on a separate sheet of paper.

Special Skills and Qualifications

Summarize special job-related skills and qualifications acquired from employment or other experience.

_____

_____

_____

_____

(Continued)

Applicant's Statement

I certify that answers given herein are true and complete to the best of my knowledge.

I authorize investigation of all statements contained in this application for employment as may be necessary in arriving at an employment decision.

This application for employment shall be considered active for a period of time not to exceed 45 days. Any applicant wishing to be considered for employment beyond this time period should inquire as to whether or not applications are being accepted at that time.

I hereby understand and acknowledge that, unless otherwise defined by applicable law, any employment relationship with this organization is of an *"at will"* nature, which means that the Employee may resign at any time and the Employer may discharge Employee at any time with or without cause. It is further understood that this *"at will"* employment relationship may not be changed by any written document or by conduct unless such change is specifically acknowledged in writing by an authorized executive of this organization.

In the event of employment, I understand that false or misleading information given in my application or interview(s) may result in discharge. I understand, also, that I am required to abide by all rules and regulations of the employer.

_____   _____
Signature of Applicant   Date

FOR PERSONNEL DEPARTMENT USE ONLY

Arrange Interview   ☐ Yes   ☐ No

Remarks _____

_____   _____
                                                              INTERVIEWER   DATE

Employed ☐ Yes ☐ No   Date of Employment _____

                                    Hourly Rate/
Job Title _____   Salary _____ Department_____

              By _____ _____
                                   NAME AND TITLE   DATE

NOTES _____

_____

_____

_____

_____

1. The enclosed application form shown (Worksheet 27) is a tool that you can use to collect all the information necessary for filling out the majority of applications. Having completed this form before you arrive for your interview permits you to copy information directly from your application to the company's employment application. As a result, you can concentrate on printing neatly and legibly.

2. Carefully review the blank application before answering any questions. This will enable you to determine the layout of the application, as they are all different. Some forms ask you to fill in boxes, others ask for information below (or above) the lines. Unless you have scanned the format, you may not catch this subtlety. You may also miss an important instruction, like WRITE IN PENCIL, and there you are printing with a neat black ball point pen! While it may look nice, you've just communicated to the employer that you overlook details and do not always follow instructions.

3. When in doubt about some question, leave it blank. You can always answer it later. If the information will not harm you but you feel it is best explained in person or is of a highly confidential nature, you may always mention to the human resources person or the hiring authority that you left some things blank for personal reasons.

4. If your answers to some of the questions on the application might harm your chances of being hired, leave them unanswered or write *will explain* or *n/a* (for *not applicable*). Be prepared, however, to answer these questions verbally, if they are reasonable questions from the company's point of view. Questions which might make you very uncomfortable may be deemed to be perfectly appropriate to the employer.

5. Some of the questions may not apply directly to you (e.g., *Preferred shift*). If this is the case, make a short dash. This lets the employer know that you have, at least, read the question, but it is not relevant for you.

6. Follow directions carefully. After accuracy and neatness, the next most important step is following directions. Ask for two application forms and explain that one will be used as a practice sheet. (It is a lot less embarrassing to ask for the second form at first, than having to come up to the receptionist with a messed up application. Never write *See résumé* as a substitute for completing the application. You can always paper-clip your résumé to the application to amplify the requested information.

If you can get only one application, fill it out lightly in pencil. Then go back and fill it in ink. Wait until the ink has thoroughly dried before erasing any pencil marks. Remember to bring a copy of your filled-in sample application form (Worksheet 27).

Commonly Requested Data on Application Forms

1. Instructions

It is surprising how many people immediately begin to complete the application without first reading the instructions. Be alert to the request that you write in pencil versus type or print in black ink. Also, signatures are sometimes requested, either in the beginning or the end of the sheet; sign your full name. Please note that signing your name indicates that the information is complete and accurate to the best of your ability. Many companies have clauses on the form which state that dismissal is possible if you lied on the application form. Don't risk it. Always be accurate. When in doubt, do not hand in the application form, rather get back to the company with the correct data.

2. Referred by; Relatives Working in Company

This section may be best left blank because you do not know for certain how your personal contact is perceived in the organization even if you have asked your relative for feedback. If you have relatives employed by the company, leave the space blank. Some have unwritten policies against hiring relatives of current employees. It is best to interview on your own merits first, then reveal your connection if you feel that omitting the data misrepresents you.

3. Personal Information

Be prepared to indicate your name, address, telephone number, height, weight, physical limitations, and citizenship. Regarding the **TELEPHONE**, make sure that a prospective employer can easily reach you or leave a number on an answering machine. If your phone is constantly busy or if someone cannot leave a message, you will be considered "off the market" by an employer or a search firm. Avoid cute telephone messages with bells, beeps, or horns. Get "call waiting" or a second line installed for the duration of your search so you can effectively field incoming calls. Don't miss opportunities which come your way.

Companies are interested in your **HEIGHT** and **WEIGHT** for two reasons. First, if you are really overweight, you pose a greater medical risk for the employer than if you are physically fit. Second, if you are out of control physically, you probably are not as disciplined in your work either. Perhaps these are unfair generalizations, but people do subscribe to them, nonetheless.

Be honest when asked about **PHYSICAL LIMITATIONS** which would hinder your performance in the position for which you are applying. If you have any physical limitations which do not impact your ability to perform the position's duties, then fill in the blank with a dash or *n/a*. Again, this means, "I have read the question and it does not apply."

If you are not a **CITIZEN** of the United States, list your visa number and type. If you have applied for U.S. citizenship, list the date.

If the application asks for details concerning any **PHYSICAL INJURIES/SICKNESSES,** use a dash unless the injury directly applies to your ability to perform the job for which you have applied. This is not the time for sympathy because of illness or infirmity. The employer is looking for a responsible, reliable healthy worker and trying to spot any lingering health problems (or preexisting conditions). Employers are nervous about hiring people with a history of worker's compensation claims. **LIST YOUR HEALTH AS "EXCELLENT,"** if you can.

4. Marital Status and Dependents

If the application refers to **MARITAL STATUS,** you are either married or single. If you are going through a divorce or separation, you are still married. If you are widowed or if you are legally divorced, you are considered to be single. If you have grown children or children from a previous marriage, merely indicate the number of children you have; do not differentiate "children" from "step children." Don't get into a lot of explanations. This will help keep the information on a professional level and keep it from getting personal.

Many applications ask about **DEPENDENTS** (and their ages), especially children. If your children are under school age, you may want to leave their ages blank. Or explain in the interview that the children are no hindrance to your work (due to sickness or babysitting problems). However, if your children are older and can take care of themselves, include their ages.

5. References

As you know from Step Four, references are important and should be revealed only when it is to your advantage and when you can effectively manage the process. Most application forms ask you to identify business and personal references, including your immediate supervisor on each job. It is our recommendation that you write in a dash in the blank for Immediate Supervisor and write in the phrase *will furnish upon request,* in the section which asks you to list several references. Granted, the application *requests* that information, but you are retaining the right to provide that very valuable and confidential data when the time is right. If you do not see a mutual fit, why should you expose your references to potential nuisance calls?

MAY WE CONTACT YOUR CURRENT EMPLOYER? is an innocent enough phrase, particularly if you are openly conducting a career search. Say *No. Not at this time.* If not asked if your references are confidential—and you want to ensure that they are—you may wish to raise the issue yourself. Do not be lulled into thinking that all search firms or employers will operate discreetly. We have seen many an overzealous recruiter prematurely contact the current or former employer, which seriously jeopardized the employment status of the prospective employee and created significant litigation exposure for the potential employer.

6. Reason for Leaving

Remember, what you say in the interview is going to be much more complete than anything you can possibly summarize on the application, given the form's space constraints. So, you may wish to indicate general answers, such as "Reorganization" or purposefully vague answers like, "Will discuss." Either answer will suffice on the application, but if you identify restructuring as your motivation, you've lost that slight edge which comes from being able to present your reasons for leaving in your own way.

Do you remember Mike Commons, and what he highlighted in his Reference Summary on p. 148? Paraphrasing from it,

> **As my résumé reflects, I have been moving well within the company since I joined it in 1967. Recently, the company has found that it needs to consolidate its operations, due to slipping profitability and sales. Under the consolidation, there was no need for two senior sales and marketing managers, and I was the less seasoned manager. As there were no other challenging line or staff opportunities within the company, I've decided to pursue my career outside with the company's full knowledge and support.**

7. Salary and Start Date

In the **SALARY DESIRED** space, leave it blank or write *negotiable*. If the application requests **SALARY HISTORY,** complete as much of the data as you feel comfortable with, though leave your **CURRENT SALARY** figure blank or place a dash there. If asked to provide some specifics, you can always indicate the following:

> **I feel that my current compensation is confidential, and I am uncomfortable talking about money this early in the interview process. I would prefer to explore your needs and the career opportunities first, then talk about money. Money is important to me, but it is not the highest priority. The opportunity to contribute to the growth and profitability of your company is most critical. Don't you agree?**

Under **START DATE** indicate the first reasonable date you are available. Even if you can start immediately, you may want to write in *negotiable* or identify a specific time frame (such as 2 weeks or 30 days).

If you indicate that you can start immediately, you may unwittingly be sending the message that you are desperate with no additional employment options. You clearly want to create the image of an individual who is a valuable commodity sought by many others.

IN SEARCH OF THE PERFECT EMPLOYER

The Ricocheting Job Search

Frank Wade and his family had recently moved into their dream house in a wooded glen on the shores of Lake Erie. Away from the irritating bustle of city living, Frank found the much-needed quiet from his pressure-filled job as head of R&D for a leading health-care company. Life for the Wades seemed to be working: Frank's wife, Linda, secured her promotion to marketing research manager, Jeremy got his driver's license and made the junior varsity track team, and Frank was recently elected to his national association's board.

In May, a reorganization centralized the company with the president assuming a more active leadership role in operations and R&D. Both the president and Frank worked hard to accommodate each other's needs in the changed firm, but the conflicting opinions of how product development should be managed strained even the long-standing relationship of Frank and his old mentor. In August, Frank and his president agreed to part company, and Frank was awarded a very generous "golden parachute."

Frank's career continuation strategy was to remain in the Cleveland area in either a similar R&D management capacity or to launch a consulting firm to serve the unique product development and engineering needs of health-care manufacturers and health-care providers.

In pursuit of such an opportunity, Frank diligently interviewed with numerous executive search firms, networked into exploratory meetings with other company executives, and even pursued venture capital monies to buy a troubled company ripe for purchase. As luck would have it, Frank's interview with a Cleveland executive search recruiter was so successful that he faxed Frank's résumé to a colleague in the Los Angeles affiliate office. The LA recruiter, in turn, contacted another account executive in the firm's San Francisco office about a recently acquired search engagement in the corporate offices of a multi-billion-dollar conglomerate in Cincinnati. Although the corporate head of applications research had no bona fide opening at headquarters, the company's research center in northwestern New Jersey had a senior

*management opportunity. Frank interviewed in New Jersey, was made
an offer he couldn't refuse, and the family relocated in the autumn
with no regrets. They traded their sailboat in for two trail horses and
haven't looked back since.*

*When asked to comment on what he learned in searching for his
job, Frank would shake his head and chuckle, "You never know how or
where the right opportunity is going to come along! Who would have
thought that the search in Cleveland would ricochet to Los Angeles, to
San Francisco, to Cincinnati, to the rolling hills of northwestern New
Jersey. I certainly didn't! I've learned that because you never know
when, how, or where the perfect connection will be made, you must
continually pursue every possible search avenue, follow up on even the
most obscure leads (because people know people you don't know), and
keep confident and optimistic."*

Job Sources—Uncovering the Opportunities That You Really Want!

There are five main sources for finding a job:

- Entrepreneuring
- Advertisements
- Personal networking
- Search firms and employment agencies
- Target organizations

Source 1: Entrepreneuring

If you are interested in becoming an entrepreneur and exploring what it
would take to launch your own business, then we suggest you spend a
day at a major library or book store pursuing the many fine manuals and
books on entrepreneurship. Most major CPA firms have a small business
practice and may even suggest some additional resources many libraries
wouldn't have.

In addition, many community associations conduct workshops
(often free or for a nominal fee) on how to launch and manage a start-
up business. Perhaps the best-known group is S.C.O.R.E. (Service Corps
of Retired Executives) as part of the Small Business Administration.
Seasoned professionals, many of whom were national leaders in their
fields, share their ideas in a group setting. Many S.C.O.R.E. offices will

also provide individual counseling to help budding entrepreneurs successfully leap those first seemingly unsurmountable hurdles.

You might be a strong entrepreneurial candidate if you are committed to being your own boss, provided your motivation is more than merely getting out from under someone else telling you what to do. While it seems that "Entrepreneurial Quizzes" abound, they are of limited use in determining entrepreneurial success. So, rather than providing you with yet another quiz, we reidentified some traits or background conditions we feel are common to successful entrepreneurs so you may wish to evaluate yourself in light of these dimensions.

Common Entrepreneurial Traits

1. Family Background
If one or both of your parents were or are self-employed, you have probably been influenced toward self-directed employment options. In addition, being an entrepreneur is highly correlated with being the oldest child, having immigrant parents or grandparents, having been in several business ventures growing up, and being raised in a home where competition and excellence is common behavior.

2. Education
Entrepreneurs respect people with education but do not view education as the answer to success but rather as a tool—among many—to be utilized in pursuit of success. Entrepreneurs tend to rely more upon their own skills than education *per se* to open doors for them. Employees just completing their MBAs, for example, often feel that they should now be paid more money because they are more credentialed. Entrepreneurs view MBAs as not inherently worth more; rather the MBAs should be given an opportunity to use their new level of learning and schooling to produce more or introduce something new which will significantly benefit the company. Entrepreneurs are more than willing to increase an MBA's pay if the contribution is present.

3. Interpersonal Skills
The following have been used to describe many entrepreneurs: scrappy, confrontative, creative, driven, independent-minded, tough to manage, mavericks, socially bold, overly confident, opinionated, displaying a "can do" attitude, bright, articulate, courageous, visionary, determined, workaholic, and not particularly influenced by others. Entrepreneurs are moderate risk takers and take calculated risks in areas they know and can influence with their own skills. Entrepreneurs would be more prone

to be competitive in sports (like tennis) and less involved in things which others or chance controls (such as gambling or the state lottery).

4. Employment History, Work Traits

Entrepreneurs come in all sizes and shapes and have diverse employment backgrounds. Entrepreneurs are innovators and clearly challenge the status quo within the organizations. Because they are typically more confrontative, entrepreneurs often "blow up" relationships, and it is common for them to have been fired more than once.

Entrepreneurs generally have been on the leading edge of concepts, approaches, or technologies, even if their organization didn't want them there. Because entrepreneurs are so creative and have a global perspective, they have a pronounced tendency to be somewhat disorganized, which is the one trait they need help with: administering the details.

Successful entrepreneurs are usually not seen as highly collaborative, prone to consensus decision making, or necessarily willing to accommodate their style to fit someone else's personality. The entrepreneur is more likely to exert some energy convincing someone of the merits of his or her approach, so others may feel their opinions and feelings are often overlooked or ignored.

5. Motivations

Entrepreneurs think primarily of gaining and servicing customers versus building a large organization to fuel their egos. Entrepreneurs "fall in love" too quickly with new things or people, new product ideas, new employees, new manufacturing ideas, and new financial systems.

The successful entrepreneur is constantly looking for purpose and the bottom line in business and social encounters. Shallow issues bore entrepreneurial-type people, as they tend to be reluctant social mixers when there is no clear agenda. Entrepreneurs typically are driven achievers with a low need for affiliation with others and a moderate need for power.

Entrepreneurial Resources _____

We recommend that you identify some entrepreneurs in your geographic area or industry and ask them if they would recommend any programs or resource materials to help you in your quest. You may wish to consider purchasing some tools to help you map out your business venture. Through a program offered by *Entrepreneur Magazine,* you can acquire many of the tools you need to start, develop, and succeed in your own part-time or full-time business. This *Be Your Own Boss Master System* encompasses audio tapes of diverse business and market experts, a 350-page manual (filled with specific information covering virtually every phase of start-up, development, and profit, and an outline featuring over 175 "hot" business start-up opportunities). The *Entrepreneur Start a Business Store* in Sacramento, California at (916) 366-0505 is one such resource for securing entrepreneurial material.

Many fine programs on the market today can help prepare you mentally and emotionally so you can succeed in any business you choose. If you are ready to seriously explore becoming an entrepreneur, then perhaps these programs may be right for you. Further entrepreneurial information is contained in the bibliography.

Proven Ways to Get Connected

Responding to ads, or getting connected through search firms involves what we call the "visible job market," in that opportunities are known to exist, they are "visible." The "hidden job market" deals in the realm of possibilities and potential—not in certainties, as in a bona fide job opening. Career opportunities are "hidden" in the hidden job market and are uncovered through the avenues of personal networking or marketing to selected target companies. For you to be able to conduct a well-rounded effective career search, it is critical that you become intimately familiar with the various job hunting strategies outlined here and become skilled in the use of each one.

The way Frank Wade changed jobs certainly supports this contention:

You never know exactly how you are going to get connected!

Invariably, as soon as we have figured out how our candidates for reemployment are going to get connected—the source through which the best offer will come—we are invariably surprised. We now operate only out of the realm of possibilities—anything is possible. Frank Wade had what we call a "ricochet search"; he successfully bounced from one connection to another.

Getting a Job Is a Simple Process

Getting a job really is a simple process. Besides, you already know how to get a job. If you've been zapped, you got zapped from a job which you previously secured. If you are going back into the marketplace after an extended absence or this is your first professional job out of school, chances are you have held at least some kind of job to earn money. If you are still employed, see our point? You followed one of the four main avenues to get hired previously.

You identify your talents, skills and accomplishments, create a meaningful and realistic career focus, put together a powerful results-oriented résumé, construct some cover letters which help market your résumé, pursue all four avenues of your career search in a balanced manner, effectively interview, secure offers, analyze your offers, effectively negotiate a better compensation package (if appropriate), accept the offer, and start work. See, it is simple and straightforward.

Securing the right job for you can be very simple, and it can also be one of the most challenging tasks you've ever managed. It is not the major things that you do or don't do that will make the difference in your campaign. It will be the subtle things, like learning how to manage your own emotions in a way to always have a sense of positive expectancy and contagious confidence or finding an appropriate way to recontact your personal contacts for a third time to get more leads or being seen by your target organizations as the only logical candidate, as a result of your persistent follow through and consultative interviewing style with its value-added perspective.

Getting a job is a simple, though not easy, process. It requires you to be at your best so you can secure the best job for you.

The Hidden Job Market

Opportunities within the hidden job market emerge, largely, out of your own efforts. You uncover them by diligently networking with your *personal contacts* or by identifying *target organizations* (companies that you really want to work for) and effectively pursuing the hiring authorities.

More than 70 percent of all jobs are found through the efforts in the hidden market, yet most people spend the majority of their time in lower yielding activities such as responding to ads and writing "cold call" letters to companies with no intention of follow-up. Why, you ask? Because effectively conducting a campaign in the hidden job market is more difficult and requires more persistence—not more skill or talent. Just more guts and personal commitment.

Your challenge is to effectively balance your efforts in both the hidden job market and the visible job market.

The Visible Job Market

The visible job market almost explains itself. When an employer places an ad in a newspaper, posts a "Now Hiring" sign on the plant gate, or

Table 6-1. Effectiveness of Job Search Methods

Methods of Obtaining Jobs	Percent of Jobs Obtained	Your Job-Hunting Goals
Personal networking	41%	Contact 8 to 15 people daily
Apply directly to employer, target companies	32	Send résumés to 100 to 300 target firms
Want ads	14	Send résumés to 6 to 10 firms per week
Search firms, employment agencies	13	Send résumés to contingency firms (10 to 25 firms) and retainer firms (25 to 225 firms)

Note: Because your circumstances may differ and your success may vary from these methods, please use these as guidelines, not absolutes. The data on the jobs obtained was from job-seeking methods as reported by U.S. Department of Labor, Bureau of Labor Statistics. Percentages are rounded off.

registers a job with a *search firm, employment agency,* or *state employment bureau,* you know that the company is hiring.

About 80 percent of all job seekers read the want ads and apply for jobs they find there. That is as far as they go in looking for a job. If you restrict yourself to responding only to want ads, you are going to miss many of the jobs waiting to be filled. Unfortunately, only 14 percent of all available job openings are filled by ads (see Table 6-1). And in a city where unemployment is at, say, 10 percent, a lot of people are looking at want ads. Imagine the competition for those visible jobs.

Just the same, 3 jobs out of 20 are in the visible job market, and the following pages provide helpful tips for pursuing those jobs. The visible market includes three primary sources:

1. Want ads
2. Search firms, employment agencies, recruiters: retainer search, contingency search, state or province employment services, and nonprofit agencies
3. Federal employment

Career Search by Level and Avenue

Many people ask us what is the expected probability of success by organization level for the various career search avenues (personal networking, search firms, target organizations, and advertisements). Although *all* avenues work and should be utilized, the following reflects our experience of people getting connected:

	Personal Networking	Search Firms	Target Organizations	Advertisements
Executive	High	Very High	Moderately Low	Low
Managerial	High	Moderately High	Moderate	Moderately Low
Professional-Technical	High	High	Moderately Low	High
Administrative-Secretarial	Moderately High	Moderate	Low	High

Source 2: Advertisements

Fundamentally, there are two types of ads: *blind ads* and *open ads*. Blind ads do not reveal the company's name or the recruiter. Open ads identify the company and, most often, the name of the recruiter from the human resources area.

The following are some tips for following up on want ads:

- Read all the ads in the "Help Wanted" section.
- Take a pen and circle all the want ads that interest you.
- Make a note of what kinds of employers are hiring people with your skills.
- Look through the rest of the paper. Want ads may be in sections other than Help Wanted. Look for companies that are hiring or expanding in other job areas. They may need your skills later.
- Read the business section for news of plant, office, or warehouse expansions or news of new facilities. You can be first in line if you write now.

Do not get discouraged when an ad calls for experience in a field where you have a skill or interest but no direct experience. We recommend that you respond anyway, as your background may create some interest. An employer might want to find somebody with experience, but often nobody is available with the exact experience desired. Your employment skills and interests may be the closest thing the employer can find to fill a position you would like to have. Also, do not identify your salary when you respond to an ad, even if the company wants to know it. Having people provide salary information is an easy method of screening out candidates. Do not give the company a reason to exclude you.

In responding to blind ads:

1. *Wait three days* after the ad's appearance before sending your letter and résumé to the box number in care of the paper in which the ad appeared. (Your résumé will not have as much competition for the reader's attention.)

2. Get a 3-ring binder and tape a copy of the ad to a sheet of paper to allow for note taking. Do not tape more than three ads per page. This will be part of your filing system. To effectively stay on top of all your activity, *review your files daily*. Indicate the date of the ad's appearance (and newspaper), when your letter and résumé were sent, and three weeks after the ad's appearance to allow for a second mailing.

3. If you are worried about confidentiality and do not want your résumé to be received by a given company, place your résumé in an envelope marked with the name of the firm you wish to avoid. Most newspapers running blind ads will honor your request. Use wording such as, *"If Box XYZ is Company ABC, please discard this envelope."*

Responses to blind ads are forwarded to the hiring company for a period of 30 days, **not a day more,** by the newspaper. If you send out a second résumé response within this four-week "window of opportunity," your letter and résumé will stand out above the competition. Conversely, if you do not "make" your four-week window, your résumé and second letter will be discarded. For effective language that could be used in a second mailer, please refer to the letter examples at the end of Step 3.

In responding to open ads:

1. When the organization is identified, we recommend that you call the company and ask for the name of the person who heads up the department or function in which you most likely would work. If possible, probe the decision maker regarding position demands and company needs.

2. Send your résumé and letter to the department head, not the person identified in the ad (most likely someone in human resources).

3. Again, tape a copy of the ad in your 3-ring notebook and send a second mailing within four weeks or, better still, follow up with a telephone call to the decision maker and discuss your capabilities.

Ads That Want Salary Information

When ads request salary information, the preferred procedure is ***not*** to provide the data, but there is a risk either way you go. On one hand, if you respond and the salary is too high or too low, you can be ruled out by a résumé scanner for being over- or underqualified without really reading your qualifications. The risk on the other hand is to be rejected by a clerk who is screening résumés using the arbitrary ruling that will reject people if they do not send salary information with their résumés.

Companies request salary data for a number of reasons. Generally, they may be looking for a fast means to sort out résumés or sometimes they want to see if the salary range for the job is in the ball park. Whatever the reason, if you ignore the request, you can always handle it later when you call to follow up or write in 20 days on a blind ad.

A good sales person always likes to talk about the value of the product before talking about price. You are looking for the opportunity to "show up" powerfully with a company. You want to introduce yourself well and powerfully and to respond to the needs of a company with your abilities which can contribute many times your salary to the company in profits. Keep doing that confidently and you will be successful.

However, if you still sense you really need to respond to the request, here are some suggestions you may wish to incorporate in your cover letter. Do not ever write on your résumé. It looks tacky and unprofessional.

Some sample language for your consideration:

My compensation requirements are open and flexible for a position which has advancement potential, challenge, and provides an opportunity to contribute directly to profits.

I am seeking a position with an overall compensation package, including benefits and incentive, in the low $_____'s.

"My current salary is $_____, and I am seeking a salary in the mid $_____'s.

Select from and adjust these suggestions to suit your preference.

Tips from the News Pages

While you are circling want ads, do not forget to read the rest of the paper. Often a news story will give you a clue as to where employment might be found. Consider this news story as an example:

INDUSTRIAL CYCLONE ANNOUNCES MAJOR PLANT EXPANSION

Industrial Cyclone Corporation today announced that construction will begin next month on a 2-million-square-foot factory addition at their Northfield Park facility. The new addition will be used for the manufacturing of steel window and door frames for the industrial market.

This article is a tip-off that people with construction experience, draft persons, and engineers will be needed right away for the construction work. The potential for quality control supervisors, material and manufacturing managers, or sales people is excellent in such a firm, both locally and corporately. You can contact them now to be proactive on future needs. Local suppliers such as cement contractors will need drivers and laborers. Paving companies will have to pave the parking lot, and fencing contractors will be needed to fence the property. Electricians, bricklayers, glass installers, ceiling finishers, welders, laborers, and carpenters will be needed by the building contractor. Because the company is expanding, they will soon be hiring production line workers, warehouse stockers, clerical help, drivers, draftspeople, accounting department employees, secretaries, word processors, safety and security personnel, food service employees, and all the people necessary to staff and run a manufacturing operation.

When you see a story in the newspaper that might mean new jobs, check it out. Make a point of visiting the company's employment office to fill out an application, phone long distance to the company to see how you may apply for work now, or send them your résumé with a cover letter in the mail.

Do not wait until the company places an ad, as you may find yourself standing in a line with 150 other applicants.

Source 3: Search Firms and Employment Agencies

Search firms and employment agencies fall into three categories:

- Retainer search firms
- Contingency search firms and employment agencies
- State or province employment services and nonprofit firms

Retainer Search Firms

Executive search firms work exclusively for an organization and *not* for an applicant. These firms are paid on a retainer basis to locate a qualified executive for a particular position. They receive their fee regardless of whether they are successful in their search. Executive search consultants are often called "headhunters."

Contingency Search Firms and Employment Agencies

Contingency firms or employment agencies, however, are paid a fee only upon their locating, and the organization's hiring, a person they presented.

Ten Strategies for Dealing with Search Firms

1. *Never pay a fee!!* The fee for these services should always be paid by the employer. If you are asked to sign an agreement or pay a portion of the employer's fee up front—walk away. If you feel you must use an employment agency that has a contract, then have a qualified attorney take a look at it.

2. Retainer firms mainly work at the middle management to executive management levels and highly technical specialties. Contingency firms and employment agencies work mainly at the middle management level down. Although some contingency firms may also effectively recruit for executives, they do not do so on a regular basis. So, pick your level, develop your plan of attack, and execute your plan.

3. With contingency firms and employment agencies, your résumé may cross the desk of a hiring manager more than once. There is a fine line between too much exposure and too little.

4. Should your background match the needs of an ongoing search assignment, the search firm will usually contact you by telephone. Letter responses are generally used to inform you that there is no current client assignment matching your background. Many of the larger and better-known firms receive such a volume of mail from individuals announcing their availability that they use postcards and form letters to respond.

5. During the initial phone contact and even during the first interview, the identity of the client firm will probably not be divulged. Nevertheless, sufficient information will usually be given to enable you to get a rough idea as to a possible fit (i.e., size, industry, geographic location, etc.).

6. Use your personal contacts to network into 8 to 12 search firms daily. However, if you don't have a lead into a search firm or employment agency account executive, do not telephone to follow up on your mailing. It is seen generally as an annoyance to the recruiter. Do not walk in and expect an interview.

7. If asked about income, tell the recruiter straight away your base and bonus, if appropriate. Do not try to defer revealing salary data, as

the search firms are only trying to identify the level of suitable jobs. Certainly, you can indicate that you are open and flexible with regard to total compensation and how/when it gets configured.

8. Although most retainer search firms do not send unsolicited résumés to a company, some do. Contingency firms, on the other hand, certainly send résumés unsolicited to companies. Contact search firms and employment agencies again within four to six months if you are still in the market. Do not take the salary minimums listed by a search firm too literally—merely use them as a general guide.

9. If an executive search firm (or a company) asks you to travel some distance to meet with them, and you incur some expenses, these expenses should be reimbursed. Your appropriate response may be:

> **How do you want me to handle these expenses? Do you want to have your travel agency send me prepaid tickets, or should I just put this and other travel-related expenses on my credit card and bill you after the trip?**

10. The recruiter, as a professional, must respect the confidentiality of your situation. If you have any doubts, do not venture out. There is always a remote possibility of a slipup, so you need to assess the risk of exposure.

Should you use retainer search firms, contingency search firms, or state, province, or federal employment agencies? Actually, there is something to be said for each, and the job hunter seeking maximum exposure should certainly be in touch with different kinds of recruiters.

Outplacement Firms—Pros and Cons

Just as there are two forms of search firms (retainer and contingency), there are two categories of outplacement firms (corporate-sponsored and retail).

Corporate-sponsored outplacement firms provide careering assistance exclusively to individuals whose fees are paid by their organization. No fees are accepted from the candidates for reemployment, and the work is usually highly customized, if being provided on an individual basis, or if groups of employees are impacted, a multiple-day workshop is tailored to meet the needs of the employees. The Association of Outplacement Consulting Firms (AOCF) sets the standard for the 250 or so outplacement counseling (OPC) firms of which there are less than 60 AOCF members, internationally.

Retail outplacement firms provide careering assistance to individuals who pay their own fee. Unfortunately, the retail outplacement firms have a spotty reputation, so individuals have to be responsible for creating their own quality support. Even though people may pay $2500 to $8500 out of their own pockets, there are no guarantees that sound advice may be provided, given the "churn and burn" operating style of many retail careering assistance firms. That is not to say that corporate-sponsored outplacement firm counselors might not have a full schedule, they might very well. What we are saying is that most retail outplacement personnel are paid a commission on business brought in rather than on business serviced. To that end, the retailer is encouraged to do a quick turn of individuals paying for the service. So to protect your hard-earned monies, be very clear about the scope and extent of the services provided.

Corporate-Sponsored Outplacement

1. Corporate-sponsored outplacement is a corporate service which helps an organization to plan and accomplish individual terminations or group layoffs.

2. Corporate-sponsored outplacement may be defined by *what it is not*. Outplacement *is not* a service through which job openings are offered, *nor* do outplacement firms act as executive search firms or employment agencies. Corporate-sponsored outplacement firms do not provide any services which are paid for by individuals. *The corporation is the client of the outplacement firm, not the employee.* Interestingly enough, there are far more misconceptions about the outplacement industry than there are about the search business. The greatest misconception is that outplacement firms are in the "placement" business, setting up interviews for people and getting them jobs. Because of the myriad nuances of a search for the perfect job, it would be a tremendous disservice to the individual if the outplacement firm took on the responsibility for the search and, in effect, secured the job for the individual.

3. Corporate-sponsored outplacement services are retained by the corporation because of substantial advantages which outplacement provides to the organization itself. Outplacement services:

- Reduce the overall cost of terminations to the employer
- Reduce the corporation's exposure to litigation
- Ease the stressful job of termination for the manager
- Provide for timely, confident, decisions to release employees who no longer fit the organization's needs
- Improve relationships between departing employees and their former employers
- Maintain morale and productivity among remaining employees
- Promote a positive image of the corporation to its various constituencies

- Accelerate the time to secure a job by partnering with displaced employees

4. The quality of corporate-sponsored outplacement firms, like search firms, is related to the quality of the individual consultant, not solely the firm's reputation on past assignments. Periodically, you'll read articles which "bash" outplacement as not worth the money, saying that displaced employees had to find their own jobs, that the advice was "canned," or that administrative support was nonexistent. Granted, some abuses exist, and you can't satisfy everyone, but to accept a generalized smear against all corporate-sponsored outplacement firms as fact is the same as believing the premise that *all* journalists report the news poorly by not allowing the truth to stand in their way of a sensational story.

The following are dos and don'ts for handling corporate-sponsored outplacement issues:

- *Don't* sign anything, no matter how innocent it looks, until you have an attorney review the document.
- *Don't* get lulled into thinking that an outplacement firm (especially retail) will get you interviews or find you a job. You are ultimately responsible for your career and its outcome.
- *Do* in-depth reference checks on any retail OPC firm that wants you to invest your money in a job-hunting campaign. Take down contact information on any testimonial letters that are offered as a glowing recommendation. If the firm has a good track record, they will welcome inquiries and be proud to have you contact their graduates.
- *Don't* be mislead by advertisements in the papers that imply they have bona fide position openings with headings such as "Career Development Consultants," "Executive Career Planning," "Executive Marketing Search-Outplacement" or "Job Hunting Made Easy." No corporate-sponsored outplacement firm that we know of advertises like this—only retailers. Retailers will be happy to review your résumé, sell you a mailing list, and have you invest in an expensive career search program. Be careful.
- *Do* ask questions, such as:
  - How long have you been in business and what qualifies your firm to provide careering assistance? What is your background?
  - Who will be my counselor, how often and how many times will we meet? May I meet that person now? If not now, when?
  - Tell me, who are your current candidates? Titles and industries, please.

- What major assignments do you have currently underway or do you anticipate in the near future? How do I know I'll be well served?

- Who have you counseled at my level within the past six months? May I contact them, please?

- What did you actually *do* for these people?

- What kinds of people, levels of position, industry, and functions does your firm handle?

- Tell me about three engagements that did not work. Why didn't they?

- What kinds of resources do you use for your database for mailings to search firms and target companies? How often do you update your database and by what methods?

- What kind of campaign would you recommend I launch, using what strategies?

- What will you commit to doing if my early attempts to secure employment do not work? What is the extent of your services after I launch my campaign?

- What percentage of my mailings to search firms and target companies will you guarantee gets to the decision makers?

- What will you do if a higher percentage of my mailings are rejected than your minimum return? Will you pay for additional résumé and letterhead printing costs as well as postage?

- What services are at my disposal, such as office and telephone usage and secretarial support? Any restrictions on usage?

- To what extent do you provide corporate-sponsored outplacement? (Please note: if it is less than 100 percent it is a retail firm.)

- *Do* go back to your organization and ask if it will provide some level of corporate-sponsored outplacement support. If your organization will not sponsor a full program, ask if it would fund some level of support, at least, on a *per diem* or workshop basis.

- *Do* ask to what extent your outplacement consultant will counsel you on an ongoing basis, especially after interviews, as well as for the duration of your campaign.

State or Province Employment Services

The obvious reason for using the services of your employment office is that employers do register jobs with them. About 5 percent of all job seekers find employment this way. Remember, these employment service officers see hundreds of people every week. They work hardest for those that stand out, those who are friendly and cooperative, not

Fundamentally, there is a 180-degree difference between how executive search firms and how outplacement firms support job seekers and approach key issues. Table 6-2 shows but a few distinctions.

Table 6-2. Ten Critical Differences between Search Firms and Outplacement Firms

SEARCH FIRMS	OUTPLACEMENT FIRMS
1. Relationship to Job Seeker Their role is to screen you out if you are not suitable for the opening. Loyalty is to client company who pays fee, not you. There is no obligation to help people searching.	**1. Relationship to Job Seeker** Their role is to partner with you and equip you with the skills to be screened in. With corporate-sponsored OPC firms, the fee is paid by company, and the firm is asked to do whatever it takes to help you get connected. There is a clear commitment to help you in your job search.
2. When You Are Traumatized While you might be viewed compassionately, you will probably be seen as weak, unable to handle pressures, and not a good candidate for any searches because of your emotional upheaval. Search firms do not consider emotional candidates as viable candidates, period.	**2. When You Are Traumatized** You are viewed as having natural reactions to a tough situation. Your consultant is empathic as an objective third party who deals with high emotions daily. You will get help examining and evaluating fears and roadblocks to your success and getting emotionally and psychologically grounded again.
3. Spouse, Partner, Family Counseling Search firms clearly work for the company and have no desire or need to involve others unless that influences the screen in/out process.	**3. Spouse, Partner, Family Counseling** Outplacement firms clearly want to meet people close to you, as involving others has a significant positive impact on your ability to effectively search.
4. Career Focus and Options Search firm account executives could care less about careering options outside of their search engagement, unless an option means that you will leave the new job prematurely or a focus provides clues to your vision and resolve. Part of recruiter's role is to limit your options.	**4. Career Focus and Options** Your consultant helps you develop a meaningful career focus or vision, given your talents, skills, abilities, commitments, and marketplace conditions. His or her role is to expand options, leveraging one opportunity against another.
5. Providing Straight Feedback It is not the job of the recruiter to tell you when or how you have screwed up so you can rehearse it again. They are judging you on how you are	**5. Providing Straight Feedback** Your outplacement consultant should be constantly adding value each time you meet through straightforward, open, candid, and insightful feedback.

operating now, not when you are not beat-up.

6. **Résumé**

Your résumé will be considered if it represents a specific fit and seems to match the corporate culture and company style.

7. **Interviewing**

Recruiters will be looking to screen you out and pass over your strengths to uncover your weaknesses. Recruiters will ask "killer questions" and try to take you by surprise while hiding the corporate skeletons.

8. **Offers**

Since recruiters work for the company, their intention is to reduce your options or flexibility by extending offers with tight acceptance deadlines while signaling that you are the top candidate before an offer is extended.

9. **Negotiation Strategies**

Recruiters are interested in cutting the best deal for the company by speeding up your acceptance, limiting the offer package, and by completing the engagement with the best possible candidate.

10. **Final Disposition**

The final outcome for a search firm recruiter is to complete the assignment and reject the other candidates not accepted for the job.

Such feedback should help you fine-tune your interviewing skills and presentation style to be more effective.

6. **Résumé**

Your resume will be written to reflect both what you have done as well as what you can do while appealing to diverse companies in multiple industries.

7. **Interviewing**

Your OPC consultant will equip you with skills so you might be "screened in" while capitalizing on your strengths. You will learn to portray your weaknesses as overplayed strengths and handle tough interview questions with ease. Your ability to effectively present your credentials will be seen as a joint responsibility with your OPC consultant, which includes helping you uncover those corporate skeletons the company and search firm would like to disguise.

8. **Offers**

Your goal is to improve competitive offers, leveraging interview trips and offers against one another. In addition, your OPC consultant will show you how to discreetly handle phone calls from other search firms, even after you have accepted an offer so as to keep your network strong.

9. **Negotiation Strategies**

OPC consultants are interested in your getting the best deal which may also include expanding the offer package while delaying some offers and speeding up others. Hopefully, you will fulfill your career path goal and create opportunities beyond this specific job.

10. **Final Disposition**

Beyond the offer acceptance, you and your OPC consultant should evaluate what you learned in the process and develop contingency strategies for how to build your new career and the "next step."

grouchy, and those who clearly state their skills. Also, see if you can follow up without becoming a nuisance to the counselor assigned to you. You may wish to clarify the best way to do this with your employment counselor.

Federal Employment

Your local, state, province, and federal government are among the largest employers in the country. To find out about government job opportunities, you must visit the employment offices for the federal agency in which you are interested. These offices have lists of job descriptions, and you might find your skills qualify you for such a job. You may be required to take a civil service test to see if you are qualified for employment. The public library and many book stores carry materials written to help you study for civil service tests. If you qualify for a job, you will be put on a list of names. When your name reaches the top of that list, you will be called in for an interview. Because this may not happen for a long time, apply early in your job search for government employment.

Using Other Nonprofit Agencies

Other agencies can serve you in finding a job, particularly if you are in a special age group or have a specific disability. Here is a list of some of the special needs which may be filled by agencies. You may want to find out about other social service agencies in your community on your own. You may find them listed in the Yellow Pages under social service agencies.

- Your local YMCA (for men) and YWCA (for women) may be active in your community in offering job-seeking programs.
- Armed services veterans, people over 55, people with felony convictions, and immigrants can find special help through agencies dealing with their specific needs.
- Your area may have programs for handicapped and people with medical limitations, programs such as those provided by the Bureau of Vocational Rehabilitation designed to help handicapped people find jobs.
- Many people are surprised to find out that they may qualify for programs due to lower-than-average income. Check to see if you qualify.
- For those under age 21, local, state, province, and federal youth job programs are available in many areas with some schools providing classes.
- You may qualify for special job support funds through federal, state, or province programs such as MA-3, OJT, JPTA, or others. Inquire with your state or province employment service or city jobs program people.

Search Firm, Employment Agency Mailings

1. You may wish to secure a copy of the most recent edition of *The Directory of Executive Recruiters,* either from the library or purchase it directly from the publisher, Kennedy Consultants, (603) 585-2200. The cost is nominal, and you will have your personal copy of over 3000 retainer and contingency firms across the United States.

2. For those search firms you know of in your industry but might not be in the *Directory,* write down the contact information on 3-x-5 cards. Consider those factors that you feel are relevant in selecting a firm by geographic location, your industry, your function. If you do not have any idea as to how to sort out these search firms, be generous and include firms you have never heard of. Why? Your goal is to create visibility and exposure for yourself. If you restrict your contacts to those firms you know have jobs, your contact list will indeed be short.

3. How many of your résumés should you mail out? 10? 100? 1000? The answer depends on a number of factors, including your job and level in the organization: If you are a senior executive open to relocating anywhere in the world, and your compensation is in excess of $100,000, then you probably will zero in on national retainer search firms handling engagements above $75,000, nationally. That is about 430 or so firms. Our advice is to send résumés to them all. If, however, you are a highly qualified technical expert and your income is $48,000, then you probably should identify about 50 firms in the $40,000 to $60,000 range. It is a waste of your time and your money to send your résumé to all retainer or contingency firms, even though some other authors recommend sending out 1000 résumés. We wholeheartedly disagree with this blanket, mass mailing approach, as it is impossible to network into and follow up with more than a handful of the key firms. Besides which, if you fall significantly below (or above) the minimum stated range of the searches the firm might be involved in, your résumé runs the risk of summarily being discarded.

4. Use your personal contacts to open the doors into as many employment offices and search firms as you can, with the intention to initiate a follow-up contact within one to three months if you have not heard from the firms.

Help from Friends and Relatives

Think about how you got your last few jobs. Did you answer an ad? Did you go through a search firm or the state employment service? Or were you referred to the company by a friend, relative, or neighbor? If you were referred, you were really using the hidden job market, and the practice is *networking*. If you have previously connected by writing directly to a company, you used a *target organization approach*.

When you network, let people know that you are looking for employment. Tell them what kind of employment you want, and ask them if they know of anyone whom you should inform of your skills, abilities, and availability. Do not write letters to your personal contacts, initially—this is a waste of time and money. Call them first, then write them and include your résumé.

Just a word about asking your friends and personal contacts about job opportunities. Do not feel that you need to put them on the spot, by asking them if they "know of any openings." You are not asking your friends for jobs rather for information about companies or people they would contact if they were to look for work. If they freeze up, it's likely they felt you were asking them directly for a job rather than for names of companies or contacts.

Source 4: Target Organizations

Five Steps in Identifying Your Target Organizations

Target organizations are those organizations which you target or identify as a viable company in which you could contribute. Fundamentally, you determine your market, your audience—those organizations most receptive to your experiences, accomplishments, and capabilities. Certainly, you will be considering such things as type of industry, kind of products, manufacturing processes, forms of distribution, marketing channels, company size, geographic location, operating styles, corporate culture, and general reputation.

By way of example, think of an inverted funnel, narrow at the top and increasingly wider at the bottom. Developing your target organization list of 200 to 300 companies is similar. Your primary list of companies is very specific and very focused and is composed of core companies. You broaden your list of companies by adding organizations related to your primary career focus.

The five steps in developing your target organizations are:

1. Identify the *standard industrial classification (SIC) codes* for your current organization (and all previous companies). SIC codes are found in many of the resource directories identified in Table 6-3.

2. Identify the *major competitors* of your current organization (and all previous companies) and the SIC codes for all their operating units.

3. Identify companies (and their SIC codes) in *related industries* or *related product lines*.

Table 6-3. Library Checklist

FINANCIAL DIRECTORIES

Standard & Poor's *Register*

Value Line

MANUFACTURING DIRECTORIES

Billion Dollar Directory
 (and Corporate Families)

Million Dollar Directory
 (volumes I, II, III)

Corporate 1000

Moody's Index

Directory of Corporate Affiliations

State Directory of Manufacturers

International Directory of Corporate Affiliations

PAPERS, PERIODICALS

Chronicles of Higher Education

Metropolitan Sunday Papers

Crain's Chicago/Cleveland Business

National Ad Search

Federal Career Opportunities

National Business Employment Weekly

Federal Jobs Digest

Predicasts F/X Index

PRIVATELY HELD FIRM DIRECTORIES

MacMillan's *Directory of Privately Held Companies*

Ward's *Directory of U.S. Private Companies*

SERVICE DIRECTORIES

Directory of Consultants and Consulting Organizations

Directory of Executive Recruiters

Dun's *Directory of Service Companies*

TECHNOLOGY, R&D DIRECTORIES

Directory of American Research and Technology

VENTURE CAPITAL DIRECTORIES

Pratt's *Guide to Venture Capital Sources*

Venture's *Guide to International Venture Capital*

MISCELLANEOUS

Annual Reports

Encyclopedia of Associations

Directories in Print

Trade Publications

---

4. Identify companies (and their SIC codes) with *related manufacturing technologies* or *related distribution channels*.

5. Identify companies (and their SIC codes) in your *preferred geographic region* through the use of your library's resources, the public library's directories, area Chamber of Commerce listings, Yellow Pages, etc. If you are looking locally, your goal is to create widespread visibility for your availability, regardless of the industry.

Standard Industrial Classification: Business Code Numbers

When you are researching businesses, the Standard Industrial Classification (SIC) code is one of the most valuable tools available. This explanation of the SIC code system is intended to help you understand how to use the industry cross-reference more effectively.

The U.S. Government developed the SIC code system in conjunction with the private business sector. Prior to its development, no system was available that comprehensively captured U.S. industry. Describing our economy by defining its types of activities, the SIC code is a universal system of comparison through which we can study today's businesses.

SICs are an integral part of any business study. Marketers and advertisers rely on them to pinpoint the kinds of businesses they want to reach. When economists study business segments, they use SICs to identify and compare industries—especially when they are analyzing changes or trends in business and the economy. Job hunters use SICs to identify appropriate or interesting prospective employers. Finally, SIC codes are used for hard copy and computer-assisted searches in business and research everywhere.

Standard Industrial Classification codes divide all economic activity into ten major divisions. These business segments are represented by the first two digits in the SIC code:

Agriculture, forestry, fishing	01-09
Mining	10-14
Construction	15-17
Manufacturing	20-39
Transportation, communication, and public utilities	40-49
Wholesale trade	50-51
Retail trade	52-59
Finance, insurance, and real estate services	60-67
Business services	70-89
Health, social services, and public administration	91-97

Each line of business is placed within one of these 10 divisions and is assigned a code. A four-digit SIC code is the most widely used, but some systems define businesses to six or seven digits.

The first two digits describe the general line of business. The third and fourth digits further pinpoint the business activity:

22   Manufacturing—textile mill products

227   Manufacturing—floor coverings

2272   Manufacturing—tufted carpets, rugs

Virtually anyone who touches the business world will find the SIC system invaluable in locating the right kinds of businesses.

To illustrate a use of SIC codes, let us develop a list of target organizations for our fictitious job changer, Mike Commons:

Background Profile: Midwest Regional Sales & Marketing Manager for TCA Corporation (not his real firm) since 1967.

Step 1:   Mike identified the SIC codes for TCA and all its subsidiaries: 2032, 2038, 2041, 2043, 2045, 2047, 2099, 3944, 3589, 2037, 2064, 2066, 2098, 5145, 5149, 2033.

Step 2:   For each of TCA's SIC codes, Mike identified major competitors and the SIC codes for all of their operating units. Mike Commons captured the SIC codes for canned products (2032 and 2033), frozen specialties (2038), flour and cereal products (2041, 2043, 2045), food service equipment (3589), consumer products (3944), confectionery and groceries (5145 and 5149). Competitors of TCA in flour and cereal products are:

Flour and Cereal Products	2041, 2043, 2045
Con Agra	2011, 2041, 2092, 2099
Pillsbury	2024, 2033, 2037, 2038, 2041, etc.
General Mills	2092, 2038, 2026, 2043
Kellogg	2034, 2043, 2053, 2049
Ralston Purina	2043, 2091, 2047, 3692, 5063
General Foods	2037, 2043, 2035, 2087, 2095, etc.

Step 3:   Mike identified companies and their SIC codes in related industries or product lines. For instance, although Gerber Foods is not a direct competitor to TCA, they are in the canned food business. Likewise, most companies in the 2000 series of the SIC codes

would be potential target organizations as they are all food related.

Step 4: Mike identified companies (and their SIC codes) with related manufacturing technologies or distribution channels. Mike Commons's familiarity with high-speed food product handling, packaging, and distribution can likewise be applied in many other fields.

Step 5: Mike also identified companies (and their SIC codes) in his preferred geographic region of Chicago through the use of library directories, Chamber of Commerce listings, Yellow Pages, etc.

SIC Code Database

After you have identified your SIC codes for focused target organizations and before developing an extensive list of target companies on index cards, contact your local library. Quite possibly, they may have many of your target organizations in an on-line computerized database for your use. Sometimes, there is a charge for the retrieval of such information. Before you blindly pay for a lengthy database printout, ask to examine a sample run. Then you can determine if it meets your specific needs.

Guidelines for Contacting Organizations

Call key decision makers (persons who can hire) in your target firms. These are usually the department heads in whatever function or department you would be in. See if you can talk to a manager at least two levels up from where you would report. Why? If you contact the individual to whom you would report, you might pose too much of a threat; also, that person may not have the same broad-based exposure to organizational needs as a more senior executive.

Unless you are a personnel or human resources professional, avoid sending your résumé to the human resources department. Human resource staffs are trained to screen out résumés. Your goal is to create a lot of visibility with a broad-based mailing and an aggressive follow-up telephone campaign. Consider 10 to 15 calls a day a good "stretch" goal. (This does not include your daily calls to 8 to 10 search firms.) Instead of viewing these as cold calls, maintain the perspective which considers these to be marketing calls to organizations predisposed to your background and experiences.

Guidelines

1. Quickly introduce yourself, your area of expertise, your referral source (if appropriate), and your reason for calling:

> Mr. Samuels, my name is Mike Commons. I'm the regional sales and marketing manager for TCA Company. I met you several months ago at the Institute's meeting when you spoke. Your remarks meant a lot to me, as I also believe in many of the same issues.
>
> As you may have heard, TCA recently reorganized, and my department was affected. Although I probably could have stayed at TCA, I elected not to put my career on hold for another three to five years. To that end, I am coming out of TCA with their full knowledge and support. As I put together a list of the companies I wanted to work with, your company was in the top-10 group.

2. If the company previously sent you a rejection letter:

> Recently I sent you a letter with my résumé informing you of my intentions which you graciously forwarded to Human Resources. They got back to me indicating that while there are no current openings, they would keep my résumé on file for future opportunities, as they were intrigued with my background. I appreciate their willingness to do that beyond a standard form letter.

3. Indicate the reason (reject letter or not) that you have selected this company to write to (or call) and what value you feel you can bring to the firm. Include some of your skills, abilities, or accomplishments that may fit the company's needs:

> I selected your company as a prospective employer for three reasons. You are a highly visible company with a reputation for having quality products, excellent customer relations, and a commitment to expect the best from your employee. I feel I possess many of those same qualities which have helped your company grow, namely, a results-producing focus, team orientation, strong leadership capabilities, and excellent interpersonal skills.

4. Ask for the opportunity to meet for purposes of introduction so that, should a need arise, they will already know of your abilities. Suggest a date in the next few weeks when it might be possible to meet briefly.

> While I recognize that you do not have any bona fide openings, I would still like to meet for purposes of introduction. In your recent speech, you indicated that your company is always on the lookout for new ideas *and* the right people to develop new products, save money, and enhance customer relations.
>
> I *can* make a difference, and the one thing I know about business is that things change. The time to learn about the availability of new technology *and* new people is before a

crisis hits. To that end, I would like to meet, introduce myself, and if your company requires an individual with my background in the future, you will have already known about me. Can we meet sometime within the next four weeks, or would the month after be better?

5. Don't accept a no too readily. Respond with phrases such as:

I understand that your schedule is full, however, my skills are excellent, and I know that I can be a valuable part of your succession plan. I can be brief and would very much appreciate a few moments of your time.

6. If you don't get an interview with your target company:

Well, I understand. I do appreciate your consideration. I would like to check back with you periodically to see if your schedule frees up in a month or so. Would that be all right?

May I also send another résumé for your center desk drawer in the event that you should encounter a need within the near future? Thanks.

By the way, is there someone else who should know of my status, (possibly the staffing manager or vice president of Human Resources), so the company will remember my interest in the event something else appropriate develops?

7. Write a thank-you letter. After all, you have introduced yourself, told the person what you are interested in, described your qualifications, and asked for an interview. Write a follow-up date on your calendar, describing the nature of your next contact. Then, make the call!

The Public Library

Your public library has books and brochures which contain useful careering information. Out-of-town newspapers at the library may be a source of employment in nearby areas. Industrial directories list employers in your geographic area which might have a need for your services.

Librarians are delighted to assist you in finding the materials you need. Ask for help in locating job sources and job-search information. Most libraries have on-line (computer) services which are excellent tools in getting timely data on companies.

The following is a list of basic library resources which will provide you with a good source of employers who may be able to use your skills:

1. *Daily newspapers* with Sunday editions are excellent sources for local opportunities.

2. The *National Ad Search* reprints a representative sampling of classified ads from 74 different newspapers from across the United States, including Anchorage, Alaska.

3. The *Directory of Executive Recruiters* lists both retainer and contingency search firms throughout the United States and has several valuable sections including breakouts by geography, industry, and the function of a position.

4. The *Directory of Corporate Affiliations* and the *International Directory of Corporate Affiliations* tell you who owns the smaller divisions, domestically and internationally, and provides information not available elsewhere.

5. *Dun's Directory of Service Companies* identifies nonmanufacturing firms which provide forms of support services to the public nationally.

6. The *Ward's Directory U.S. Private Companies* identifies privately held firms in your city, state, and industry.

7. The *Million Dollar Directory* lists major publicly held companies.

8. The *Manufacturer's Directory* for your state lists employers by SIC code, city, and alphabetically.

9. *Trade publications* and other *trade directories* are geared specifically to your industry, function, or field of expertise.

10. The *Federal Jobs Digest* identifies public sector jobs and ways to apply.

Format for Collecting Target Company Data

The following format will enable you to collect valuable company information in a standardized manner. Since your company mailing goal is several hundred companies, you will need to photocopy this format, then cut the formats out and tape them onto index cards for ease of use. Having this information taped on cards will allow you to alphabetize companies easily.

Company name:

Address:

City:

State:

Zip code:

Attention name:

Title:

SIC code:

Employee count:

Telephone:

Annual sales:

Salutation:

Source 5: Personal Networking

Simply put, *personal networking* is contacting business colleagues and personal friends you know and involving them in your career search so you might expand your circle of acquaintances who are providing assistance in your job-seeking efforts. *Effective networking* is considered key to a successful job search. Regardless of your position or organizational level, the success of your campaign is directly related to your comfort and success in networking. It's not surprising that you may feel a lot of pressure around networking, how to do it well without exploiting your personal relationships.

Step 7, "Using the Telephone to Capture Leads and Interview Powerfully," presents many helpful tips on networking. Please feel free to adapt any of these suggestions to make them work better for you. If you have a technique that works well for you, please write it down and mail it to us. We'd be pleased to receive it, as it may be something we want to pass along to others.

Four things you absolutely must do with your personal network contacts:

1. Inform them of your status.
2. Ask for help—leads or opportunities they might know of.
3. Legitimize by sending your résumé and having follow-up contact.
4. Follow up immediately on leads.

Inform Contacts of Your Status

Briefly inform them of your situation, provide them a career focus, highlight several things about what you have done and can do, and let them know what kind of job you are looking for:

As you may be aware, my company recently went through another reorganization centralizing its operations, and my position was eliminated. Although I might have had the opportunity to remain in the organization in a lessor capac-

ity, I was not interested in putting my career on hold for three to five years. As such, I am looking with the full knowledge and support of the company for a challenging sales and marketing management position.

In my capacity as regional sales manager, I am skilled in new-product introduction, field sales, account penetration, and dealer development. My strengths lie in creating distinctive promotional campaigns and training approaches which quickly produce results and improve sales and profits.

Ask for Help

After you have reestablished contact and validated the reasons for your call, ask your contacts for their assistance in the form of leads and contacts. Try to solicit these leads and information according to the major avenues of careering: personal contacts, executive search firms, and target organizations. Your goal in networking is not to secure a job but rather to create *visibility* for yourself and your campaign. If you are able to maintain the perspective that enables you to make telephone calls "for purposes of introduction," the pressure to perform perfectly in your networking is diminished. When calling contacts, seek information about *target organizations:*

1. Ask your contacts to suggest some good companies (in your geographic area or industry) to whom you can send your résumé so these companies will know of your availability as future needs arise.

2. Have your personal contact respond to *your list of target organizations.* Show your contact your list or read off your top 20 to 50 companies. These companies represent your highest priorities and are the ones into which you most want to network.

Also ask your contacts about *executive search firms:*

1. Ask if they have any experience with search firms that they would recommend. If they do not have any direct experience, ask if they know of others who have had good experiences with search firms and get their names and telephone numbers. You may wish to secure the name of the head of human resources or staffing in your contact's company.

2. Upon contacting the vice president of Human Resources, ask if he or she would give you names of the search firms the company uses, based on your referral from your contact. Follow the recommended three-step process of inform of status, ask for help, and send your résumé with the Human Resources executive and search firms provided.

Finally, follow these last guidelines in developing *personal contacts:*

1. Ask if they can give you the names of several friends who might be able to suggest other leads or companies which may be appropriate to contact. Have a goal of securing three to five additional names per contact person.

2. Ask if they will remain alert to employment opportunities and let you know if they hear of a lead. (You might provide one or two additional résumés, which they might give to someone if they think it might help.) CAUTION: Never lose control of your campaign. Do not rely upon others to blindly distribute your résumé.

3. Always follow up with friends volunteering to send résumés out on your behalf. If they volunteer to create a mailing for you, it is best for you to have your friends write the letter and for you to do the mailing. This way, you have the ability to recontact these people because you have a list of people and you know exactly when the mailing went out.

Send Your Résumé

As you close your conversation, get the OK both to send your résumé as well as to periodically follow up to inform your contact of your search's progress and to solicit additional leads. Most people will readily agree to that strategy, if only to get you off the phone. However, it is a great opportunity for you to have a second, even more enthusiastic conversation. Ironically, you will find that some of your contacts will identify leads for you only after you have demonstrated success in your search. Be patient and understanding. Create that image of success by being focused, confident, enthusiastic, open, socially bold, and forthright in your dealing with others.

Follow up Immediately on Leads

Always contact your *secondary network* contacts as soon as you can (see Table 6-4). These people are the individuals whose names your personal friends have given you. This is not cold calling. It is simply following up with people who will be happy to talk with you on the basis of your mutual friend's suggestion.

Networking . . . It Works If You Work at It

Your personal contacts will begin to ask their friends and relatives about job leads and company information for you. Your chances of finding a

Table 6-4. Approaches to a Secondary-Level Network Call

Dealing with Secretaries

"I'm calling concerning a personal matter regarding (name of mutual acquaintance)."

"I'm calling as a result of a recent conversation with (mutual acquaintance). Please have Ms. _____ call me back." (What's the nature of the call?) "It is a personal matter concerning Mr. (your contact). Please have Ms. _____ contact me at her earliest convenience."

Dealing with Secondary Personal Contacts

"I was talking with (name), whom I understand is a mutual acquaintance. She suggested that I get in touch with you on a question I had and that you might be willing to help me."

"I am (title) with (company) and I am exploring a new career opportunity in (your industry). I have skills in _____ and _____. (Name) suggested that since you know a lot of people (or are well connected in the industry), that you might be able to suggest the names of some people who might hire someone like me. Do you know anyone that I might get in touch with? Would it be alright with you if, when I call (name), I mention that I have talked with you?"

"Why don't I send you my résumé so that you can take a look at my credentials? I'll plan on getting back to you in a week to see if you thought of anyone as an appropriate contact."

job this way are truly greater than other methods, although you must use all methods in your job-search campaign.

Your coworkers—superiors, peers, and subordinates—in all your employers are an excellent starting point in building your network. Add to this list the consultants, vendors, suppliers, and customers you might have come in contact with from your job. Remember, the sales people who call on you also call on a number of other companies and have access into some executive corridors you do not.

Your pastor, priest, rabbi and your church directory are excellent sources of job information, as are members of social clubs (the VFW or the Moose, for instance). Do not forget people you deal with—your neighbors, doctor, dentist, merchants, or even your barber or hairdresser. How about people on your Christmas card list or other holiday list? It's a good place to start.

And when a friend does give you a job lead, ask if you can mention his or her name to help you open the door to an employer's office. When such leads result in an interview or a good contact, get back to your contacts and thank them. It may result in additional leads.

WORKSHEET 28
My Personal Contacts

Without considering if a person would be an *A* or *C* priority contact, write the names of business colleagues or personal friends as fast as you can. Your list is written on paper, not carved in granite. You can always delete a name after you've captured the data the first time. Make as many copies of this worksheet as you need.

Name	**Name**	**Name**

Developing a Networking Contacts List _____

Begin brainstorming and make a list of your personal contacts: business colleagues and personal friends (see Worksheet 28). List everyone you can think of who might know about other business professionals, companies, or hear of a job opening. This network of friends and acquaintances is your best source of job information.

As you develop your list, do not exclude people whom you may question if they will be a source of solid leads or contacts. Work on developing a large list of names (50 to 200 people). After you have identified every individual you know, go back to the beginning and prioritize every person according to an *A, B, C* priority basis. *A* individuals are those people you see as very well-connected, who know you well, and who would welcome a call from you. *B* contacts are those reasonably well-connected who would be receptive to a call, and *C*'s are people with whom you are not so close and yet they might know one or two people for you to call.

On index cards, write out the contact information on *A* priority persons, (then *B*'s) and make it a practice to get in touch with them every two to four weeks. With your *C* contacts, you may wish to write them to inform them of your changed employment status, then follow up with a telephone call at some later date.

USING THE TELEPHONE TO CAPTURE LEADS AND LAND INTERVIEWS

A Small Change Makes a Big Difference

Donna Samuels was a fine interviewer. She knew her résumé backward and forward and could field tough questions better than the majority of our clients. In fact, she seemed to long for an aggressive interviewer so she could "strut her stuff." She never failed to delight us, as she recounted the specifics of her interviews and how she effectively managed the interview, asking penetrating questions which "peeled back the layers" of one company after another during her search.

While Donna was a great interviewer, she was terrified to pick up the phone and initiate a call. She was comfortable networking only with her closest friends. As she repeatedly called them, she found their support waning. Even though Donna knew she had a great résumé and was effective face-to-face, she sabotaged her efforts to network on the phone.

After observing her in action and tape-recording her side of the conversation, we recommended she stand up and gesture as if the person she was talking to was actually in the room. This change in physical posturing strengthened her voice projection and ability to present a summary of her résumé naturally and conversationally.

With these initial successes, Donna's confidence soared as she overcame her stage fright. She shortly became as effective in telephone networking as she was in face-to-face interviewing.

Overcoming Stage Fright

Donna's paralyzing fear of the phone and her inability to break through to decision makers is not all that uncommon. And yet, she knew she needed to become comfortable. Almost without exception, the telephone will be the means of *personal* contact concerning career opportunities, regardless of how you become introduced to the organization. If your background generated interest and there is a possible fit, you will receive a call rather than a letter. Telephones are extremely potent search tools. Although the telephone can be your greatest ally, it can also stop you dead in your tracks before you get to first base.

Presenting yourself professionally and clearly over the telephone is a critical marketing skill which must be learned by serious job seekers. Before looking at the techniques and skills needed to make the presentation, let us first address the fact that many of us have serious reservations about using the phone to generate leads and interviews.

To effectively market yourself on the phone, you need to be willing to:

- Be open to the idea that you can be a successful self-marketing telephone caller.
- Carefully prepare to do well on the phone.
- Practice raising your comfort level about using the telephone.

Eleven Guidelines You Have Probably Forgotten _____

1. The telephone can be your best means of covering the job market. It is so fast you can get in touch with virtually anyone, anywhere, in just a few minutes. Consider: How long would it normally take you to meet 10 to 15 prospective employers if you talked in their offices or wrote them a letter?

   - You can reach 10 to 15 employers *every day* just by picking up the telephone and dialing.
   - You can gather information faster and easier by using the telephone.
   - You are more likely to reach the person doing the hiring if you call instead of visiting.
   - **Making a phone call can be 100 times more effective than writing a letter.**

2. Avoid lengthy telephone interviews. At least 50 percent of the data you would give in a face-to-face interview are lost because you cannot pick them up over the telephone. Not only can you *not* read body language over the telephone, but you cannot project your own either. Also, since hearing is the only sense channel being used, *how* you sound is very often more important than *what* you say. Over the phone, your *vocal* self will be distorted. Excitement and enthusiasm may be misinterpreted as nervousness or tension. Practice developing a well-modulated voice.

3. A prospective employer forms an impression by the sound of your voice and the questions you ask. You can also learn a lot about a possible employer by the way you are treated on the phone.

4. Your main objective in making personal contact is to get the employer interested in meeting you. If an employer calls you regarding a position in which you are clearly not interested, gracefully decline consideration and provide leads of other people, if appropriate.

5. If called, do not reveal more than your Verbal Résumé* which follows this list without getting some information in return on the organization and the position opening. If there is some mutual interest, press for the interview.

6. If you feel that you are being dragged into a full-blown interview over the telephone, you need to regain control. One technique is to say something like the following:

> **Since it sounds like we have some mutual interest in exploring this further, let us establish a convenient interview time. While we have covered some excellent ground over the telephone, I feel a face-to-face discussion would enable us to get to know each other and the situation better. Do you agree?**

7. When talking to the executive's secretary, try to have obtained her name in advance and use it. Be confident, positive, firm, and polite. As a general rule, do not discuss the nature of the call other than to say that the executive is expecting your call (this is true; in your letter you told the executive that you would call). Or use your current job title to get by the secretary.

8. Be prepared to answer some reasonable questions, e.g., "How does your background relate to this position?" Again, avoid a full interview over the telephone.

9. The executive typically will attempt to reject an interview gesture. Since executives are busy people, you expect to hear: "We have no appropriate openings now. What do you really want to see me about?" Come back with a simple statement indicating that your main interest is to meet for purposes of introduction, if and when something develops.

10. If denied an interview, politely indicate your disappointment and ask for names of individuals who might be approached.

* The concept of the Verbal Résumé℠ was developed by Robertson Lowstuter, Inc., 104 Wilmot Road, Deerfield, IL 60015.

11. Become more comfortable on the phone by doing the following:

- Call various businesses to check out the names of managers or supervisors in your field of interest. Or, you can call prospective employers to get a better idea of the types of questions they will be asking you. You might even ask, "What are some of the tough questions *your company* asks?"

- Leave the best prospects for the last and call them when you feel comfortable on the phone. Practice your telephone presence with friends or others whom you know are also looking for a job until you are able to talk comfortably.

- Making a lot of calls as you look for a job may not be easy. If you believe it will be easy or difficult, you are right. What you believe is what you get. Confidence and self-esteem are what will get you through these tough times. The right job is out there, if you have the patience and perseverance to find it.

- Make it a game. How many "nos" does it take before you can come up with a yes? A *yes* is really all that matters. Rejection is a normal part of everyone's job search. We have learned that if you get one yes for ten nos, you are doing just fine!

The Verbal Résumé— Your Two-Minute Commercial

Obviously, your written résumé is a vital part of your job-search campaign. It covers your entire career, highlighting important aspects of your responsibilities, accomplishments, and abilities while using language that reflects your capabilities to contribute.

Your Verbal Résumé is a 2- to 4-minute, tightly worded, brief and punchy presentation that concisely presents a clear and interesting summary of you. It parallels your written résumé as it also highlights your key qualifications and how you can contribute. Think of your Verbal Résumé as an advertising commercial, quickly gaining the listener's attention and with enough interesting benefits to make it worth the person's while to continue to listen.

Just as your written résumé was scripted and clarified, your Verbal Résumé is also written out. Then it is revised and refined until it becomes an interesting, relevant, and action-oriented career synopsis which you can deliver in a nonhurried verbal style within 2 to 4 minutes.

When you practice, "deliver" rather than merely read your Verbal Résumé into a tape recorder. Practice it with your close friends, family, or friendly bathroom mirror. A great time to rehearse your Verbal

Résumé is while driving in your car to appointments. Don't worry about the cars next to you, everyone has their own agenda, and yours is to powerfully deliver your Verbal Résumé.

Many experienced job searchers make photocopies of their initial presentations to keep near all their telephones as visual support. They find that these copies help their self-confidence and reduce worry about what to say next on the phone.

When you do not have eye contact with an interviewer you miss the guiding signals of body language and facial expression available in a personal interview. A written summary gives you more freedom to listen even more intently on the telephone to what the interviewer is saying and to notice voice changes or important leads.

The Six Elements of Your Verbal Résumé

Your Verbal Résumé consists of six distinct sections. Follow this format as you write out your Verbal Résumé:

1. Introducing Your Verbal Résumé

In order to take advantage of the first few critical moments of an interview in which first and lasting impressions are made, it is recommended that you seize the first appropriate opportunity after you have established rapport and learned something from the other person to introduce your Verbal Résumé in this manner:

> **I wonder if it might be helpful if I were to briefly sketch in my background, what I have been doing, what I'm looking for in my next position, and why I am leaving my company. Would that be helpful?**

In most situations your focus is very much appreciated and will meet with an immediate approval. Proceed immediately to deliver the rest of your Verbal Résumé as follows.

2. Career Focus

In a single sentence, concisely focus your primary career orientation. If you are an accountant you might begin by saying, **"I have a strong financial and accounting background and over 10 years' experience in managing general accounting."** If you are an engineer you might say:

> **I'm a registered professional engineer with 15 years of mechanical and electrical instrumentation experience.**

Or, if you are changing career focus, you might say something like this:

> **Although I have yet to manage my own sales territory, I have excellent work experience. I am able to successfully present ideas to managers, I'm persistent, and I have quickly learned every job I've been given.**

3. Born and Raised

In a single sentence, briefly outline where you were born and raised. Do not go into detail. The purpose is to focus yourself geographically (East Coast, Midwest, West Coast, for example).

4. Education and Special Training or Skills

Briefly state your degrees, major subjects, and school name in about 5 seconds. Do not elaborate on your college experiences or choices unless you are a recent graduate. It is not necessary to fit this information chronologically into your presentation. Quickly cover the information here, so that you can concentrate on your experience. This handles your credentials.

> **I have my Bachelor's in psychology from Aurora University and my Master's in labor relations from the University of Illinois.**

You may also wish to cover special credentials in this section such as a CPA, PE, or RN. Relevant special nondegree or noncollege training can be included such as seminars or workshops. Be careful to include only those items that are relevant to this interview, as this can take up valuable time.

If you have not completed your formal education, this section is ideal to focus your best skills and talents gained through on-the-job experience or apprenticeships.

5. Work History and Significant Accomplishments

Unlike your written résumé, your Verbal Résumé starts at the beginning of your work career and proceeds chronologically up to the present, without mentioning every position change and dates. The reason for reversing this procedure is to quickly skip through your early years so that you can finish your presentation by talking about your most recent work experience. Of the time allocated to this section, spend two-thirds of the time on the last five to eight years of your career and one-third on all preceding time. If your earlier experience is more important to the position you are seeking than your last five to eight years, then, of course you should shift your emphasis accordingly.

Begin with your early position or positions in summary fashion and move up to the current time, listing companies, titles, key responsibilities, and accomplishments. A good rule-of-thumb for accomplishments is not to provide more than about four results for your entire Verbal Résumé. If you provide more, you will probably get bogged down in detail, and your delivery will lengthen unnecessarily. The accomplishments you select should be significant and provide a clear link to the needs of the particular job opportunities in this organization.

Pay particular attention to your transitions from company to company. They should be reasonable and believable. Refer to new skills, responsibilities or experiences that each new job provided. Keep track of your time. Two to four minutes goes by quickly, so diligently watch your tendency to provide more data than are needed when the interviewer reinforces you with a comment or an affirming smile, if you are face-to-face.

6. Reasons for Leaving

Until you discuss your reason for leaving your current employer, the entire interview remains under a cloud. If you do not bring it up, the interviewer will. When the interviewer raises the issue, it will often be asked in an investigatory manner which may sound as though there is some suspicion about your circumstances.

If you bring up your leaving, the issue of your departure is presented voluntarily and you are able to use language which clearly reinforces your candidacy. The result is usually quick recognition and understanding of economic, political, interpersonal, or organizational events, and you have the freedom to continue the interview, further exploring your abilities and the company's needs. Plus, your credibility is greatly enhanced in the interview. The employer knows that if you confidently reveal this potentially damaging information, everything else you say probably is believable.

Also, since most résumés indicate that the applicant was still employed at the time the résumé was written, this section allows you to "clear up" what has happened since you wrote your résumé and to clarify your current status.

Conclude this section by offering a concise statement about what has attracted you to this particular company or position (if possible) and an inquiry of the interviewer to see if she or he would like you to expand further on any of the areas you have summarized.

The following example illustrates how J. Michael Commons introduced his reasons for leaving his current employer:

I have had a very challenging career with the TCA Company. I've been involved in every stage of the sales and marketing function and have advanced to national sales manager.

The business has recently consolidated its operations, with my division being impacted. As such, the need for two sales managers is not present. So given the limited opportunities now, I've decided that it's a good time to move on.

I've discussed my concerns with senior management. They have been very understanding and have provided excellent support to me in this transition. My obligation to TCA is now complete, and I am available to start as soon as possible with a growing organization such as Becklon Products.

In conclusion, the six elements of a Verbal Résumé for your use in designing your introduction presentation are:

1. Introduction
2. Focus
3. Born and raised
4. Education, training, skills
5. Work history and accomplishments
6. Reasons for leaving and current status

Before preparing your Verbal Résumé (see Worksheet 29) review the example on p. 208 of an introductory summary utilized by another job seeker. At no point, should your uninterrupted Verbal Résumé be longer than 4 minutes. You'll have time for greater elaboration later, but this capsule summary of your credentials must be short. The speaking time of this example is approximately 2 minutes and 55 seconds. Read this example out loud, with a watch, so you can experience an optimal delivery speed.

Eight Helpful Tips for Breaking Through to Employers

Now that you have both your résumé and Verbal Résumé together, let's look at readying yourself for contacting employers or search firms.

1. *Prepare an opening statement.* Write down your statement on paper and see how it sounds to you. Make it interesting and attention-getting. If you bore the listener, chances are they will either politely dismiss you or hang up. Be prepared.

2. *Practice delivering your Verbal Résumé* until you can recite it without sounding sing-song or monotonous. If you get someone on the telephone who is interested, you can launch into it. Learn how to enthusiastically delivery your Verbal Résumé with the same high-level energy you use to talk about something of great importance to you.

A VERBAL RÉSUMÉ EXAMPLE

I am an experienced corporate photographer with experience in all aspects of technical, product, advertising photography, and lab work.

I was born in the Kansas City area and was raised in California and the Midwest.

My education includes Photo Journalism at UCLA, and Commercial/Industrial Photography at Dresden School of Professional Photography and at Kodak Educational Center in Rochester.

My first assignment was as a photographer with the *News Tribune* in Long Beach, California. I covered news, sports, and fashion events and developed a strong sense of urgency in meeting deadlines. It was a challenging and creative position, but it didn't give me much variety, so I applied to several publishing companies.

I held several positions with publishing houses, completing many on-location commercial assignments. I also had the opportunity to manage a photography department with Durant Drug Company, where I also had supervisory responsibility and retail sales duties. I enjoyed managing the department as well as the special photography assignments.

I have a strong personal attraction to photography, especially in scenic and natural environments, and I have had exhibits and a one-man show of my work in New York.

Since 1974, I have been corporate photographer for Acco Brothers Co., a leading manufacturer in the specialty chemical field. I have managed all corporate in-house photography including:

- Catalogue, product, and advertising photography
- Public relations and executive portraiture
- Extensive on-location field assignments for product shots

I am experienced with most photographic equipment and in both black and white and color lab processing.

Recently Acco Brothers has chosen to close its corporate photography department and use outside services as a cost reduction move. I am affected by this transition, which allows me the opportunity now to look for another excellent company that has a strong interest in having a quality, in-house photographic capability.

I'm most interested in Frampton Corporation's growth and products, and I believe I can provide significant cost savings and efficiencies in your photographic work as a corporate photographer. I look forward to learning more about Frampton in this interview. Are there any particular parts of my background on which you would like me to expand?

WORKSHEET 29
My Verbal Résumé

Using the guidelines of the preceding pages write out your Verbal Résumé.

_____

_____

_____

_____

_____

_____

_____

_____

_____

_____

_____

_____

_____

_____

_____

_____

_____

_____

_____

_____

_____

_____

_____

_____

_____

3. To get interviews, you must *pick up the telephone* and *ask for interviews*. But this means knowing who you would like to speak to, what you want to ask them, and where they can be reached.

4. After you have decided on your *plan of attack*, prepare specific questions and decide how you will answer some of the common questions you may be asked.

5. *Record a few calls* on your tape recorder. Listen to your voice and decide how you can improve your phone manner.

6. *Be relaxed* on the telephone, listen, and react to what the person on the other end is saying. Take notes that you can read and refer to later. You need to get the facts the first time. Do not be afraid to have a person repeat a name, the spelling of a company, or an address. These facts are crucial to your job search.

7. *Describe who you are,* what you want, and what you have to offer. Keep in mind that all you will be asking for is an opportunity to meet for *purposes of introduction and networking*.

8. Communicate *your commitment to follow up* on this initial phone call within a few days to either confirm the interview schedule or press for another meeting "for purposes of introduction."

Building Telephone Confidence

Preparation is the key to building self-confidence in telephone self-marketing. Successful telephone communication is not achieved by luck. Rather, it is achieved by anticipating, preparing, and practicing.

You never know what people may say when you call them. If you are not prepared or have not practiced telephone techniques, some of their responses can stall you and limit your successful introduction. Review carefully the following four-step approach used by many job searchers to build their confidence on the telephone.

1. Research
2. Primary network contacts
3. Secondary network contacts
4. Target organizations

Research

Build your confidence early in the job search by using the telephone for nonthreatening, low-risk information gathering or research. You are going to need a quality target list of companies to contact about your availability, including such specifics as name of decision maker, title, telephone number, perhaps even sales size of company. Clearly, you would not want to send out your résumés to organizations on an impersonal "occupant" basis. You know how you treat such mail. Knowing that you are contacting the right person by name is a great confidence builder. Contacting the right person also significantly improves the quality of your contact, the company's perception of you, and the rate of response to your résumé.

So begin by calling companies. Utilize the receptionist, other department people, or clerical people to get the correct name and title of the person you wish to contact later:

This is the RL Research Group, and I am verifying some data on your company. Can you please tell me the name of your company president? Can you spell that last name please? And his correct title, please? Thank you very much.

As you research your target firms in this manner, you will begin to feel your comfort level improving and your telephone skills becoming stronger. With very little risk on your part, you are able to get the feel of how to introduce yourself and your purpose quickly, to be creative in overcoming objections, and to use the telephone as a job search tool.

Primary Network Contacts

Begin using the phone to inform your primary network of personal friends, and business and professional colleagues, neighbors, and acquaintances of your status and your career objectives. These people are not strangers. They are people you know well who would want to help you succeed. Introduce your job skills quickly to them. Ask them if they have any information or can provide leads into target companies, search firms, personal contacts; ask them if they know of any specific employment opportunity.

Refresh your networking skills by reviewing once more Source 4: Personal Networking in Step 6. This is not begging for a job. **Do not even ask them if they know of anyone who is actively hiring.** If you do a good job describing your skills and abilities, you will not have to ask. If they know of something current, they will volunteer that. Remember, if your contacts seem to "stiffen up" and say "we are not hiring," you have somehow miscommunicated your intentions. You need to clarify that: "I am not asking *you* for a job. I am sorry if you feel as if I was putting you on the spot. Rather, I am interested in whether you know any companies (and search firms and leads) I should contact."

What you are after now is contacts: companies and people who might, from time to time, have a need for people with your skills. Here are the key things to say to your network contact which parallel the advice provided about personal networking in Step 6:

1. Crisply focus your basic skills, abilities, and career objectives.

2. Ask if your friend can suggest good *target organizations* that you should include in your target list which might have a future need for someone with your skills. Your friend may even know the right person to contact by name or someone who would be able to "introduce you to the firm."

3. Ask if your friend knows anyone in *your list of target organizations*. Again, these organizations are ones you specifically want to have a relationship with, even though there might not be any current openings.

4. Ask if your friend can suggest any *search firms* or *employment agencies* through personal experience or through his or her company's personnel department.

5. Ask if your friend would provide *personal contact* leads for you.

Use Worksheet 30 to create your network introduction. When you have called 20 to 30 friends and discussed your abilities and goals with them, you will find your competence and confidence level reaching new heights.

Secondary Network Contacts

It is now time to contact your secondary network contacts. These people are the individuals your personal friends have told you about. This isn't cold calling. It is simply following up with people who will be happy to talk with you on the basis of your mutual friend's suggestion. When you call, immediately make the linkage to your mutual friend. This makes your contact a bit easier and more comfortable. Then follow the same steps you used with your personal friends in establishing your primary network.

Let's review how one of our job searchers, Jean Dorn, introduced herself to a secondary network contact:

Hello Mr. Reynolds, my name is Jean Dorn. You don't know me, however, I am a friend of Bill Gentry. He suggested that you might be able to briefly help me on a subject he and I were discussing. Have I caught you at a good time?

Mr. Reynolds, I am an experienced manufacturing manager, with an excellent engineering background and a solid track record of increasing productivity and reducing manufacturing costs in the consumer packaged goods industry.

WORKSHEET 30
My Network Introduction

Using information from the following example, write out your own introduction to your network contacts. Use additional sheets of paper as necessary.

As you may be aware, my company recently went through another reorganization centralizing its operations, with my position being eliminated. While I might have had the opportunity to remain in the organization in a lesser capacity, I was not interested in putting my career on hold for 3–5 years. As such, I am looking with the full knowledge and support of the company for a challenging sales and marketing management position.

To recap, in my capacity as Regional Sales Manager I am skilled in new product introduction, field sales, account penetration, and dealer development. My strengths lie in creating distinctive promotional campaigns and training approaches which quickly produce results and improve sales and profits.

_____

_____

_____

_____

_____

_____

_____

_____

_____

_____

_____

_____

_____

_____

_____

_____

_____

Because of some recent ownership changes over at Drexel Corporation, I am going to be looking for a new assignment. Bill said that you have good knowledge of your industry and he thought you might be able to suggest some good consumer product firms that I should send my name to so that they will know about me in case they have any future openings.

Continue making secondary network calls in this manner until you have made 20 to 30 calls. Since the use of your mutual friend's name minimizes resistance, concentrate on quickly introducing your skills, abilities, and accomplishments. Concentrate also on smoothly and comfortably shifting from introduction to your request for information. You are now a seasoned telephone networker. Now follow through on all solid secondary contacts throughout your campaign.

Target Organizations

Prepare a written outline to help you make direct contact phone calls to potential employers. Place it by your phone and refer to it to get started or if you think you might forget something.

Stand up and gesture when you talk to people, especially on the telephone. People will catch your enthusiasm and sincerity. Smile. Imagine the interviewer as a friend. If you knew you could not fail, how would you act? The following is an example of a written outline for calling potential employers:

Hello, my name is (name). I am the (title) at (company).

Recently my company has _____ and my job has been impacted.

I am interested in a position as a _____ or a _____ because of my experience and skills. While you might not have any appropriate opportunities at this time, I am interested in becoming known to your company should a need develop.

I am an experienced _____ skilled in _____ , and my strengths lie in _____ and _____ .

As I am just now beginning to conduct a job search, I have identified your company as one I would like to get to know better. That is why I am calling. I am interested in (company) and any current or future needs you might know of within your company or others in our industry.

Highlights of my accomplishments include _____ ,
_____ , **and** _____ .

Can we set up a brief meeting on _____ **or**
_____ **of this week, or would next week be
better for you?**

Thanks very much. I sincerely appreciate it.

The ABCs of Telephone Contacts to a Company ————————

A telephone contact has three parts:

1. Identifying who you are
2. Positioning what you want
3. Adding value

Identifying Who You Are

Letting an employer know who you are is crucial. Pronounce your name
slowly and understandably. Start with a greeting. For instance: "Hello,
my name is (name). I am the (title) at (company).

Positioning What You Want

Get to the point quickly with an employer. Do not keep him or her guess-
ing. Indicate that you either want to be considered for a position inside
the company, or you are calling to network because your company is
restructuring, (or whatever reason). Be specific and get to the point:

> **Recently my company has** _____ **and my
> job has been impacted. I am interested in a position as a**
> _____ **or a** _____ **because of my experience and
> skills. While you might not have any appropriate opportuni-
> ties at this time, I am interested in becoming known to your
> company should a need develop.**

Read this out loud to yourself and be certain that you can be clearly
understood. Speak up clearly. When you make the first few calls you may
be nervous. However, after several practice calls, you will probably find
your introduction becoming more relaxed, natural, and conversational.

Practice, practice, practice will get you relaxed and feeling powerful.

Adding Value

Adding value is the most important part of your conversation. The
employer needs to see your potential as a valuable contributor. If you
add value, doors will open.

- What do you have to offer that this company cannot do without?
- What are your skills, experiences, good qualities, and results achieved?
- How are you different from all of the other job seekers?

Tell the employer what you have done, what you can do, and what you would like to do. Use the qualities that you have already assembled, but *present them conversationally*—as if you were talking to a friend:

> **I am an experienced _____ skilled in _____ and my strengths lie in _____ and _____ .**
>
> **As I am just now beginning to conduct a job search, I have identified your company as one I would like to get to know better. That is why I am calling.**
>
> **Highlights of my accomplishments include _____ , _____ , and _____ .**

Read the qualities you have listed out loud. You may want to make some changes in wording so that they are easier for you to repeat.

Note: People take their cues from you. If you believe in yourself—that you can contribute significantly to an organization, regardless of your role or level—then others will believe in you also. You will get what you create in life and in your job search.

Telephone Follow-up

An integral part of your initial conversation with prospective employers or networking contacts is positioning yourself for follow-up phone contact. Often, your first connection with people will not yield the results you would like, and you need to recontact them to gain meaningful leads or exploratory interviews. At the close of your conversation, ask if you may follow up with a second call to keep your contact posted on the progress of your search. When you do this confidently, provided you have not pressured your contact into providing leads, most people will graciously indicate their acceptance of a recontact.

Answering Reject Letters

It may be appropriate for you to recontact some of the firms that sent you reject letters. Now, don't misunderstand—we are not talking about contacting every single organization that sent you a "boing" letter, rather only your top 10 percent.

If the reject letter is from one of your top organizations, then recontact the person to whom you originally wrote and thank them for getting back to you (themselves or through a human resource person). That's right, thank them! Few firms today take the time to respond to résumés and contacts. Let the person know that you appreciate his or her thoughtfulness. Indicate that the executive's thoughtfulness reconfirms your high evaluation of their company when you selected them as an organization you would like very much to work for. Following up on rejects will distinguish you from your competition, as few people take the time to do so.

If the reject letter said that there are no current openings, but your information would be kept on file for future needs, you can ask for an interview. Request the opportunity to meet personally, "for purposes of introduction," on the basis of your excellent abilities.

Such a brief introductory meeting might be valuable in the event that a future need arises. If that happens, they will already know of your abilities and can call you. Actually a large number of excellent positions are filled by candidates who have already qualified themselves before the actual opening occurred.

Your first goal in these calls is to establish a warm, professional, and comfortable contact with someone who can potentially hire you. Even if this is all you achieve this time, you have done well for a first contact.

Your second goal is to meet the manager briefly, for purposes of introduction, so that you are no longer a faceless name on a résumé. This distinguishes you from the thousands of job searchers who depend primarily on their résumé to get them a job.

Don't be overly concerned with being rejected again in the follow-up calls. **Your goal is not to get a job but to develop a large "no" list.** All too often we do not initiate a follow-up call because it is uncomfortable and we want the call to be perfect. Do not worry about perfection, your aim is to create visibility and exposure for yourself in these introductory calls.

Follow-up on "No Replies"

What about those top target organizations to whom you sent résumés and from whom you received no reply? Follow up on them too. Tell the executive (who would be most likely to actually hire you if there is a need) that you recently sent a résumé, not because there is a current opening, but because you believe that your experience, background, skills, or industry knowledge can make you a valuable candidate for future opportunities with the organization. Tell the executive about your credentials. Ask for the opportunity to meet briefly for an introductory meeting, so that the company will be aware of you and what you can offer as future business needs develop.

Telephone Answering Machines

You need a reliable telephone answering machine during your job-search campaign. Sometimes people object to having one of these devices, and phrase their objection as, "I don't like those machines," or, "I hate to get one of those machines when I call someone." Be that as it may, *consider your home phone as your business phone.*

Think about the last time you called a local merchant for a business purpose only to find that no one answered the phone. The second or third time that this happened, you probably called another store. The original store lost your business.

That is what corporate recruiters, executives, and search firm people will do. After three "no answers," they move on. You will have lost a job opportunity. If they can leave a message, they will go to other things, save time, and be confident that they have reached you. Get an answering machine and connect it.

What kind of machine should you get? A wide variety of machines are available at costs from $25 to $100. We recommend a machine that has two tapes, one for receiving messages and one for your recorded message. This feature reduces the time callers must wait to record their messages and requires only one tone sound instead of two before they can begin their message.

Machines that simply state your message and don't allow the caller to leave a message are worse than no machine at all. Ideally a machine which automatically activates the "on" feature is preferable, so that you will not forget to activate it manually before leaving the house.

If you are away from home frequently, you may wish to be able to call in to your machine from a remote phone and receive your messages. There are excellent "beeperless" systems available which do not require that you carry a beeper device.

In addition, a good option to select is a toll saver feature. You can set the machine to ring four times before the first message is recorded and two times on each subsequent call. If you call your answering machine at home, you can hang up on the third ring and save long-distance or toll charges when their are no messages.

Finally, make your message brief, clear, professional, and businesslike. Avoid informal greetings like "Hi" and attempts to be humorous. Before recording your telephone answering machine message, read the recording instructions carefully and practice recording. Next, sit quietly by the machine for a few moments and listen for distracting sounds. Arrange for people, pets, clocks, fans, and other sound producers to be silent during your recording. When you record your message, "deliver" your message in a courteous and businesslike manner. Speak directly into the microphone, with your mouth about 8 inches from the unit. Do not rush — speak clearly. Smile and sound friendly.

Examples of messages you can use or adapt are as follows:

Thank you for calling. I am sorry we are not available to speak with you personally. Your call is important and we would like to get back to you. Please leave your message, name, phone number, and time you called after the tone, and we will get back to you shortly.

Thank you for calling the Smith residence. None of us are available to take your call at the moment. If you would please record your name, message, phone number, and time you called, after the tone, we will see that your message is delivered as soon as possible and that your call is returned.

Summary

As you have seen in this step, you *can* raise your telephone comfort level. By beginning at the relatively low-risk research communication stage and by developing a comfort level at each successive stage through repetition, you will become more confident, bold even, in your use of the telephone.

It is critical that you learn how to talk comfortably to a company's representative about yourself and your abilities as a valuable resource for a firm's future needs. Using the telephone as an integral part of the campaign is a powerful marketing approach designed to specifically improve your success in securing an appropriate job for you in the least possible time.

INTERVIEWING POWERFULLY: BEATING OUT YOUR COMPETITION

STEP 8

Visualizing Success: Creating Personal Power

"Visualize success—see yourself answering the tough questions successfully and confidently. If you saw yourself being successful, what would you be thinking as you entered the interviewer's office? If you knew, beyond a shadow of doubt, that you had the power to manage this interview exactly as you wanted it, how would you act?" These were the questions we posed to Roger Dalton, a middle-aged operations manager and former marine sergeant, who had been generating initial interviews with ease but who had very few second interviews.

We suspected that Roger's underlying insecurity, coupled with his assertive and blunt manner of speaking, was turning off employers. Although Roger was an excellent maintenance engineer, he possessed only moderate skills as a manager of people, a role in which he was increasingly frustrated and committed to leaving. As he no longer wanted to be a round peg in a square hole, Roger began interviewing for nonmanagerial opportunities outside of his company.

"Identify an individual that you know or suspect would have terrific interpersonal skills and would interview confidently. Have you identified that person? Can you visualize that person, physically, in your mind? Good. Let's have that person go on one of your interviews. Visualize your person getting ready, driving to the next interview, greeting the receptionist, being ushered into the interviewer's office, commenting on the surroundings, asking several initial leading questions to establish rapport, volunteering information, fielding tough questions, making observations about the company's growth, and effectively probing further into sensitive areas concerning organizational politics.

"Feel the reactions of your person when he or she is asked a particularly difficult question and confidently responds, 'I'm sorry. I've never been asked that question before and I've drawn a blank. May I come back to this question later, when I can better formulate a response?' Visualize the interviewer and your person continuing to comfortably converse, exchanging information on a mutual 'I talk, you talk' basis. Sense the interview drawing to a comfortable close. Visualize your person beginning to summarize the interview, thanking the interviewer for the opportunity to learn more about the company, expressing a mutual fit, appropriately asking for feedback and the 'next step' and exiting the building.

"With your eyes still closed, repeat this interview process only with yourself in place of your person. Don't strive to have your words and actions be identical to your person, rather be confident and relaxed as you greet the interviewer, ask and answer penetrating questions, handle with ease those questions which have always 'derailed' you previously. See yourself as poised, confident, gracious, genuine, interpersonally warm, and technically competent.

"Visualize the interviewer becoming enthusiastic about your candidacy and asking about your availability for a second round of interviews. See yourself comfortably managing the interview's summary and close, asking for and giving appropriate feedback, and exiting the interview. Given your visualization process, describe how your body feels right now. Fine. Describe your mental state as you were visualizing a successful interview. Describe how you are feeling right now. Where did you get in trouble in your previous interviews and what can you do to prevent its reoccurrence?"

Equipped with new skills and heightened interviewing awareness, Roger excitedly "visualized" his next interview. He reported back to us that the interview went far better than any interview previously and that it felt as if he was interviewing with an old friend. "Déjà vu," is how Roger described it, like he had been there before . . . for indeed, he had.

The Three Questions Asked by All Employers

The interview is the key to being hired. Roger knew that and so do you. Your networking, marketing letters, or résumé may get you the interview, but you will get hired because of the solid job you do in the interview. Ultimately, the employer is interested in the answers to three fundamental questions:

1. *Can you do the job?* Do you have the technical background, training, education, capabilities, and experiences to perform the work, short-term as well as long-term? Do you have a track record of results which match the opportunity?

2. *Will you fit in?* Do you have well-developed interpersonal and organizational skills? Are these skills sufficient to interact well with the team? Do you exhibit an operating style and a level of flexibility which would accommodate changes? To what extent are you able to gain the widespread endorsement and advocacy of others?

3. *Do you want the job?* How enthusiastic are you? How well prepared are you for the interview? What do you know about the company, the competition, or end users? Did you ask to receive company literature before the interview? To what extent did you challenge the interviewer through observations, comments, and questions? How did you communicate your desire to contribute to the business?

If you and another candidate have the skills to perform the job, the employer will hire the person that she or he likes the best. If you both meet the minimum requirements, it is just common sense to go for the person who might be more personable on the job. It is true that *people hire people they like.*

Preparing for the Interview: 16 Recommendations

The following are 16 recommendations for preparing for the interview:

1. Take a trip to the local library and ask the librarian for reference directories in which you can find information about the company, its competitors, its vendors, and its industry. Contact the local Chamber of Commerce, also.

2. Request company literature (annual reports, employee newsletters, promotional material, or product brochures) that would help you prepare for the interview.

3. Call the placement offices of area colleges or ask friends and neighbors who work at the company where you are interviewing. You need to find out what the company does, what sorts of equipment are used, what a person in your position might be doing, and if the company has growth potential.

4. *Anticipate, prepare, and practice.* It is essential that you anticipate questions that may be asked of you, prepare solid responses which are truthful and credible, and practice responding in a relaxed and confident manner. Practice, practice, practice answering the interview questions which are located near the end of this Step in Handling the Tough Questions: Role-Playing. Read them out loud in

front of a mirror or have someone else ask you the questions. Don't forget to smile, speak up, speak clearly, and practice using gestures until you feel and look natural and genuine. Although we are somewhat joking, you should become so skilled at interviewing that you can "plan out your spontaneity" in the interview.

5. Maintain your perspective! Remember, there is the potential for mutual benefit. *The company has as much to gain from hiring you as you gain from being employed. Don't give up your personal power.*

6. Ask probing, penetrating questions. *Effective interviewing is a two-way street.* A candidate who does not ask leading questions is generally seen as weak, indecisive, or uninterested.

7. *You have "rights" as an interviewee.* You have the right to be treated with dignity and respect in the interview. If you are being intimidated in the interview and you find it impossible to turn it around to your advantage, you have the right to terminate the discussion. If you are being greatly inconvenienced by an unusual interview schedule, you have the right to ask for some accommodation to your own schedule.

8. When interviewing, your instincts reveal significant pieces of information which should be considered. Most people do not seriously evaluate the data they collect from their intuitive "selves," believing that how they are intuitively reacting to a person or a job opportunity is not a valid source of information. We have known people who have been so excited about the monies being offered that they ignored what their "gut" was telling them. Invariably, three to six months into the new job, they complained of taking a "nonjob" and left soon after. You may be tempted to accept the first decent opportunity which comes along. Given the uncertainty of the future, it is very easy to rationalize yourself into a position while blindly ignoring your gut instincts that might very well be saying, "Whoa!"

9. Dress conservatively for interviews. You want to stand out from the crowd in a positive manner. Hair should be conservative. If you have a beard or mustache, it should be neatly trimmed or shaved off for the interview. You can always grow it back after you have been hired. Men should aim for a clean-cut appearance.

10. Dress appropriately for the interview. Napoleon Hill once said, "You will become what you think about." Fine clothing, which fits comfortably and flatters, helps instill confidence. If you think confident thoughts, so shall you act. Women should wear a business suit, an attractive dress, or a skirt/blouse with a minimum amount of jewelry and perfume. Men should preferably wear a suit, or a nice sports jacket at least. A suit or a sports jacket would seem out of place in some areas of the country so use your own judgment. When in

doubt, overdress slightly. You are trying to make a positive impression. Remember: *You never get a second chance to make a good first impression.*

11. Do not chew gum in an interview and do not smoke, even if the interviewer offers you a cigarette. Get a good night's sleep so you can be fresh for the interview.

12. *Arrive early.* Be sure you are close, but do not go into the building until about ten minutes before the interview. Being punctual is very important to a prospective employer. It gives him or her an idea of how responsible and reliable you are. If you come too early, you may have to wait for the employer, and it could be awkward.

13. In all that you do, *be enthusiastic and confident.* Your body language should reflect your positive attitude that says, "I *can* make a difference."

14. Be cordial to everyone you meet on your way to the interview. Secretaries and other employees can have a positive (or negative) influence on the person who is conducting the interview. Many employees know that a position is open and people will be coming in for interviews. They also can spot strangers and will form an impression. A good impression passed on to the interviewer can only work in your favor.

15. If you are overweight, begin a conservative exercise and weight loss program. Like it or not, physically fit people appear more "together." The employer may unfairly assume that if you are undisciplined regarding your physical being, you probably are also somewhat undisciplined on the job. You didn't put those extra pounds on overnight, and it is impossible to shed them overnight, as well. Regarding exercise, consistency is more important than the occasional hard workout. The key to any exercise program is the ability to build up your physical stamina, gradually increasing the intensity of the workout.

16. *Visualize success! If you knew you could not fail, how would you act, think, and feel?* Truly successful job changers visualize themselves actually going through an effective and powerful interview. They create sensations in their mind as if they were on-site, at the employer's office building, responding to tough questions, as well as asking probing questions in return.

Three Stages of the Interview

Each interview is composed of three stages or phases, be it with an executive search firm or a target organization:

STAGE I.   Building rapport

STAGE II.   Discovering needs, creating linkages

STAGE III.   Summary and close

I. Building Rapport

Even though you've researched the company and are prepared for the interview, it is appropriate to both develop rapport quickly and get the interviewer to talk about the organization's *past* successes, *future* plans, and *present* resources so you have a "context" for the interview. Then you can vary your responses specifically to the unique demands of the interview.

Keep in mind that your goal is to manage the interview, not to dominate it or control it. An extremely effective tool is to ask several strategic questions immediately—upon sitting down—to develop rapport and focus. These questions center on establishing perspective about the company's past, future, and present:

Past, Future, and Present Perspective

Past: "Thank you for the opportunity to interview. I have always been impressed with the company and even more so after I took the liberty of doing some research on the company. Your growth rate in the past five years was impressive. What were the main things you would attribute your success to?"

Future: "Thank you for that historical perspective. Since you've grown rapidly in the past, how do you plan to continue that growth in the face of changing technology and increasing competition?"

Present: "Given where you have come from and your ambitious plans for the future, how well-equipped are you now, in the company and in your department, to meet these challenges?"

"Verbal Résumé"

After the interviewer has shared with you some things about the organization, it's your turn to share. Remember, your time limits on your Verbal Résumé and your goal—to create a context for the interview and establish rapport. Your lead-in could sound something like this, "Thank you for sharing about your organization. Would you like to hear a summary of my background and the results achieved?" At that point you can highlight your track record in the context of the information provided by the interviewer.

II. Discovering Needs and Creating Linkages

You will be spending the majority of your time in Stage II, the "body" of the interview. Later in this Step, in "Handling The Tough Questions:

Role-Playing," you will encounter questions commonly asked in the body of the interview.

Discovering Needs

This is the time in which *you* will have an opportunity to uncover needs, discover possibilities, and create linkages. One of the most powerful interviewing approaches is to create a "consultant's perspective." Imagine that you've been hired by the organization with whom you are interviewing to provide top-quality advice on how to address the challenges in the open position's job description. This is a time for you to be listening, observing, asking probing and penetrating questions, and reflecting on things you have seen and learned in the organization.

As an interviewee, you may think of yourself as not having as much power as the interviewer. You may even unconsciously grant more power and credibility to the company representative than to yourself, as a potential employee. However, this is a time for a mutual exchange of ideas and information to see if there is a fit. Remember, you have as much to give any company as they have to offer.

Creating Linkages

Linkages enable you to ask questions or respond to issues in ways that allow you to effectively transition from one topic to another. For instance, if you ask a question of the company decision maker, presumably he or she will respond with some information. You can either use that information to "bridge" to a new topic of discussion, provide supportive information from your own background, or make an observation which encourages the interviewer to continue the discussion. Interview linkage enables you to operate on a mutual "give and get" basis, which will feel more balanced and make the interviewer more comfortable.

III. Summary and Close

Managing the interview means you know where you are and where you want to be in the interview. Given that, it is appropriate to create some closure to the interview and to get some idea as to how you are fitting into the candidate pool. It is recommended that you do the following:

1. Summarize the interview, acknowledge your interest, and express your appreciation for the opportunity to interview:

> **Ms. Jones, we have covered some very good points in our interview. I sincerely appreciate the time you spent with me and the care with which you outlined the position. I am very interested and excited about this opportunity.**

2. Acknowledge a mutual fit, or nonfit if appropriate:

Based on what you and your colleagues have described, it appears as if there is a very good fit. I am particularly pleased with how well you and I seem to work together and the values we seem to have in common.

3. Ask for feedback as to how the interviewer sees the fit:

How do you see the fit with my background, skills, and abilities?

4. Ask, **"What is the next step?"** Listen to what occurs next. You may learn extremely valuable information on the timetable of the decision and the status of other candidates.

5. Commit to a timetable to get back together for a second round of interviews, a psychological appraisal, reference checks, or a physical examination.

. . . that ought to put us about the twentieth of the month for the next step? Great! If we have not confirmed our schedules by then, I will give you a call to see how plans are developing. Would that be all right?

6. Follow through with thank-you letters to all the people with whom you interviewed. Yes, each and every one.

7. Several days after the round of interviewing and after your letters have been mailed, you may wish to follow through with a call back to the decision maker and the respective human resource representative to see if they have any additional feedback.

Let's drop in on Mike Commons summarizing one of his successful interviews:

Thank you for the opportunity to meet you and your team. I sincerely appreciate you making this possible. I thought we covered some very interesting things both about the company's long-range growth plans, your departmental needs, as well as how my background seemed to relate with your sales and marketing strategies.

I see a "fit" from my perspective; what do you think? Are you interested in taking the next step? What do you think our time frame should be to get back together again? Given that you are going to be out of town for the next two weeks, are there some other people in the organization I can interview with while you are out? This might be one way to keep up the momentum. What do you think?

Great! I look forward to hearing from you this week. Since I have a number of business appointments, as well, I will plan on calling you Friday, early afternoon, if you haven't reached me. I look forward to our next meeting.

During and after the Interview _____

During the Interview

1. Tips

Smile, have a firm handshake, stand erect, sit up straight, maintain eye contact (especially with difficult questions), don't take notes, enunciate, speak clearly, answer questions concisely and directly, do not ramble, ask questions, create linkages from one topic to another, be enthusiastic, do not take criticism or pointed questions personally, legitimize objections, add value, and keep visualizing success.

Be genuine and let the positive aspects of your personality show through. If you have a sense of humor, reveal it; do not force it, and, by all means, *never* tell jokes. Remember, interviewing is a two-way process with the opportunity for you and the company to be of mutual benefit. If you have trouble remembering names, repeat the person's name several times immediately after meeting the person and several times throughout the course of the interview. The exchange of business cards is an effective way to reinforce your remembering a person's name and title.

2. Money, Money, Money

If the interviewer asks how much money you would like to make, tell him or her that the job and opportunity are more important than the starting pay. If you are pushed to name a figure, know how much the job should pay (again, your preparation before the interview should help here), and figure in your experience and know-how. Then suggest a range.

I have been looking at opportunities from \$_____ to \$_____ because, as we discussed, I am more interested in the job and potential than the salary. How does this fit with your expectations?

3. Asking for Feedback . . . and the Job

When you feel the interview is coming to an end, tell the interviewer how much you have enjoyed the meeting and acknowledge that you feel there is a fit and would like to take the next step. Ask the employer if he or she feels the same. Offer a firm handshake. Smile. Ask how soon a decision will be made. Ask if you haven't heard by that date, if you can call and check. Employers like honesty. Ask for the job if you want it.

4. A Poor Interview

If you feel that an interview went badly because you were nervous or you did not understand a question, acknowledge that you were nervous and probably tried too hard to make a positive impression. Ask how you could improve and see if the employer will offer you another chance at an interview.

After the Interview

1. Thank-You Letters

After the interview, make notes on how you felt about the interview, using the Interview Critique sheet at the end of this Step. The Interview Critique sheet will help you strengthen your presentation skills and significantly improve your ability to anticipate tough questions.

Write a different letter to each person with whom you interviewed, thanking each for his or her time and consideration. This will refresh people's memories and serves to put your name in front of them again. After all, they may have been talking with quite a few people and may get you confused with someone else.

You may want to bring up any unsolved problems for the interviewer and how your skills and abilities match the company's needs. Remind each person what a good employee you would be, and bring up any new information that you have come across since your last meeting.

2. Follow-Up Phone Call

Wait a few more days after the interview, then give the interviewer a call. Thank that person once again for the interview, ask when a hiring decision will be made, and indicate that you have some additional questions (if appropriate) about the job, the organization, the department, whatever. At the end of the discussion, let the employer know that you are considering other offers (if you are). For instance,

I have been interviewing with other companies and I may need to make a decision by the first of next month. I would really like to work with you. When will you be making a decision? Shall I call on Friday?

3. Keep Interviewing

Following the interview, set up more interviews. Keep working at your search. Try to schedule one or two interviews every day. Many job offers will improve your confidence and enhance your candidacy to a prospective employer.

Keep interviewing until you accept a position with which you are happy. You may wish to continue to interview with companies even after you start work, if the new job is really not what you want. If the job market and your finances are extremely tight, you may need to accept an *interim position.* An interim position is a transitional job you are planning to keep only in order to meet your financial obligations as you continue your job search. If the job is clearly transitional and not permanent, you probably do not want to be in this interim position more than 12 to 18 months. Beyond 18 months, people might accuse you of settling for something considerably less than your skills if you do not position it as a consulting assignment.

Handling the Tough Questions: Role-Playing

Role-playing is a good way to anticipate what an employer may ask in an interview. Role-playing will also help you to think about an answer. The object is to consider a response so that it will come out naturally. You do not want to memorize your answers and sound robotic in an interview. Much of the fear of an interview comes from not being fully prepared or practiced. We recommend that you go on at least four "throw-away" interviews so you can practice handling difficult questions prior to the interview for your ideal job.

Think about the types of jobs the company has to offer and review your skills, abilities, and results achieved. Then try role-playing "out loud" with yourself or a friend. Have a friend play the role of the employer, asking you questions. Have your friend be tough. It will be good practice for you. Then, after you have run through it this way, switch roles. Maybe you can come up with some good employer questions.

People Hire People They Like

Many employers decide in the first few minutes whether they are interested in you. Remember, offers go to people who may not, technically, be the best, but rather, are best at job hunting and interviewing. So, go through the following questions (Worksheets 31 through 52) and write out how you would answer them. Consider the response you will have and how you might elaborate on it or make it better.

Expand Your List of Questions

Develop your own list of questions. Keep track of the questions asked of you in all your actual company or role-play interviews and practice answering all of them.

WORKSHEET 31
Why Are You Leaving Your Company?

To this tough question, employers are favorably impressed with a clear, concise, direct and positive response. Do not be vague or hesitant. Is your explanation reasonable and logical? Employer concerns include:

- Are you a job hopper?
- Were you let go for a cause?
- Will you stay long enough to contribute?
- To what extent might you be running away from a problem?
- How is your relationship with your boss and company now?

Sample response:

> **My company was recently acquired and a number of functions were consolidated with _____ people leaving their jobs. My position was among those impacted. While I had the opportunity to look for another position within the company, I elected not to put my career on hold for three to five years. As such, I am looking with the full knowledge and support of my company.**

Your response (refer to your Verbal Résumé in Step 7):

_____

_____

_____

_____

_____

_____

_____

_____

_____

_____

_____

WORSHEET 32
Tell Me about Yourself

This is your chance to make a strong first impression that will greatly improve your chances for an offer. This is a very important question that deserves careful preparation. Build on the material developed earlier to respond to this question. Companies are interested in your ability to present your ideas in a rational and straightforward manner. They are interested in knowing if your career has been upward, mobile, and logical. Have you progressed during each move, and how have your moves added to your career?

If you have had frequent job changes, talk about the experiences in terms of your career expanding. Give evidence that you are stable and dependable and would like to find a firm to which you can make a serious long-term commitment. Companies are also keenly interested in your interpersonal or operating style. Will you be compatible with other employees or will you become disruptive?

Again, this presentation has five parts and should cover no more than 4 minutes:

1. Career focus
2. Where you were born and raised
3. Your education, your special skills, or military training
4. A chronological listing of the key jobs you have held with key companies; list one or two accomplishments per job, if not too lengthy
5. Why you are leaving your company and why you picked the company you are interviewing with now.

If you have not done so, prepare a written summary of your answer to "tell me about yourself." If you have completed your Verbal Resume, now is the time for you to practice this response in earnest.

_____

_____

_____

_____

_____

_____

_____

_____

_____

WORKSHEET 33
What Are Your Greatest Strengths?

This is probably the most common question in the interviewing process. Virtually every interviewer wants to know how you view yourself and what you consider to be your greatest strengths. Since you are not really sure if the interviewer is asking about your personal strengths or technical strengths, you can presume the question to be open-ended: "I would like to talk about both my technical strengths and my interpersonal strengths." Proceed to your technical strengths first, then your people-to-people strengths.

Why will interviewers throw these potentially unnerving questions at you in the interview? What do they really hope to gain and what do they hope to hear you say? These "impossible questions" are usually open-ended and designed to see how quickly and flexible you can think on your feet. Open-ended questions provide an opportunity for you to create a context that is appropriate and which relates to the previous discussions. These kinds of questions test how fast you think and how concise and articulate you can be when the pressure is on.

Prepare in advance at least five job-related strengths. Rehearse them and shrink them to one or two sentences. Then support each with a good example with a quantifiable result that you can cover in under 30 seconds. Sample response:

> **I am collaborative, technically competent, have a broad experience base, able to effectively develop and lead teams of managers and professionals, able to generate wide-spread endorsements for me, and my ideas. I am bright, ambitious, and set high performance standards for myself and others.**

Review your personal self-description in Step 2 and then write your response to the question, "What are your greatest strengths?"

_____

_____

_____

_____

_____

_____

_____

_____

WORKSHEET 34
What Are Your Greatest Weaknesses?

First of all, don't be intimidated by this type of question or even the trick question, "What are your top five weaknesses?" The interviewer is interested in knowing that you are able to handle difficult questions as well as to reassure him or her that hiring you would not be a mistake. Don't be fooled into thinking that because the interviewer asked you for five weakness that you have to respond with five. Give your top one or two weaknesses and leave it at that. Ironically, that trait that you deem to be your greatest strength will be viewed by others as your greatest liability or weakness, if you overextend it or use that strength inappropriately.

To this question of weaknesses, the interviewer is looking for a serious and appropriate response, and does not appreciate any joke about your weaknesses. Responses such as, "I have no weaknesses" or "I don't golf too well" are unacceptable responses and can portray you as an individual who is inappropriate, flippant, or who has little insight into yourself. Remember: *Tell the truth, but not the whole truth*. Keep your responses nice and tight and concise in your responses. When you do, you will be all right.

The formula for identifying weaknesses without damaging yourself is:

- State your strength.
- State the excess of the strength (in other words, your weakness).
- Tell how your strength shows up.
- Tell how you manage your strength so that it is not a significant problem.

Sample responses:

Strength: "I am driven by goals and deadlines, that is a strength of mine."

Excess: "I am aware that I can become a bit intense if we are not meeting goals and deadlines."

Shows up by: "When that happens I tend to work longer hours and do not relax which sometimes shows up as my being tired or irritable and I have a tendency to push my people to perform."

Managed by: "So, I have learned that when I have reached my limits to relax more, work smarter rather than harder, while delegating optimally. That's something that comes with seasoning. And it works."

(Continued)

Review the section on personal weaknesses in Step 2. Now write an answer to the question, "What are your weaknesses?"

_____

_____

_____

_____

_____

_____

_____

_____

_____

_____

_____

_____

_____

_____

_____

_____

_____

_____

_____

_____

_____

_____

_____

_____

_____

_____

_____

_____

This question is similar to the question asking about your strengths and your operating or managerial style. Employers are interested in knowing two things when they ask this question. One, do you know yourself well; second, is your personality as you describe it, compatible with the department's and the organization's culture? Even though you might be technically qualified to do the work, if you're not able to get along with people with whom you would interact, it would be unlikely that you would be hired because the decision maker is not interested in the organizational "clutter" that always accompanies conflict. In addition, by describing your personality style, you would have an opportunity to describe your values and work ethics. Keep these general, at first, and then if the interviewer is interested in specifics, you must be prepared to either define your traits or provide examples of them, as appropriate. The following is a sample response to the question, "What is your personality style?"

In terms of my personality, I can best be described as open, gregarious, straightforward, ambitious, and enthusiastic. I see the big picture and develop trends from many pieces of information and still can effectively operate at a very fine level of detail. I am intellectually curious and thrive on challenges. I am result-oriented, approachable, personally warm, and supportive of others.

Now write *your* response:

_____

_____

_____

_____

_____

_____

_____

_____

_____

_____

_____

_____

WORKSHEET 36
Why Should We Hire You?

Another form of this question is, "In comparison to other candidates, why should we hire you?" This borders on a trick question and is somewhat difficult to answer if you try to answer it as asked. Respond as if the question was asking about your strengths, abilities, or accomplishments. Talk about things the employer probably sees as valuable, given those insights which you have already gained in the interview. Here is a sample response:

> **You should hire me because of my knowledge, skills, and abilities. The challenges and opportunities that this position represents fit nicely with my track record and my interests. The long-term plans for your organization in this function closely parallel my personal and professional growth plans. You should hire me because of my ability to secure widespread endorsement in ways that probably will enable this operation and team to be more effective.**

Now write your response to the question, "Why should we hire you?"

_____

_____

_____

_____

_____

_____

_____

_____

_____

_____

_____

_____

_____

_____

WORKSHEET 37
What Went Wrong in Your Company? Were You Fired?

Why you are looking for employment outside your company or your reasons for leaving are always areas of great concern for employers. They want to know if you are merely transferring your problems from one organization to another, to what extent you have any personality quirks or technical flaws which would get in the way of you performing effectively. Although things may have gone wrong in your past (or current) company, this is not a time to reveal everything. *Wrong* denotes error and, quite possibly, something bad. It is appropriate to reveal only those things that were correct and justifiable which have led to your seeking employment elsewhere. So, keep it general and develop a story consistent with your references. A sample response to the question is:

> **Nothing went wrong in my former organization. As I mentioned, the organization was restructuring, and the streamlined operation eliminated a number of duplicated functions and positions, including mine. I was offered the opportunity to remain with the organization in a lesser capacity, but I did not want to put my career on hold for three to five years. As you well know, separation from a company is increasingly becoming a way of life. Sometimes it is necessary for the economic survival of the organization. I view this as a "no-fault separation" in which neither party is to blame and in which all parties are amicably separating. If you are interested in exploring the reasons for the separation and my coming out of the organization in more detail, I would be most happy to supply references that would confirm what we have been discussing, when it is appropriate.**

Now write your response to the question, "What went wrong in your company?"

_____

_____

_____

_____

_____

_____

_____

_____

_____

How Do You Feel about Your Company's Eliminating Your Position?

Be careful not to be drawn into a discussion in which you and the interviewer criticize terminating managers and share experiences of being "zapped" and in which both of you express sympathy for each other's unfair treatment. It can be a subtle trap. Even if the interviewer is regaling you with stories of his or her own termination and how difficult it was to find meaningful employment, do not agree or say, "Yes, that certainly is the way it is for me too." Maintain a respectable distance with any discussion that sounds like dissatisfaction or anger. You may wish to consider saying something like:

> **Although I am disappointed in the situation, I fully recognize the need to make that decision. If I were in the identical decision-making role, I would certainly have made the same choice. I hold no animosity toward the organization. My separation is very amicable and extremely supportive. I could not ask for a better relationship. As I have said, I am disappointed that I will not be able to continue working with such a fine team of professionals because we contributed a significant amount to the organization. It seems to me that every organization goes through a life cycle, with my company going through restructuring and downsizing. I understand that, I fully accept it, and am interested in getting my life and my career back on track. I am positive and confident in my ability to do that; that is why I am so pleased with the opportunity that you and I are discussing because it certainly seems to fit those things in which I am interested.**

Review your Worksheet on organization and culture in Step 2 and then write your response to "How do you feel about your company's eliminating your position?"

_____

_____

_____

_____

_____

_____

_____

_____

_____

WORKSHEET 39
Why Are You Interested In Working for This Company?

This question gives you an opportunity to apply some of the information you uncovered in your research on the company prior to the interview as well as in the actual interview. Consider relating back to your earlier responses or "strengths" and your ideal job. Employers are interested in hearing about your desire to contribute to the company, and not your desire for job stability, compensation, and benefits. In fact, issues of wages, hours, and working conditions should be the last items you talk about. A sample response is:

In researching your company and when speaking with some of your vendors and employees, I have heard only praise. Your innovative products, emerging technologies, and attention to quality are all things I believe in. When I put together the list of the top-ten companies I would like to work for, you were among the top five. In addition, I am excited about the opportunity to contribute to the company's growth and profitability.

Now write your response to the question, "Why are you interested in working for this company?"

_____

_____

_____

_____

_____

_____

_____

_____

_____

_____

_____

_____

_____

_____

_____

Here's an opportunity to speak realistically and positively about your former or current organization. Do not criticize your organization or find fault with it unless specifically asked to do so. Even though you may have had a bad experience with your company or with several executives in it, now is not the time to vent your frustration. The only thing that venting does for you is diminish your professionalism. Remember, "If you throw dirt, you only lose ground."

Be positive and realistic, keeping your responses somewhat general. If you become too specific, you run the risk of not identifying dimensions the interviewer will relate to. Be watchful of becoming flowery. Present your observations in a positive, enthusiastic, and almost quiet basis. Otherwise, you run the risk of not being credible. A sample response is:

> **My organization could be best described as a professionally managed organization with talented individuals in key roles. We have a good product line, are well respected in the industry and in the marketplace, and take quite a bit of pride in what we do. The organizational environment is one in which people are able to communicate openly and straightforwardly with each other. It seems as if the good of the organization takes precedent over individual needs and that we are all operating in a team basis, with no one person's interest ahead of the team's goals. If you talk to other individuals from my company, you will discover that there is a great deal of dedication and loyalty for the philosophy and mission of the company. I am only sorry that the streamlining of the organization is creating a surplus of individuals, including myself. While I am disappointed that I have to search for employment, I have been flattered and pleased with the kinds of results my job search has produced so far.**

Your response to the question, "What did you like *best* about your company?" is:

_____

_____

_____

_____

_____

_____

_____

Your response should be similar to the previous question, "What did you like *best* about your former company?" Guard against being drawn into a more detailed discussion of what you felt was wrong with the company. Keep your responses general, upbeat, positive, *and brief!* For example,

> **As you can tell, I am an enthusiastic supporter of my company. The company has been able to produce a good product, establish a worldwide network of qualified sales agents and distributors, compete in an extremely tough marketplace, and create an environment in which people have an opportunity to grow and to learn to the best of their ability. I don't have a whole lot to say negative about the company. I guess, if pressed, the thing that I would indicate was that the organization was reluctant to hire people unless the need was more than justifiable. Although I do not dispute that, it meant that we worked very hard with not much extra staff.**

Write your response:

_____

_____

_____

_____

_____

_____

_____

_____

_____

_____

_____

_____

_____

_____

_____

_____

WORKSHEET 42
What Did You Like *Best* about Your Former Position?

Like many of the other interview questions, this question requires that you answer positively and realistically, providing the optimal amount of background information without revealing areas of major concerns. For example:

> **I liked the challenge and that I was able to structure my job pretty much the way I wanted it, with guidance from my boss. I welcomed the challenging stretch goals which forced me to reach deep within me and to perform to the best of my abilities. I worked in an environment that was demanding, professional, warm, and supportive. My coworkers set high performance standards for themselves and others. We operated as a team and had the right to confront each other on poor performance if it was going to damage the team. I like that caring, supportive, and straightforward environment in which people helped each other.**

Review the section on position and duties in Step 2 and then write your response to the question, "What did you like *best* about your former position?"

_____

_____

_____

_____

_____

_____

_____

_____

_____

_____

_____

_____

_____

_____

_____

WORKSHEET 43
What Did You Like *Least* about Your Former Position?

Again, be careful here! Make sure that your answers are positive and very support-ive of your current or former boss and organization. Issues such as "constant 70-hour work weeks" or "90 percent travel" are softer areas to reveal than "I did not have enough to do" or "my organization was in chaos and it drove me crazy!" A sample response is:

Well, as you can tell, I am pretty sold on the organization and position that I had. I do not really have much to complain about. I think the only downside about my position is that I had too much work to do. That, coupled with my tendency to be a bit of a workaholic, made for some very long hours. However, two personality traits reinforce that. One, is that I have difficulty saying "no" when an individual comes to me for help. Second, I know that I am experienced and have the ability to gen-erate quite a bit of work, and I know that at some point I will be able to get it done.

Write your response to the question, "What did you like *least* about your former position?"

_____

_____

_____

_____

_____

_____

_____

_____

_____

_____

_____

_____

_____

_____

_____

_____

WORKSHEET 44
Describe Your Last Boss

Never say anything negative about a former employer. Your prospective employer will probably assume that if you like to complain now, you will assuredly continue complaining if and when you are hired. The interviewer will be evaluating your ability to assess the "big picture," which certainly includes the dynamics of an interview. Portray your boss in a positive and realistic manner. The interviewer will appreciate your candor and insight. A sample response is:

> **She was very strict, which worked well in our area, given the time pressure to generate results. You always knew where you stood with her and she set very high standards of performance for herself and others. I liked that. I believe people should get straight feedback on how well they are doing.**

Review Step 2's section on supervisors and bosses and then write your response to the request, "Describe your last boss."

_____

_____

_____

_____

_____

_____

_____

_____

_____

_____

_____

_____

_____

_____

_____

WORKSHEET 45
What Have You Accomplished in Your Career?

Respond to this open-ended question by choosing two to three major accomplishments that reflect the breadth of your experiences and talent and which complement the company's needs as expressed by the interviewer. Sometimes, this type of question is asked, "What is the single most important accomplishment that you have achieved in your career to date?"

A sample response is:

> **What I'd like to do is talk about my accomplishments in a broad manner and then provide specific examples which support my broad-based contributions, if that's alright. I feel that my single greatest accomplishment or skill is my ability to quickly diagnose a situation, present practical and cost-effective recommendations, help others to implement these options, and to manage things in such a way as to quickly improve productivity or set the stage for additional development or growth. Examples of this are . . .**

Review and memorize your résumé! Now write your response to the question, "What have you accomplished in your career?"

_____

_____

_____

_____

_____

_____

_____

_____

_____

_____

_____

_____

_____

_____

WORKSHEET 46
Would You Explain the Gap in Your Job History?

If you have an employment gap, explain it as briefly and convincingly as you can. Most employers understand your need to conduct a job search if your position was eliminated due to a consolidation. For example,

After the reorganization, I was working on a part-time consultative basis while conducting a job search, which delayed me in getting a job. My career search took longer than I would have liked, but the part-time work helped me explore many dimensions of my target company while contributing as a consultant.

Write your response to the question, "Would you explain the gap in your job history?"

_____

_____

_____

_____

_____

_____

_____

_____

_____

_____

_____

_____

_____

_____

_____

_____

_____

_____

_____

WORKSHEET 47
How Do You React to Criticism on the Job?

Employers are anxious to know if you are able to learn from your mistakes or do you get defensive easily. Choose a criticism that was made to which you have responded and use a good accomplishment to show that you grew from it. If you are hurt or angry about anything in your old job or company, you will always injure yourself in interviews because this question may rekindle an upset that previously happened and which may have led to your separation. Get the emotional ups and downs handled before the interview, before you permanently injure your career success.

Begin taking control of your upset by clearly recognizing that you are the person who keeps generating all that emotional energy every day, not anyone else. Other people just do what they do. You are the one who adds the emotional kicker to it. Ask yourself what you are "getting out of" your upset (like sympathy, attention, proving that you are right). Ask what it is costing you to hold on to your upset, and how long you are willing to pay that cost for yourself and those about you.

A sample response to the question, "How do you react to criticism on the job?" is:

I respond favorably to constructive criticism, as I know that I am able to grow from the experience if I pause and reflect on what is being said. Even if I do not feel the observations were accurate, it is up to me to clarify another person's perception of a problem, rather than disregard their belief or reaction. I feel that it is important to see another's point of view as being valid. Ultimately, it is my responsibility.

Write your response to the question.

_____

_____

_____

_____

_____

_____

_____

_____

_____

_____

Discussions about compensation are often awkward and uncomfortable. You may even feel that you and the employer are adversaries in that you feel you are worth more than what the company is willing to pay. While questions about salary are asked many different ways, your answers should be uniformly consistent, as outlined in the sample responses.

If asked *early* in the interview about salary, try to defer revealing specifics (unless with a search firm) until later in the interview, when you have more information. Two possible responses are:

I am somewhat uncomfortable talking about money this early. I would like to defer talking about my specific compensation requirements until later in the interview, when I have a better handle on the scope of the job and we can see if we have mutual interest.

Thank you for asking about money requirements. It's important and I want to discuss it, but I would like to do so in context. Of first importance to me is that this is an important career step for me. I am looking for a firm which will provide challenge to my skills and opportunity to grow and develop. Would it be all right if we looked into this area first a bit deeper before we get into the money? If these things are right, I'm flexible on the economics.

If the person agrees to defer the discussion, immediately ask several exploratory questions about the greatest needs in the company in your area of expertise, the expectations for the job in the next year or two, and the position's most significant challenges. This gives you an opportunity to develop needs of the company and to respond with your matching abilities.

If you cannot defer salary discussions, or if asked LATER in the interview, see if the employer will reveal his or her intentions first. Some possible responses are:

You have asked about compensation, what do you have in mind?

I am currently in the $35,000 range with a management incentive and generous benefit package. Money is important to me, but it is not the only consideration. The opportunity to contribute to the growth and profitability of the firm is most important, as well as opportunities for advancement, personal satisfaction, and long-term stability. How does that fit into your expectations?

(Continued)

My total compensation is in excess of $100,000, and I am currently looking at career opportunities less than $75,000 and also considerably higher than that, depending on the job, company, and location. As I indicated, while money is important to me, it is not the only consideration. Minimally, I am interested in remaining whole, salary-wise, over a 6-, 12-, and 18-month period. What kind of income did you have in mind?

Write your response to the question, "What salary do you want?"

_____

_____

_____

_____

_____

_____

_____

_____

_____

_____

_____

_____

_____

_____

_____

_____

_____

_____

_____

_____

_____

If you are told by an interviewer that you are "underqualified" upon revealing your compensation, it is appropriate to make several key points *only after you get some specific feedback from the interviewer:*

> **Oh, why do you feel that way? Is it because of my compensation or is there something specific in my background or experiences that leads you to conclude that?**

Practice asking questions which counter objections in a manner that does not appear to be threatening to the interviewer nor defensive on your part. A sample response is:

> **Thank you for being candid. Regarding compensation, I would like to make two key points. First, I recognize that I have been behind in compensation, but I have not been willing to relocate out of the company nor push for additional monies. I felt that the experience that I was gaining was well worth the investment of deferred income. While money is important to me, it is not the only consideration. Second, I have always been promoted into positions of increasing responsibility and been able to assume these greater roles with little difficulty.**

Write your response to the statement, "You are *underqualified* for this position."

_____

_____

_____

_____

_____

_____

_____

_____

_____

_____

_____

_____

_____

You Are *Overqualified* for This Position

Being told you are overqualified poses a similar kind of challenge. If you reveal your compensation requirements early in the interviewing process, you cannot effectively counter the charge of being overqualified, because you may not have enough information about the position or the organization. If you defer discussions about compensation until later in the interview, you will be in a much better position to talk about being *fully qualified* versus overqualified. Accordingly, you will have a much better basis to discuss your credentials meeting specific needs of the employer. The following is a sample response to the statement, "You are *overqualified* for this position."

Thank you very much for acknowledging that I am well compensated and have good credentials. I am very proud of what I have been able to accomplish, and my company has consistently rewarded individuals who have performed in an outstanding manner. Although I am interested in remaining whole, compensation-wise, experience has shown me that it is more important to be in a position in which you are well qualified, having fun, able to significantly contribute, grow in the function, and learn from other individuals. That's what turns me on, that's what's important to me.

You mentioned overqualified. I really do not believe that I am overqualified. Rather, I see myself as "fully qualified," given that you need someone to contribute immediately and assume positions of increasing responsibility. Since you currently do not have the staff on board to do the kinds of things you need to have done long term, and you're willing to recognize and reward outstanding performance, I don't see that I have anything to worry about long term. This is exactly the kind of environment in which I thrive and would love to participate.

Write your response to the statement.

_____

_____

_____

_____

_____

_____

_____

_____

WORKSHEET 51
What Do You Know about Our Company?

This question is almost always asked. The more prepared you are, the more you will stand out from others applying for the same job. Most job seekers do not do an adequate job preparing for interviews. If you do prepare, you will really shine. Refer to the Library Checklist at the end of this step for good library resources you can use. Consider researching and commenting on dimensions such as sales size, number of employees, type of product lines or business groups, locations, competition, legislative trends, if any, and future company plans. A sample response is:

> **I know that you employ 150 people and that you are well rooted in the community. The company has been here for 75 years which says to me that it is a good strong organization. The company's general reputation is solid and is known for challenging its people to perform up to their potential. The product line is varied and seems to meet a growing market need. In addition, your company is consistently developing new products and technologies. While I know some things about your company, I would certainly like to learn more about it today.**

Identify important dimensions you want to explore and then write your response to the question, "What do you know about our company?"

_____

_____

_____

_____

_____

_____

_____

_____

_____

_____

_____

_____

WORKSHEET 52
Do You Have Any Questions about Our Company?

Ask some questions that you already know part of the answers to — then elaborate on them. People are usually proud of their company and want to talk about it. There is a list of sample questions later in this chapter. A few possible responses might be:

How did your business get started?

How have you earned your international reputation?

How does business growth look for the next year or so?

Have you had any recent layoffs or do you anticipate any?

To what would you attribute your success?

Why is this position open?

What has gone well (not well) in this position?

What do you see as areas needing improvement?

Write your questions.

_____

_____

_____

_____

_____

_____

_____

_____

_____

_____

_____

_____

_____

_____

_____

1. What are your current job duties?

2. What were the biggest decisions you have made in the last 12 months? Tell me how you went about making them and what alternatives did you consider?

3. Tell me about a major project with which there were problems. How did you resolve them and what were the results?

4. Describe one of the best ideas you ever sold to a peer or supervisor, including your approach and result.

5. How have you gotten around obstacles that prevented you from completing projects or assignments? Describe the conditions under which obstacles most often occur for you.

6. In your job, how is performance measured and what constitutes doing a good job?

7. What would make up a typical day for you? How long do you usually work? To what extent is it possible to organize your day?

8. Give me examples of different approaches you have used when persuading someone to cooperate with you.

9. When dealing with individuals or groups, how do you determine when you are pushing too hard? How does it look, and what do you do about it?

10. Tell me about some times when you were not very pleased with your performance. What did you do about it?

11. Tell me about some projects you generated on your own. What prompted you to begin them, and how did they do?

12. Why have you chosen this particular field? What do you feel are the biggest challenges facing this field? This industry?

13. What are your long-range goals? If we hired you, what are the top-three goals you would like to see this department achieve?

14. What can you do for us that someone else cannot do?

15. If you could start your career over again, what would you do differently? What unfulfilled goals do you have and when will you achieve them? Why are they still important to you?

16. Are you creative? Give me several examples. Are you a leader? Give me several examples.

17. Do you have any health problems or physical limitations that might prevent you from performing the job as described to you, including travel, if required?

18. What interests you most about this position?

19. How long will you stay here in our company?

20. What aspects of your current job would you consider to be crucial to the success of the business? Why?

21. What was the least relevant job you have held? Why? How did you feel about it and what did you learn?

22. How long will it take for you to make a contribution?

23. What would your greatest business *opponent* say about you?

24. What would your greatest business *proponent* say about you?

25. Describe how and when you get stressed. How do you display it or act it out?

26. How long have you been looking for a position?

27. Have you ever been criticized unjustly? Why?

28. How have previous jobs equipped you for greater responsibility?

29. How did you manage to get the time off for this interview?

30. Let's role-play. Pretend you are a consultant hired to assess me and the organization. You have concluded your work. Describe my operating style and those of all the people you have interviewed. Also, tell me how I should change the organization.

Illegal Questions: How to Handle Them and What to Do

Surprisingly, well-intentioned interviewers still ask questions which are blatantly discriminatory or close to being considered so. Companies who allow this practice to go unchecked not only run the risk of turning off well-qualified candidates but also unwittingly expose themselves to discrimination litigation.

If you find yourself in an interview in which you feel you are being asked discriminatory questions, do not stiffen up immediately. Rather, make a mental note to verify that this is, indeed, the case. Employers are legally constrained from making employment, salary, promotion, and termination decisions based on age, race, sex, religion, national origin, or physical handicap.

For example, you may get asked about your age, about the age of your children, or about how your husband views you working for a company. You have three choices when this occurs. The first one is to close out the interview. The second is to meekly comply and give the answer. You may not wish to respond in either of these two manners. The first loses a good possible job opportunity because of a poorly prepared interviewer. The second may harm your self-esteem and reinforce negative behavior.

There is another choice. The third way is to look behind the bad question for a good question which you can answer in such a way that you respond to a genuine and legitimate concern of the interviewer. For example, you may be asked about your age. Consider that behind that question may be a very legitimate concern about older people sometimes not being active and having stamina for long hours or tough, "hands-on" work. A professional response to this discriminatory question is to pause briefly and then state:

> **It must be difficult for you to ask me about age, as it is for me to answer, for all the obvious reasons. However, I think I know what you are getting at. If you are concerned about my ability to be energetic and have stamina and staying power, you bet I do. I have learned to work smarter. I make very few errors in my work and have not missed a day of work for illness in four years. Does that answer your question?**

Or, if you are asked about your husband's view of working wives or some similar, obviously sexist questions, you could respond by saying the following:

> **Your question about my husband's view of my working must be a difficult one for you to ask, as it is for me to answer, for all the obvious reasons. However, I think I know what you're getting at. I am a very committed career person, and we are very supportive of one another. You will note that I've had three promotions since returning to the work force and stayed with my last firm for six years. You can count on me, if we reach a fair offer, to be very committed to Globe Corporation. Does that answer your concern?**

Or, if the interviewer should be so thick as to persist in the question, a stronger approach is to say:

> **I am frankly a bit puzzled about how that information is important to my job performance. If you could ask the question another way so that it relates to the job itself, I'm sure I can give you an answer which would reflect how I can provide value to your company.**

Your Turn: Questions You May Ask in the Interview

The interview should not be a one-sided affair with the employer dominating the questioning. You have to know about the job, the company, and the people in your future employment situation. It is necessary to use your judgment to determine how and when to ask questions in an interview, as well as the number of questions.

Asking open-ended, penetrating questions helps you "peel back the layers" of a company and demonstrates that you're interested and capable. It will also help distinguish you from other candidates. Obviously, you will not be asking all these questions; if you did, the interviewer would feel interrogated. We recommend that you study these and select the ones with which you are most comfortable and that are most important for you.

Position Definition

1. What is the scope of the position's responsibility, authority, and accountability, and how challenging is the position? What is needed and wanted in this job? How is performance measured and by whom?

2. To whom will I report? What's his or her background and management style?

3. Why is this position available? How long has it been open? Can I speak with the person who had this job previously?

4. Are there any other people in the company under consideration for this job? If I get it, how will they feel and act?

5. What is the organization of the department, what are the travel requirements of the job, and where is the job located?

6. What are the five most significant things that need to be accomplished by this position, within the first year, and what are the major hurdles?

7. What career growth and promotional opportunities are present beyond this position?

8. How would employees describe the extent to which they are informed, involved, developed, and promoted?

9. How are decisions reached in the department and in the company, and to what extent will I be involved?

10. What support do I have from other functions, and how do I negotiate for this help?

11. How does my background meet your needs? What is not present?

12. When will a decision be made on this search?

13. What is the next step?

Organization Structure and Operating Philosophy

1. Outline the organizational structure.

2. Describe the corporate culture or "personality" of the company.

3. Who are the key executives in the organization and what are their personalities, backgrounds, abilities, accomplishments, and professional and personal goals?

4. Describe the nature of the present decision-making process and the level of risk taking throughout the organization.

5. To what extent does the corporation encourage and reward entrepreneurial managers?

6. Will the company's *future* business require more emphasis on professional managers than on entrepreneurial managers?

7. Describe the company's philosophy on human resources, its programs, and how the philosophy is being achieved.

8. To what extent are managers results-oriented, tough-minded, and uncompromising regarding business and people issues?

9. To what extent is ROI a major measurement of management performance?

10. How much does management rely on management practices such as MBO, total quality management, open systems organization, and participative management?

11. How effective are managers in recruiting, hiring, and training quality personnel? Rate their effectiveness in identifying poor performers and coaching them to an acceptable level of performance or taking the necessary action to replace them.

Corporate Objectives

1. What are the corporation's primary financial objectives and performance measures?

2. To what extent are these objectives uniform across all product lines? What are the company's primary strategies for achieving its financial objectives?

3. What is the obligation of the corporation to its shareholders? What is the obligation of the corporation to its customer regarding product quality, value, price, consumer safety, and customer satisfaction?

4. What emphasis does the corporation place on short-term results as opposed to long-term successes?

5. What are the corporation's primary sources of capital and plans for expansion?

6. What is the company's attitude toward profitability and reinvestment in equipment, facilities, and people needed to stay ahead and abreast of changing technology and competition?

Business Prospects

1. What is the history of the company, including present and past product lines and the markets that they serve?

2. To what extent will the company's business strategies emphasize growth in the current product lines as opposed to development of new product lines or acquisitions?

3. Who are the corporation's major competitors? In product and service markets? In the labor markets? To what extent does the competition vary by product?

4. How does the corporation anticipate maintaining its current sales levels? Its profit margins?

5. To what extent might the company's competitive situation make it vulnerable to loss of key personnel or a possible takeover?

6. What is the scope of the company's domestic and international operations in terms of revenues and employees? Total numbers and percentages?

7. What are the company's 1-, 5-, and 10-year sales objectives?

8. To what extent does management support and emphasize investing in the development of target business areas and in the divestiture of marginal products or business groups?

9. In what stages on the "growth curve" are your products?

Strategic and Operating Plans

1. Describe the nature of the planning process and how decisions concerning the budgeting process are made.

2. Identify the key corporate participants in the planning process, both short and long range.

3. What operating guidelines are used to monitor the planning process and the results?

4. What is the system of accountability to ensure the attainment of the operating and strategic plans?

5. How often and in what form does the company report its results internally to employees?
6. How are results acknowledged and rewarded to the managers and staff?
7. What are the repercussions of having a significant variance to the operating plan?
8. What is the company's typical response when a business unit manager does not make a plan? How does this response contribute or inhibit to the attainment of the business plan in the future?

Dealing with Company Founders and Owners

1. How would you describe the company you'd like to leave your heirs in terms of sales size, employee size, number of locations, profitability, asset base, etc.?
2. What are your aspirations for the company during the next five years? Ten years?
3. What role do you want to play? Strategic? Operational? Financial? Legal?
4. If for any reason you are unable to be CEO, how would you like to see the company managed? Is this known, understood, and agreed to by your heirs? Is it in writing?
5. Have you considered the degree to which you want your heirs to have strategic or operational influence in the company until one of them is ready to assume the role of COO or CEO?
6. What are your thoughts about sharing the management of the company you created? Have you defined the scope of the COO and the accountability and authority attendant to that role? To what extent are you committed to having a COO help you run your company?
7. It has often been said that founders and owners of businesses are extremely reluctant to truly share the management of the companies they found. What assurances do I have that you are committed to the COO's role?
8. To make our working relationship successful—something we both want—we'll need to be sure we have good chemistry together. How might we determine that and then what action would you see us engage in to build that relationship?

Interview Critique: Fine-Tuning Success _____

Your ability to learn from your interviews will be greatly enhanced if you critically evaluate each meeting in terms of each interviewer's needs, the company's demands, and how you can contribute in the role. We recommend that after interviewing in an organization you complete Worksheet 53, the Interview Critique Sheet (page 264). Before another interview, your review of these sheets will reinforce those things that went well and raise your awareness (and resolve) to eliminate the negatives.

If you keep these critiques current and diligently review them, you will find that you are able to master interviewing in a way you never thought possible. Your responses will be tighter, your answers more crisp, your confidence raised, your credibility enhanced, and your enthusiasm contagious. Remember . . .

You never get a second chance to make a good first impression.

WORKSHEET 53
Interview Critique Sheet

Following each interview, complete these three questions. Use the information below when you write your thank you letters and prepare for your next interview. Fill out this information immediately. Many interviewers fill it out in the car before driving away from the interview. *Do not* wait until the next day to complete this; your memory will grow stale.

1. What is the one significant thing said by each person I met which could be a "hook" I can refer to in a follow-up letter?

   Name   Title   Statement/Need

   _____

   _____

   _____

   _____

2. What are the most significant company "needs" raised by each person I interviewed that my skills can match?

3. What should be mentioned in any follow-up letters which might improve my candidacy? This might include things to reinforce something about me or cover something that was omitted.

KEEPING YOUR JOB SEARCH "ON TRACK" AND "ON FIRE"

Plan Your Work and Work Your Plan

"If I make 10 really solid networking calls a day, I'll probably create at least one interview. Fifteen to twenty calls per day will probably yield 2–3 additional visits, not counting the estimated thirty additional leads of companies, personal contacts, or search firm executives. Given this level of activity of being able to get an interview for every 10 calls, I should be able to generate at least two to three bona fide interviews a week without any trouble.

"Based on national statistics, if I successfully complete 10 interviews, I'll generate at least one offer of employment. Since my objective is to produce three offers so I can negotiate effectively and pick the best opportunity for me, my goal is minimally 30 interviews. That means, I have to make 300 networking calls to reach this level — with no guarantees, of course."

George Pratt was an engineer and was very analytical. He needed some sense as to the magnitude of a typical search and wasn't going to be comfortable until he had established some parameters and probabilities for his own search campaign. Large, complex tasks didn't bother George; they were his training and his early experience in project management.

George's credo: "Determine your goal, calculate the resources required to achieve it, factor in some slop, plot the timetable, commit yourself to the task at hand, and never, never give up."

Managing Your Search versus Having It Manage You

If you are like most people, you are probably feeling a bit overwhelmed by all the steps in this career-planning, job-getting process. George Pratt was feeling overwhelmed until he organized his activities into smaller pieces with definitive outcomes and timetables. Yes, there is a lot of "stuff" involved to getting the right job for you. Although you do not have to do all the work suggested to be successful, you will find your campaign more organized and easier to manage if you do.

A good friend of ours, George Morrisey, international business consultant and well-known author, likes to define *management* as "The effective use of limited resources to achieve desired results." As it relates to your search campaign, the effective use of your resources (time, energy, talent, and money) will mean the difference between success and delayed success. The central theme of this Step is goal setting and the achievement of your goals.

Why Establish Career Search Goals?

> ALICE: Please sir, can you tell me the way?
>
> CHESHIRE CAT: Where are you headed?
>
> ALICE: I don't know.
>
> CHESHIRE CAT: Then any road will take you there!

Rather than have you wander aimlessly like Alice in *Alice in Wonderland,* we want to help you develop a strategy to get what you want. To achieve your career search goals, you obviously need to know:

- Where you are headed
- How to get there
- A timetable for accomplishment
- Contingency plans for problems
- A method to measure when you're successful and when you're not

Plan of Action

How well you achieve your search goals will depend on how committed you happen to be and how well you develop a detailed plan of action. Contractors would not think of building houses without detailed blueprints and material specifications, regardless of how experienced they might be. Yet, it is rather ironic that people, perhaps even yourself, launch a career search with hardly any advance planning. If you identify your desired outcomes, become committed to successfully reaching these goals no matter what, and diligently work your plan, you greatly increase your chances of success.

Record Keeping

Maintaining accurate, up-to-date records will greatly aid you in keeping organized and increasing your search momentum. Nothing is more embarrassing than receiving a phone call from a prospective employer and not being able to link up the name of the caller with an organization. However, if you establish a simple, easy-to-use system early on, you will not have to create a system once you actively begin interviewing.

Things You Can Do

1. Read Step 9 managing your campaign in its entirety.
2. Make several copies of your goals and post them in conspicuous places, to reinforce your commitments. Place cards in your car, on your bathroom mirror, or on your refrigerator.
3. Inform people of your commitments and enlist their help in keeping them.
4. Remember to follow the proven adage, "plan your work and work your plan."

Five Ways to Get Your Search Moving and Keep It on Track _____

1. Be committed to your success. Don't let anything distract you from your goal. Experiment with some of these recommended job-changing ideas, even though they may have never worked for you before or you have heard negatives about using a particular job-changing method.
2. Acknowledge that your job hunting probably takes three times as long as you would like and requires ten times the patience you thought you had.
3. Follow the daily activity guidelines on the next few pages.
4. Read, then reread, the section, "Getting Unstuck and on Top of Rejection," later in Step 9.
5. Create a support team for yourself. Enlist the aid of several close friends, relatives, or mentors who can provide encouragement, allow you to nonjudgmentally vent frustration as it occurs, and be an objective third party to help keep you motivated and on track.

Your Daily Activity Guidelines for Success

In order to conduct an active search, one which yields results, we recommend you create a significant amount of activity around your availability. As reminders, pursue each of the four main avenues of how to get a job:

1. Personal contact networking
2. Target organization mailings
3. Advertisements
4. Search firms and employment agencies

Personal Contact Networking

- Never write when you can call. Never call when you can see someone in person. Personal communication is the best way to network.
- Make a complete list of everyone that you know—*50 to 200 people.* Look up names of people you know from work, school, church, relatives, neighbors, vendors, consultants, and salespeople who call on you.
- Make up to 10 to 20 calls per day, connecting with people.
- *My commitment is _____ conversations per day.*

Target Organization Mailings

- Mail your résumé, with cover letter, in waves of 100 to target organizations. Why only 100 organizations and not the 400 you've identified all at once? If you mail to more than 100 at any one time, you will not be able to effectively follow up with phone calls. You can certainly mail out to all 400 organizations, eventually. Depending upon your industry focus (health-care companies only, for example) or geographic focus (any northside Chicago manufacturing companies, for instance), the size of your list will vary considerably.
- Your mailings to organizations should target the specific individual who is the department manager or someone else likely to make the final hiring decision and list your skills, abilities, and responsibilities while identifying your reasons for writing the company.
- Do not depend on computer lists to get you a job. They don't work. You select the firms through research, networking, and personal knowledge. That way you have a personal commitment to follow up on them.
- By making follow-up calls to the specific individuals identified at each target organization, you will be able to considerably expand your networking base. Have a goal to never hang up without at least one lead.

- Experts in direct mail marketing are delighted with 1 percent return on a mailing. Letters are not a high-return resource unless there is direct solicitation follow-up. Don't settle for a quick, easy answer on selecting your target list. A mailing without accuracy or follow-up is very low return activity. With follow-up such activity becomes extremely powerful.

- *My commitment is to mail my résumé to _____ organizations and to follow up on the _____ organizations.*

Advertisements

- Respond to a minimum of six ads per week.

- Look for and respond to ads that fit your objective. Blind ads are OK. Respond to those that fit, highlighting in the insert sections of your cover letter the things that the ad specifies. Write out your response immediately so they don't pile up! *Date your cover letters four days after the ads appear* and mail your letters at that time.

- Search box ads for leads and intelligence on companies that should be added to your target list for future needs.

- *My commitment is to respond to _____ ads per week.*

Search Firms and Employment Agencies

Retainer Search Firms

- For a national search, contact 150 or more retainer search firms. For a regional search, contact 30 or more retainer search firms.

- Maximize your list of those you inform of your candidacy. Contact people after a few weeks to ensure that they have your résumé and that they have it filed under your area of expertise. Ask for an appointment to meet for purposes of introduction.

- Use your personal contacts to open the door into 8 to 12 search firms per day, connecting with key account executives.

Contingency Search Firms

- For a national search, contact 25 to 30 contingency search firms. For a regional search, contact 5 to 10 contingency search firms.

- Contact as many firms as you can manage well. Ask questions to be sure that they have worked with people with your background and organizational level. What companies do they work for? How will they represent and position your résumé to companies? What data will they provide you before you go out on an interview?

State or Province Employment Services and Nonprofit Agencies

- Contact the state employment service on a regular basis. Many firms list good positions with them.

- Do some research to determine if there are any nonprofit agencies set up to service your needs. Don't overlook this or any methods that might help to locate that "right job" for you.

- *My commitment is to contact _____ search firms or employment agencies by phone and _____ through mailings.*

After Your Mailing

The following are nine ways to create job search momentum:

1. Each evening, identify the 10 most interesting firms you want to work for. Write them down and gather contact data, including why you might be a good fit. Also, select three new personal contacts to call.

2. The next morning, first thing, research the target organizations (using networking, books, phone calls to the firm's receptionist, etc.). Develop a file of reprints on your "core" target companies, the competition, and the industry. Use this competitive information in your correspondence or conversations with your target organizations. Identify the key contacts in your target company and possible areas of interest or concern to them. These would be the people you would most likely be working for if hired.

3. After getting your research together and getting organized (before 8:30 a.m.), begin calling your key contacts and briefly introduce yourself, your capabilities, and your interest in meeting for purposes of introduction.

4. Begin also to call your network contacts to get names of search firms, additional leads, and target companies. Remember, follow up on the leads your contacts give you immediately and periodically get back to your contacts to keep them posted on your success with their contacts. They will appreciate it.

5. When you contact your target companies, try to set up an interview with each key contact, again for purposes of introduction. Failing that, secure a commitment to a follow-up phone call sometime in the near future, even if it is to periodically inform them of your status. Before ending this conversation, add value about your credentials and capabilities.

6. Develop a personalized thank-you letter for each telephone interchange you have. If you spent time on the telephone with one of your key people, that is, a legitimate contact, and a thank-you note is appropriate. Keep in mind, only a fraction of job seekers write thank-you letters. Become the tough competitor to beat by doing something which distinguishes you from others.

7. Go on interviews. An introductory meeting is counted as an interview even if there is no immediate, visible opening. After each interview, write a thank-you letter individualized for each person you saw. Why separate letters? Because correspondence is often routed amongst all the interviewers. You don't want to be perceived as a person who uses one approach to all situations, do you?

8. Set up a follow-up plan including next-step strategies, specific dates on which you will telephone, write, or visit. Mark the dates on your calendar. Commit to executing your plan and following through on your dates.

9. Select ten more firms and contacts. Start the process again. If you didn't make your goal, don't be discouraged. Just keep focused and committed to moving forward each day.

Use Worksheet 54 to record your progress.

Twenty Search Tips to Empower Your Campaign

1. Be open to the possibility of successfully getting connected utilizing any one of the job search avenues, not just the way you connected the last time you looked for a job.

2. Take complete responsibility for follow-up to your contacts or companies. Don't accept, "Don't call us, we'll call you."

3. Use the want ads as only one source of contacts, recognizing that it usually has a low yield.

4. Spend 70 percent of your time on those activities which generate 70 percent of the action.

5. Do not give up on one (or more) of your prime target organizations after they tell you, "Sorry, we do not have any openings."

6. Use the positive feelings that you have after a super interview to aggressively pursue additional opportunities because you want multiple offers from which to choose.

7. Contact your target organizations more than once.

8. Write timely thank-you letters which provide value and make the reader think about what you have said and the position you espoused.

WORKSHEET 54
My Daily Search Progress   Date _____

Record your daily progress on this chart. As you "keep score" faithfully, you will discover that your search focus will be enhanced and you will begin to develop insight into how to generate search momentum. It's simple—make lots of contacts and your search will be active.

	Personal Contacts	Search Firms	Target Organizations	Advertisements
Goal	_____	_____	_____	_____
Actual	_____	_____	_____	_____

Name/ Title	Company	Phone #	Status

Note: You may wish to reproduce this sheet for a daily progress record with our compliments.
Copyright © 1990 Robertson Lowstuter, Inc. (708) 940-4400

9. Do not become "cocky" in the second and third interview, thinking "the job is mine."

10. Always remember that you are up against very stiff competition so you need to always look to create additional positive exposure for yourself.

11. Always evaluate the impact your words have in the interview so you are constantly assessing your "story" against how it might sound to an employer.

12. Remember: Executive search firms and employment agencies work for the employer.

13. Become known in companies as a talented person *before* there are openings.

14. Write individualized thank-you letters to multiple interviewers in the same company.

15. Develop a consultant's perspective while interviewing, which will enable you to write mini-proposals thereby creating a significant distinction between you and your competition.

16. Do not identify salary data in a letter in response to an ad that states, "only résumés with salary history and requirements will be considered." If your background is interesting, you will get called.

17. Do not believe that blind ads necessarily mean jobs—the ads may be placed by search firms wanting to "round out" their files or by companies seeing who is on the market.

18. Respond to advertisements a second time within 30 days if you have not heard back from your first response.

19. Use a bad experience from one interview to reaffirm your commitment to always be prepared. See this experience as a valuable learning opportunity, not a defeat.

20. Discreetly continue to go on interesting interviews even after you have accepted a new position so you are always developing and nurturing your network.

Turnaround Strategies:
How to Get Unstuck and Get on Top of Rejection

You will get rejected for a lot of reasons—some valid, many for no rhyme nor reason. The challenge is to sort out the valid rejects from the invalid ones and turn them into your advantage. To a good salesperson, a no is almost the same as a yes, it just requires a different strategy to win. In this process of job changing, you may get stuck. You may feel as if you are off track or are not moving forward like you should. Don't worry, that is a normal part of the campaign. All is not lost; there are remedies to handle rejection and to get going again. Consider these ideas as part of your turnaround strategies.

Personal Contacts

Some people may not support you as much as you would like because they honestly may not have any contacts or leads to pass on. Even though they may genuinely want to help, they get busy and do not follow through with information for you. Some remedies are:

- Always be sure you know precisely what you want your personal contacts to do *before* you approach them.
- Give your contacts a typed list of your top 10 to 30 target organizations and ask whether they know anyone employed there or if they know of someone *else* who would know an employee.
- Prepare and practice your responses to some basic questions to demonstrate that you are composed and confident. Even with business acquaintances, be prepared to answer such things as, "Why are you leaving? What are your short/long range objectives? What are three of the most significant things you have accomplished in your career?"
- Refer to "Personal Networking" in Step 6 to refresh your memory. Remember to inform people of your status; ask for help and information concerning leads or opportunities, executive search firm contacts, and target organizations; gain commitment for you to send your résumé *and* to follow up periodically to see if your contact has any additional leads or information for you.

Target Organizations

Well-known companies receive a tremendous number of employment inquiries. Because of the time and expense involved in responding to each letter that comes in, you may not receive a personalized return letter. Be mindful of your probable emotional response when you get a postcard acknowledgment of your résumé: "If this is how they treat people, I do not want to work there." Ironically, *that* company may be the best place in which to work, given its reputation. After all, look at how many people write to them! Here are some remedies if your pursuit of target organizations has stalled:

- If your reject letter was personally written by the decision maker you wanted to reach, write a follow-up letter. See "Follow-Up Letter after

Being Rejected by a Target Company" in Step 3. By doing so, you will definitely be in the minority of candidates responding a second time.

- Follow up on your letter with a call approximately a week later to establish a relationship and solicit leads. In effect, you turn the prospective employer into a personal contact. Will you get rejected often? Sure. But when you strike a lead—great!

- Acknowledge to the employer that although the company might not have any current openings, you would like very much to be at the top of the résumé pile when something develops.

Ads

Ads generally represent the lowest yield for job candidates. However, since clients at all levels have successfully connected by responding to ads—open and blind—we recommend that you continue to respond to them. Remember: It may only take one lead to introduce the ideal job to you! Use the following tips if your follow-up on ads is not working:

- If you have not gotten a response within 20 days, respond again with your résumé. They may have misplaced your original correspondence and your résumé. Refer to Step 3's section Second Ad Response Letter to renew interest.

- If the ad identifies the company, call the company and ask to speak to the head of the department. Explain your situation and express continued interest. Go for it! You have nothing to lose and everything to gain!

Search Firms

Retainer search firms do not seem to be interested in you unless there is a potential match with one of their current assignments or if they want to learn more about your previous employer. Ironically, when you are looking for employment it can be pretty tough to get a call back from a search professional let alone secure a lead into one of your target organizations. Try the following:

- Ask your personal contacts for the names of account executives they respect and would recommend. Use your contact's name to obtain a personal discussion. As search firm executives are inundated with candidates seeking a personal audience, you will need to persevere.

- Maintain or update your file on open positions in which search firms have used you as a network resource. You are simply calling back for a return favor.

Employment agencies are much like search firms in their attitude, except their motives are slightly different. They do not make any money unless *their* candidate gets the job, and "their candidate" is only theirs if they are the first agency to introduce him or her to the company. Since their fee is not guaranteed, they probably will not take the time to research the company's needs in depth. Try the following:

- Call the agency person back once or twice to let the recruiter know that you are really interested, but then back off unless you have time to burn and you really want to talk. Recognize, though, if the recruiter does *not* return your calls that the chances are slim there is anything very interesting there.

- Concentrate on those agencies which specialize in your field. Watch advertisements in newspapers or professional trade journals for agencies who place repetitive ads for jobs within your discipline. Even if the particular ad does not exactly fit your experience, they might have something else they are not advertising.

Note: **Never agree to pay anyone a fee for finding you a job.** Standard industry practice relies on the company or the search firm to pay for all reasonable expenses.

What about Employee Leasing, Consulting, or Temporary Employment?

Part of a National Trend

As part of your search strategy, you may wish to consider consulting or temporary employment as a careering option (on a full-time basis) or as "trial employment" before either you or the company commits completely. Organizations are becoming increasingly receptive to "leasing" employees through a third-party temporary services agency or an employee-leasing firm to provide short-term project support prior to extending a formal offer. This is an excellent method of evaluating the suitability of a candidate, *and* it represents a tremendous opportunity for you to scrutinize the company, as well.

If the organization has had greater turnover than desired, or if there is a high degree of risk associated with accepting a full-time position, you may want to suggest a limited consulting contract of 1 to 30 days to provide support, assess company needs, and make recommendations for their problem resolution.

Caution: Our general rule of thumb is do not undertake a consulting assignment or temporary employment if it will not lead anywhere. Your career search momentum may be severely damaged if you consult for a company on an extended basis without furthering your career goals. However, if you have run out of money or you have been unemployed for an extended period, let's say more than 18 months, you will probably need to accept some job—any job—to earn money and get your self-esteem back.

The Stigma of a Lengthy Job Search

If you are still employed but have been actively job hunting for an extended period (let's say 12 months) your credibility may have been damaged. Your contacts, references, search firms, and target companies will begin to feel that there must be something lacking in your technical skills, managerial abilities, and interpersonal skills. What possible other explanation do you have for you being out so long? Could it be that you have not developed nor executed a results-producing search strategy?

If you have been unemployed for a long time, let's say 9 months for a mid-level manager, you may wish to begin some temporary employment or employee-leasing assignments. Being unemployed for many months is extremely stressful and also highly visible. People like people who are successful. Unfortunately, most people distance themselves from people who are not quite so successful, have trouble coping, or project an air of desperation. It is really ironic—the time you need people's support the most is when you are least likely to get it.

So, create the image of being in control and effectively producing the result you desire. Get employed—at least temporarily. It is amazing the number of leads that materialize once you are "gainfully employed" in some capacity, even temporarily. Invariably, once you are connected, your confidence will be greater, and people will notice and respond. It is almost as if there is a switch in their head that clicks on with the message, "Now that you have successfully concluded your search, you must be good, so I will provide some leads now."

So, rather than waiting for a bona fide full-time, permanent assignment to come along, create the same aura of success now. Think about it—how can you create it?

TURNING AROUND REJECTION, STRESS, OR A STALLED SEARCH

_____ STEP 10

Closing the Gap between Reality and Expectation _____

"I'm not being successful," Kate cried in frustration. "Things are not happening the way I know they should and the way I want them to. People don't return my phone calls, they do not pick up on my suggestions the way I'm used to—does everyone have to have things spelled out in complete detail! Don't these search firms know what a terrific commodity I am? And why does it take so long for these organizations to get back to me and make up their minds? Don't they know I'm dying out here?"

Kate Kendall was used to getting things her way. She prided herself on her ability to effectively read people and the changing political winds in her organization. She was known for her technical competence and her ability (and courage) to make bold decisive moves when others hesitated. Kate had an enviable record of successes and was thought to be the only candidate for the department head when Dr. Shu retired in 18 months. As others operated as if this promotion was a certainty, so did Kate. She became bolder, more assertive. She started to "throw" her assumed authority around more blatantly, even countermanding Dr. Shu's mandate for the marketing group. Worse still, she took liberties with her liberal travel schedule to squeeze in personal time off in exotic international regions without reporting it.

Unfortunately, the broad base of endorsement she had once enjoyed crumbled beneath her as one subordinate after another confidentially sought out Dr. Shu to address the badly floundering projects abandoned by Kate as she "trotted around the globe." Left with little recourse, for the damage was irreparable, Kate was entrusted to executive outplacement for mending and career planning.

After some very straight peer group analysis and feedback, Kate took ownership of the situation and effectively regained control of her career and her life though not completely her patience.

Patience, Patience, Patience

At this point in your campaign, you have developed a résumé that stands out from the competition and have mailed it to your personal contacts, search firms, and target organizations. In addition, you have strengthened your interviewing and marketing skills and are fully prepared to handle the tough interviews. Now is when you need to be at your best.

Ironically, now is the time when you may feel both exuberant and depressed. There is a psychological high after having "launched" into the marketplace. You wait expectantly for the harvest of positive phone calls and letters. They may come sparingly. You know that patience is required, yet you wish your situation would be different, that you would get 12 calls the next day.

Experience has shown that these calls do come but at a much slower pace than is comfortable. Regardless of the warnings, you will probably experience feelings of being let down, abandoned, even betrayed. After all, *you* did *your* part, you sent out your résumés, etc.

This part of the campaign requires you to balance your expectations with plenty of patience. Remember, a thousand people like you have been there a thousand times before. Patience! Have confidence—the process will work for you if you work at it.

Things You Can Do

1. Thoroughly read this entire section. You will find it more valuable than you imagined.
2. Work through the exercises and follow along with the visualization process to gain greater confidence and to become more "grounded" in your accomplishments, talents, skills, and abilities.

Being Highly Successful

However, if your situation is such that three days after you broadcast your job search you get flooded with calls, great! You are in the minority, and we applaud the success of your market approach, good fortune, and great timing. But even with a highly successful campaign, you need to be aware of your emotional swings from highs to lows.

Managing a highly intense job search can be very heady, very much like riding a world class roller coaster. There are some exhilarating ups and some heart-stopping plummets. Plummets occur when the number of interview trips declines suddenly, when the phone goes silent, or when you are the runner-up for the ideal job.

The point is, even if your campaign rides like a roller coaster—hang on! One never gets off a roller coaster when it is still moving. Do not operate every day as if it were a life and death matter. You have the tools to do the job. Remember, you have been successful before—you will be successful again.

Being Stuck: Recognizing Your Physical Sensations, Emotions, and Attitudes

When you are stuck, your well-being is interrupted, and you experience discord in all parts of your life. When you are deeply stuck, do not expect to be fully aware of it. Your mind knows it, though, and stress may quickly build.

You may divert your responsibility from how your career and life looks by blaming others or by making excuses for everything that has happened to you. It was not *your* fault that the first mailing did not hit the way you thought. It was not *your* fault that the interview did not produce an offer. And it *certainly* was not *your* fault that the ad you answered did not come through with anything.

At the same time, you may experience yourself finding fault with everything that others are doing (or not doing) on your behalf. The typographical error in a letter becomes extremely important. Your friend was supposed to get back to you with the key name from a major target company, and she has not. The executive recruiter has not called back yet. Things do not seem to be working.

These *are* important and should be corrected, but if you become obsessed with them, then it is a sign that you may be stuck. Your stress will consume a tremendous amount of energy that could more profitably be channeled into being optimistic, enthusiastic, and committed to a defined action plan. Let's look now at how stress reveals itself.

Common Physical Sensations When under Stress

Drained	Insomnia
Lifeless	Fatigued

Empty	Cold extremities (hands, feet, nose)
Out-of-body	Shaken
Drifting	Tunnel vision
Falling	Jittery, fidgeting
Tight	Clammy skin
Muscles clenched	Slurred interrupted speech
Teeth and jaw ache	Inappropriate behavior
Headache	Low tolerance for noise and light
Joints and muscles ache	Reddened complexion
Diminished	Pale complexion
Uneasy	Tight clothing
Nauseated	Suffocating
Weak	Frequent need to urinate
Energyless	Spastic colon
Roaring in head	Dilated pupils
Slow motion	Tingling scalp and skin
Fast motion	Lightheadedness
Clumsy	Difficulty swallowing
Under- or overeating	Lump in throat
Oversmoking	Cannot breathe
Overdrinking	Hyperventilating
Overmedication	Biting nails
Overly loud talking	Spots in vision
Overly soft talking	Not hearing words said
Load on back	Crowded

Common Feelings and Emotions When under Stress

Unloved	Apathetic
Discarded	Used
Worthless	Unappreciated
Unclean	Sexless
Impotent	Lost
Emotionless	Scolded
Alone	Forgetful
Disjointed	Sudden attack of doubt
Withdrawn	Giddy
Depressed	Hair-trigger temper

Attacking others	Indecisive
Need for neatness	Blaming others
Afraid to trust people	Ignoring differences
Attacked, threatened	Denying being terminated
Low self-respect	"Replaying" events
Low self-worth	Name calling
Sadness	Powerless, incapable
Unable to disassociate with firm	

Thoughts, Attitudes, Beliefs When under Stress

It's not my fault!

I need to defend my position.

Effective people do not get stressed!

I am not stressed!

Others are biased and prejudiced, not me!

Broken promises are the rule of the day.

There is only one way to learn—the hard way!

I will now manipulate others for my gain, that's the way.

Oh, no—not another problem! I can't cope!

If I ignore this problem, it will go away.

I have been taking on problems which aren't primarily mine.

I can't seem to say "no."

Most situations are impossible!

Can't anyone do anything right anymore?

It is not fair! How come? Why me?

Stress Comes from Change and Irrational Beliefs _____

Stress comes from the somewhat idealistic view that "life should be the way we want it to be." However, we also know that "wishing makes it so" only works in the world according to Walt Disney. While your eyes may be the window to your soul, your language (the words you use) reflects on how you think, feel, believe, and behave. Upset will emerge when you find yourself living in the context of your expectations versus reality, the way life really is. Even the trials and tribulations of everyday life can set us reeling and cause upset. See if you use any of the words under the Expectations column. You might wish to circle those words and add any other words that you use.

Expectations of Life

Must be	Should be
Ought to be	Needs to be
Has to be	Want it to be
Wish it were	Could be
Got to be	Will be

> The greater the difference between your expectations and life's reality, the greater the potential for
>
> 1. **Anxiousness**
> 2. **Frustration**
> 3. **Disappointment**
> 4. **Anger**
> 5. **Sadness**
> 6. **Fear**

Life's Reality: The Way It Really Is—Here and Now

Note: Carried to an extreme, the end result is *failure*. Reality has failed to live up to your expectation of it. The only thing constant about life is change. If you find yourself frustrated or upset, the reason is probably because something has occurred differently than you imagined.

Remedy: So, lighten up and examine both how realistic your expectations are and how you might effectively close the gap between where you are now and where you want to be.

> # The greater the difference between our expectations of how life should look and how it really is, the greater the potential for stress

---

Immediate Stress Relief

Before you can revitalize your stuck or stalled campaign, you need to reduce then manage your stress. First of all, realize that although this might be one of the most taxing experiences of your life, you are by no means the first to go through it. It is actually quite common. Then, realize that since you cannot live your life today completely free of stress or distress, it is important to develop effective ways for dealing with that stress.

Temporary Fight or Flight

- Take a break; put the search aside for a while and get out of your house or apartment. Take a long walk; exercise your muscles as much as you can.

- Breathe slowly and deeply from the abdomen, concentrating on blowing out slowly and evenly.

- Ask a friend to listen while you blow off steam in private. Say whatever will relieve your tension. It does not have to be true or highly responsible. The object is to feel relief from the stress.

- If you have been drinking a lot of coffee, reduce your intake of caffeine for a while. Same with alcohol.

- Mentally take a step back, and take a *good look* at your total job search project and recommit yourself to the task.

Imaginary Flight

- Physical remedies for stress reduction: Quietly tense your toes, legs, your shoulders, etc. and then let go, until you begin to feel better. Nobody has to know what you are doing. It can be done in a meeting without attracting attention. Grip your chair tightly, twist your handkerchief, or scarf. Take more deep breaths.

- Nonphysical remedies and humor for stress reduction: Look for the good that can come from your stress. Look for the humor in the situation. What is ridiculous about it? "How did a nice person like me get into this? I never deliberately set out to have a bad day, did I?" Look at the situation as if it is right out of the Sunday comics. Imagine yourself somewhere else—in a place where you would really love to be, a place where you always feel peaceful and relaxed.

Direct Honesty

- Take responsibility for your search. "Own" your career *and* your life. You are the source of the problems, as well as the solutions. *Recontextualize* the problem by shifting your perspective as to how you view a problem and are entangled by it.

- Admit your feelings and take responsibility for them, without blaming or accusing another.

- Admit your stress and your need to do something immediately to relieve it—and then go and do it.

- If you have made a mistake, admit it and move to correct it.

Plan Your Work and Work Your Plan

- Recognize that just as inaction is at the source of your upset or emotional distress, *so is action the best source of pushing past the feelings that hold you captive.*

- Reread the basics of how to find jobs. Put together a specific list of things which are lagging and needing action in each job source area. Plan a series of five or six action steps you can actually execute within the next six to eight hours. Ask yourself, "What are all the positive things I can do right now?" Then *do them!* It works. Success breeds success.

Lighten Up

- The time when you need to secure a job most is the time when you will least likely get it because you're probably uptight and projecting a sense of desperation.

- Soooo—relax. You've been successful before, you'll be successful again.

Handling Rejection and Becoming Unburdened _____

The Cold Reality

- You *will* be rejected. A search, like any marketing campaign, is not 100 percent successful even though you might like it to be different. When you are unable to secure an interview or you are turned down for a job you really wanted, it very much feels like rejection.

- You can be hurt deeper than you thought possible and are willing to admit.

- Highly competent and perfectly rational people will turn a deaf ear to you, even after previously indicating that they would support you.

- Secretaries will penetrate your well-rehearsed attempts to get past them to their bosses.

- People will not return your phone calls, especially executive search people.

- Your search will take three times longer and will be ten times tougher than you imagined.

- Your mailbox contains only bills and reject letters.

The Warmer Reality

- People *do* care about what happens to you—even strangers.
- Help will come from many unexpected sources.

- There will always be opportunities out there for those who believe in themselves and keep on working.
- If you are committed to your success, so will others be.
- Success may come from a phone call out of the blue.
- You *have* accomplished a great deal. As soon as these accomplishments are matched to a need, you *will* be called.

Commitment—The True Difference

Individuals involved in the search process come in all different sizes and shapes, temperament, and makeup. Why is it that some career searchers are really on fire for themselves and others seem to be limp?

The difference is commitment. *Committed people cannot be stopped.* Committed people exhibit a special kind of motivation that keeps them moving unerringly toward their goal, regardless of obstacles or issues of personal convenience. Certainly, your personality will play an important part in the level of outward display of enthusiasm, but personality is no predictor of the extent of your commitment to your success. The military has a simple phrase to express commitment to a task at hand which we would like you to make operational in your life:

> # Hunker down and move forward

Are You Really Committed to Your Success?

Do you . . . ?

1. Create challenging personal career goals and develop realistic and viable action plans to obtain them?
2. Keep in balance the things you would *like to do* against the things you *have to do?*
3. Maintain positive expectancy about your life and search efforts? Do you have the feeling you cannot fail? Do you create the same level of enthusiasm in others?
4. Distinguish between being patient and being stuck?
5. Take responsibility for those things you have control over and not feel guilty about life's circumstances over which you have little or no control?
6. Continue to work when it is easier to quit? Is your operating philosophy, "It's OK to be down, just never give up?"

7. Critically assess the status of your campaign and have the discipline to put it back on track?

8. Commit to being the best you can be?

Getting Unstuck: Thirteen Things You Can Do

1. Observe and then verbalize where you are on your emotional roller coaster of awareness, denial, anger, depression, acceptance. Be honest with yourself; this is for your benefit—no one else's. Make a copy of the five emotional stages, post it in a highly visible spot, and refer to it often.

2. Allow yourself permission to be angry or depressed and still have the capability to conduct an aggressive campaign. In other words, it is okay to be in whatever emotional state you find yourself. Having emotions and getting stuck is a normal part of life.

3. Focus your attention on the emotional state that you are in and determine what is making you angry or depressed, for example.

4. Make the distinction between your self and your behavior. While you certainly are responsible for your behavior, *you* are not your behavior.

JUST BECAUSE . . .	DOES NOT MEAN THAT . . .
Your campaign fails.	You are a failure.
Your campaign succeeds.	You are a success.

5. Ask Yourself

- Where am I stuck?
- How do I know when I am stuck?
- When do I get most stuck?
- What do I gain or lose from *me* when I am stuck?
- What do I gain or lose from *others* when I am stuck?

If you draw a blank, ask, "What is it that I am afraid to admit—the one thing I will never reveal?"

6. Recognize that you gain tremendous personal power when you control your circumstances rather than allowing your circumstances to control you. When you assume responsibility for your life, you generally will experience a sense of freedom—freedom to be yourself.

7. Concentrate on the successes you have had. Although it is far easier to zero in on failures, continue to focus on campaign *successes* and *progress*. This continued push will encourage additional successes.

8. *Focus* on target areas (personal contacts, for example). Identify goals that are measurable and represent a challenge. Try to make 40 quality contacts per week.

9. When faced with a seemingly impossible challenge *ask yourself* the question, "Although it is impossible—what are five possible solutions to the problem?"

10. Identify the smaller bits of work that could move the larger task forward and start to accomplish them.

11. Ask for support from others in being successful in your career search. The support could range from asking someone to be a willing listener during tough times to critically evaluating a business strategy you have developed. *Caution:* Most people do not know how to ask for nor receive honest feedback from others. Generally, we see it as too embarrassing, too brutally honest, or as an imposition on the person's time. If you are fortunate enough to receive honest data upon asking for it, graciously profit from it.

12. Commit yourself to the task.

13. Hang on and keep doing what you know is right and needs to be done—even when you are uncomfortable, your efforts are not showing immediate returns, or you'd find it easier to quit. Anything worth doing requires effort.

> # Success comes before
> # work only in the
> # dictionary!!

Lessons from Professional Athletes

In a recent benefit dinner in Chicago, two outstanding athletes were recognized for their achievements in their sport and for their personal contributions to life. The two honored were Mike Singletary, all-pro linebacker of the Chicago Bears football team and Nancy Swider-Peltz, a world class speed skater who is the only woman athlete in the world to successfully compete in four consecutive Olympics: 1976, 1980, 1984, and 1988. Highlights of their inspiring speeches, and Mike Ditka's introduction, are summarized below.

Nancy Swider-Peltz

1. You haven't even begun to tap into your potential.

2. Have a goal worthy of your dedication, energy, and talents.

3. Get back up after defeat—failure is not final.

4. Use victories to keep going; use the momentum to capture the spirit of winning (not losing).

5. Reject self-defeating attitudes and behaviors. Incorporate only those things in your life which promote, support, and sustain the achievement of your goal.

6. People don't really care about your problems, your fatigue, or your life's history. People care only if you "show up," try your best, are willing to risk not succeeding. People only care about you if you give life a run for the money. If you put forth your best effort, people will rally around you.

Mike Singletary

1. Focus on what you have and give thanks.

2. Be prepared to give your all in whatever you do.

3. Identify the talents, skills, and abilities that you do have and work on strengthening them. Work with what you have been given.

4. Do not worry about nor focus any time on what someone else has. Don't spend your energies on what you don't have. Grow where you are planted.

5. You miss out when you do not give everything you have. If you stop short of committing your all, then you will never know how good you could have been nor who you really are.

Mike Ditka

Mike Ditka, head coach of the Chicago Bears, introduced Mike Singletary and motivated the group with these comments:

1. To gain a lot in this world, you have to sacrifice a lot. There are no shortcuts, no pills to take, or no books to read. The only way to live life is to gut it out.

2. Discipline is the uppermost requirement to living life to its fullest.

3. You can wish all you want, but sitting around doesn't get it. You have to work hard at being successful and never let your standards of excellence down for a moment.

4. Get rid of the distracting and demotivating elements in your life.

5. *Pride* is spelled *G. U. T. S.*

Success Can Be Stressful—How to Manage It Well _____

You may feel that once you have an offer or two, your worries are over. Not necessarily. Be advised that you may be both excited and troubled by the prospect of successfully ending your campaign. In fact, you may be more anxious and troubled with two or three offers than when you first were separated.

Why? The consequences of your career move are far more significant and *lasting* than the time frame in which you conduct a career search. The time involved in a search is measured in months, but the time spent in the right (or wrong) career move is measured by years! Figure 10-1 illustrates the point.

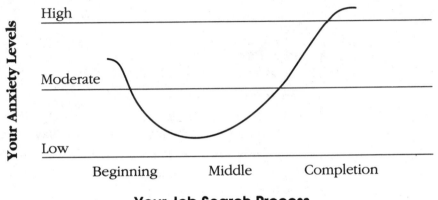

Your Job Search Process

Figure 10-1. Your anxiety levels.

IN SEARCH OF THE PERFECT OFFER

Creating What You Want Through Effective Negotiations

Leveraging up Offers and Opportunities

Sam Donovan gave everyone until June 15th, including himself. He got zapped March 16th and set as his goal a three-month job campaign. Using the organizational skills and personal discipline for which he was known, Sam plotted the time line for his career course meticulously. As the former vice president of Sales and Marketing for a $850 million organization, Sam was used to making things happen once he was focused and his mind set. He had no doubt that he would be successful.

Sam had progressed rapidly and succeeded where others failed in his company's "churn and burn" environment. The long hours, the numbing pressure to win at any cost in an intensely competitive business—all served as narcotics to Sam's addictive workaholic temperament. As Sam told us, "Until now, my working philosophy has always been this: Put me on your team, tell me my job, equip me, set an impossible task out there, and get out of my way! Even though I'd sacrifice myself and my family in the process, I'd work 36 hours a day to get the job done." Indeed, Sam had done so, for now he was physically and emotionally spent. Although getting zapped was traumatic and he was still in shock, Sam also experienced a sense of tremendous relief.

Eight years earlier, Sam was our client as well. He was in his mid-thirties and had a well-developed "ready, fire, aim" operating style which he acquired during his first company's extraordinary growth years. Ironically, Sam's career blew up for the same reason in both companies, his lack of a balanced approach to getting the job done—technically and interpersonally.

Eight years earlier, Sam was terrified about being out of work and hated the "loss of face" which he felt accompanied such a condition.

291

Imposing a severe austerity regimen on himself and his family, Sam attacked the outplacement process and the marketplace with a vengeance unlike any other client we had ever worked with. Within six weeks, Sam had five bona fide executive management offers: two offers as general manager or COO, two offers as vice president of Sales and Marketing, and one offer as a senior partner in a leading management consulting firm in Chicago.

Eight years earlier, Sam learned that he could secure a good job quickly, if he needed to; however, this was not his objective now. With 12 months worth of severance, Sam was committed to slowing down, understanding more fully how he sabotaged his efforts, and healing relations with his family and himself. "Slowing down" for Sam meant that his goal was 90 days not 45 days.

Equipped with his results-oriented credentials and network contacts, maintained through periodic luncheon meetings with search firms and other executives, Sam launched a powerful and balanced search. Declaring that he would make a decision by June 15th, Sam began to establish a negotiating position for himself immediately. People clambered to get on board; opportunities seemed to materialize out of thin air for Sam, even though other executives in a similar capacity weren't able to generate the same level of activity. Sam initiated and received a minimum of 40 calls a day, easily twice as many as our other clients. Our role was to act as business advisor, career counselor, coach, and friend as we constantly reined him in, so in his normal enthusiasm and impetuousness he wouldn't blow up opportunities or make hasty decisions.

Thirty days after Sam launched his campaign, he had 23 attractive opportunities simmering in various stages of readiness. At the 60-day mark, Sam had dropped 9 searches from his original 20, but he picked up another 6 possibilities. At day 75 Sam began to consolidate his activities into high-, medium-, and low-priority opportunities, concentrating on penetrating further into the top eight firms we identified as top prospects. On the 80th day of his search, Sam had received two offers and zeroed in on three of the remaining top jobs. At his 90-day target day, Sam had received five offers, effectively negotiating the total compensation packages for each, and by 4 p.m. had accepted the position as vice president and general manager of a $200 million manufacturer with a corporate culture which is considerably more "laid back" than his previous employers.

Sam learned a valuable lesson: Know your outcome, be committed to achieving it, work the plan, make a decision, and manage the decision and the outcome.

As you can see from Sam's example, an effective search campaign is far more than merely mailing out your résumé to prospective employers and search firms or employment agencies. It involves strategic planning, marketing, and negotiating. For you to be successful in this campaign, you must consider incorporating the following *elements of success* into your routine:

1. Know Your Outcome

What is it that you really want to achieve? Do you just want a new job? If all you are looking for is a job, any kind of job, that's easy—there are plenty of minimum-wage positions available. If you want a career move, then invest the time and energy in this activity, not unlike the time you invested in getting your education, completing a major project, or raising your family.

2. Be Committed to Achieving Your Outcome and Be Enthusiastic

Determine your life's priorities and make your campaign a top priority. What would your campaign look like if its priority was the same as, let's say, breathing. Would that change what you accomplish? Employers want to have enthusiastic people work for them. Enthusiastic people are generally more optimistic, more competitive, and willing to tackle new challenges.

3. Evaluate Everything in Your Life against Your Goal

Ask yourself the question, "What is the best use of my time, energy, and talent *right now?*" If your activity is what you deem to be a high priority and it supports you in pursuit of your outcome, then it may be something you want to keep on doing. If you suspect it is not a top priority, critically assess it and then reprioritize it.

4. Develop Personal Intensity and a High Sense of Urgency

People who achieve significant results universally have a high degree of intensity about their beliefs and possess a high degree of urgency. This burning desire to accomplish your outcome will help create the momentum you need to push beyond those times when it is convenient or uncomfortable to continue working.

5. Work Your Plan and Eliminate What Is Not Working or Adding Value

Once you have established your plan and are satisfied with its soundness, work the plan. If you find that during the course of your plan's execution you need to modify some things, then do so. When you drive your car, you are constantly fine-tuning the controls in your car to produce a desired outcome, whether to stop when needed or to successfully navigate a curve. The same fine-tuning and attention to detail is required for your campaign strategy to be successful.

6. Make a Decision, Manage the Decision, and Enjoy the Outcome

After you have an offer (or offers) you will be evaluating it against your criteria for the ideal job: position responsibilities (short term and long term), challenges, compensation, personal chemistry between you and others, and other dimensions important to you. Determine if the opportunity is right; if it is, accept the offer and don't second-guess yourself. You made a terrific decision because you made it based on all the available information you had and you agreed it was the best one to make. If you are not completely satisfied after being employed for a while, you may need to look beyond your own situation and look for ways to contribute to others. Discover what others *want* and *need* in this new relationship and continually look for ways to add value to another person, the team, and the company. Once you add value, your satisfaction will increase significantly.

Signs of Continued Interest

Ongoing interest in you as a job candidate is typically displayed in many ways:

1. A second interview visit has been scheduled, and you will be meeting the decision makers.
2. You have the commitment to visit multiple business units or facilities.
3. You will be interviewing with people who would be your peers.
4. The appointment for a psychological appraisal or other testing has been confirmed.
5. References have been or will be checked.
6. In-depth salary and compensation discussions are held.
7. You have gone on house-hunting trips with your spouse and your family.

8. You have been asked to inform the hiring manager before making a final decision regarding the acceptance or rejection of an offer.

9. An offer is extended.

Some signals that you give to indicate your interest in the company include:

1. You have sent thank-you letters after interviews you had.

2. You begin to compare all other opportunities against one position.

3. You send timely and relevant technical or managerial articles to decision makers.

4. You make follow-up calls or send letters with personal follow-up and contacts made within organization.

5. You send your references, and you inform your references of your keen interest in this position.

6. You conduct additional research on the company, its competition, and industry trends.

Receiving and Analyzing Offers

Although the employment process and job offers are clearly business transactions, you will feel like you are entering into a personal relationship. Intuitively, you understand that personal chemistry between you and others in the company makes all the difference in the world. You might be offered the "best job in the world," but if the people relationships do not feel right going in, the situation may not work.

Receiving an Offer

Follow these guidelines when you receive an offer:

- Be enthusiastic. Sound pleased. Express your interest in working with your new boss and for the new organization.
- Take notes on the starting salary, reporting relationships, title, start date, and other benefits. Feed back your understanding.
- If the offer is low, react positively and counter with a "catch-up" strategy to create the compensation package you are comfortable with starting, even though some monies may be delayed.
- Ask when the company needs your decision.
- Ask that the offer details be sent to you in writing. Until the offer is in writing, consider it "smoke" which could evaporate at any time. The

verbal employment agreement which you have so carefully cultivated with your potential boss is in jeopardy if your new boss is transferred or leaves the company. To that end, it is clearly better to have the hiring specifics in writing. If it is not company policy to confirm offers in writing, then you send a confirming letter to your new boss.

- Sign off warmly, thanking them once again for the opportunity.

Analyzing an Offer

- Refer to your notes on the Worksheets in Step 2. Examine the relevancy of those factors compared to this offer. Honestly make any necessary modifications to that list based on how you have grown and what you have learned during your search.
- Ask yourself, "To what extent does this offer and the opportunity meet both my short- and long-term needs?" Fill out Worksheet 55.

What's In the Offer—Potential Negotiable Points _____

Although most offers are straightforward enough, you might wish to evaluate your offer in light of some of the following elements. Please do not be intimidated by the length of this list, no one could possibly have every single item mentioned below.

Organization
- Title
- Reporting relationship
- Responsibilities, authority, and accountability
- Annual and long-range goals
- Performance standards and measures

Career Opportunity
- What is the likely career path?
- What is the company's promotion policy?
- What specific action can you take in the next 6, 12, and 18 months to gain the experience, exposure, and preparation necessary to be considered for the next promotion?

Financial
- Base salary
- Hiring or sign-up bonus

WORKSHEET 55
Offer Analysis

To assist you in evaluating your career options, answer the following questions:

1. What does the ideal job look like for me, in terms of duties, projects, and responsibilities? Work team and leader relationships?

2. What elements of the ideal job are present or missing in this position?

3. What do I like and dislike about the position?

4. What reasons do I have to accept or decline this job?

5. What is preventing me from accepting this position? Evaluate:

   • What other offers have been made?

   • What specific activity can I do to generate additional offers?

   • Without damaging the relationship with my prospective employer, what specific actions or "next steps" can I take (or request be taken) which may effectively delay my acceptance or rejection decision?

   • How long can I realistically delay accepting the offer before I turn off my potential employer?

   • How is my financial situation? Do I need to accept this offer to "keep bread on the table"?

   • Should I take this job now *and* continue to search?

   • To what extent is my fear of changing jobs and being zapped again getting in my way of accepting this offer?

- Bonus eligibility
- Guaranteed first-year bonus or floor of total salary
- Total compensation potential
- Annual bonus percentage or target dollar amount
- Amount and date of next scheduled increases
- Profit-sharing plan
- Tax-deferred investment plan
- Deferred compensation
- Matching contribution stock plan
- Phantom stock plans
- Broker fees or conversion costs for stock purchase
- Stock options
- Company car: lease reimbursement, operating expenses, or monthly allowance
- Entertainment expense allowance
- Country club, health club, or luncheon club
- Allowance for legal, tax, or estate planning assistance
- Low-interest loans
- Consumer product discounts
- Credit card: Watts telephone in home, air travel, car rental gas/oil, or general charge card
- Regional cost-of-living adjustment, if recognized

Job Security
- Severance pay and benefit continuation
- Outplacement services with a firm of your choice
- Consulting fees after termination
- Employment contract of minimum duration

Benefits
- Medical and life insurance: Standard and executive
- Comprehensive major medical costs
- Reimbursement of out-of-pocket and deductible provisions for hospitalization
- Acceptance of pre-existing conditions
- Vision or dental coverage plan

- Supplementary pension provisions
  - Phantom stock
  - Matching contribution
  - Contributory pension plan additions
  - Deferred salary or incentive plan
- Extended life insurance plan
- Automotive, A&D policy for family members
- College tuition assistance for children
- Salary continuation during illness
- Additional vacation days
- Vacation travel expense reimbursement
- Spouse travel: domestically, internationally
- University executive management program
- Graduate degree: tuition, fees, and time off
- Seminars

Relocation
- Relocation of household goods
- Mortgage interest differential
- Company purchase of your house
- Reimbursement of "moved from" costs (old residence)
  - Real estate commission
  - Mortgage points coverage
  - Complete relocation coverage
  - Tax gross-up on relocation costs
  - Attorney fees
  - Appraisal fees
  - Inspection fees
  - Selling points
  - Relocation of second car, boat, wine cellar, etc.
  - Lawn care
  - Mortgage prepayment penalty
  - Bridge loan
  - Relocation of carpets, drapes, and appliance "disconnects"
- Reimbursement of "moved to" costs (new residence)
  - Interest-free "bridge" loan for 6 to 12 months

- Mortgage interest differential for 3 to 5 years
- Purchase points
- Filing and administrative costs
- "Gross-up" of taxes
- Travel costs to and from new location and old residence for 3 to 6 months
- House-hunting trips (three to four) with spouse to locate housing
- Travel costs to new location during the move

Housing Cost Differential

If relocation is an option, then the cost of housing plays a significant role in your employment decision making. Although you may have received an attractive offer, it may not be fully competitive if you lose ground financially due to higher housing costs in the new location. To that end, you may wish to ask for some form of housing differential, increased base salary, or additional stock options, for example.

Leveraging Offers against Each Other

Once you have been made an offer, you may become quite anxious. For many this is the best of times and the worst of times. It is a time to do some serious evaluation of those career and life plans you have developed earlier. If the offer presented to you is truly a once-in-a-lifetime opportunity, then your choices are clear. But ironically, you will probably still have other situations you would rather have offers on. Murphy's Law!

- Objectively evaluate your employment options, the number of offers (actual or pending), how well you "fit," your sense of the company's desire for you, etc.
- Determine the longest acceptable delay and secure the OK from the company offering you a job offer. You could say:

    I am very excited about coming to work here. However, I would like to follow through on commitments to finalize my discussions with several other companies.

- Recontact organizations that had previously shown interest. For example,

    I am in the midst of receiving some fine offers and would like very much to include your organization in my decision making. Where do you stand on making a decision?

Companies drag their feet on extending offers for a wide variety of reasons. They have other business priorities, you might not be the strongest fit, the plans have changed and the position is not going to be filled, or perhaps a pending acquisition may materially affect hiring decisions. Rather than remain uninformed, contact the hiring authority and request feedback on your candidacy and the company's timetable.

What to Do When the Offer Is Low

Because salary offers feel so personal and they seem to be closely tied with feelings of self-worth, you run the risk of not responding as positively as you should or even "blowing up" the opportunity if the offer is less than expected. Receiving a lower-than-anticipated compensation package feels like rejection. You may be hurt, embarrassed, confused, and perhaps even angry. If you are like most people, you may not handle this as confidently and powerfully as you did the interview. Even though the salary or title may not be what you want, it is vitally important not to show your disappointment.

Catch-Up Strategy—Negotiating Effectively

If the offer is low, express your enthusiasm for the opportunity to contribute to the company first, and then reveal your disappointment in the job offer. Indicate your desired compensation package and ask if some form of satisfactory accommodation can be worked out for both of you:

> **Thank you for the offer. The opportunities at _____ Company sound terrific, and I am looking forward to contributing to the team. I am somewhat disappointed in the compensation package, however. I would like to explore creatively how we can reach a mutually agreeable compensation arrangement. Money is important, but it is not the only career consideration, as we both acknowledged. My interest is to remain whole, salary-wise, over a 12-month period. I would like you to consider some options which might include a hiring or sign-up bonus and/or guaranteed 6-month and 12-month salary increases. I understand that career moves like this are a "leap of faith" for both of us. I am willing to sacrifice some money up front because I am confident that through my contributions, any deferred dollars will be made up over time.**

Improving Offers by Focusing on Needs, Not Money

If the employer is reluctant to move on your compensation package, you may want to influence the decision maker by respectfully highlighting what the company will likely get (talent-wise) for the money being offered.

Help the recruiter or decision maker examine the organizational needs and challenges *first,* then zero in on the credentials required to do the job and the compensation—in that order. Remember, if the offer is less than you think you deserve and the company is truly unwilling to go higher, you may be overqualified, given their commitment. The company may clearly *need* a person with your talents but may *not want* to pay the price. Your challenge, then, is to get the employer to know the extra value that you can bring.

Here is a model that you may find helpful as you attempt to educate then shift the employer to a more generous (and appropriate!) salary offer. Although your compensation levels and background will be different than Mike Commons, let us use him as an example. You will have an opportunity to complete your own worksheet (Worksheet 56 on page 304) if you find yourself in this situation. But first, let's dissect the following model, starting with Table 11-1.

Salary Offer

The compensation package of $45,000 base salary and no performance bonus plan is very conservative, given the needs of the corporation to

Table 11-1. Assessing an Offer

Salary Offer	Company Wants, Needs, Requires
$45,000 salary $5,000 relocation benefits Medical benefits—complete 401K plan No car allowance No performance bonus Limited relocation benefits	National Sales Manager 10–15 years sales management experience Experienced sales manager with track record of building and leading highly motivated sales teams who will penetrate accounts, increase sales and profits, and turn around troubled company Ability to build sales from $200 million to $500 million while handling national accounts Succeed retiring Vice President of Sales in 2 years
Company Likely to Get	**Optimal Offer**
Territory management experience 5–8 years selling experience Limited supervisory experience Medium-sized company background	$55,000–$65,000 base salary Performance bonus Car allowance Complete relocation benefits

turn around the troubled sales organization, revitalize sales, and balance the product mix.

It is appropriate to fully identify what is included in the salary offer, including often overlooked details such as deferred tax or compensation plans like 401K plans and comprehensive medical and life insurance plans. As Mike will be required to relocate to accept this job, the $5000 relocation benefit is much too conservative. A more realistic relocation benefit is one with no limit on the costs associated with real estate commissions, transportation, and "points" on both ends with about 60 to 90 days temporary living allowance. Also, given the required senior sales management role, a car allowance and incentive bonus are normal and customary.

Company Wants and Needs

Through in-depth interview discussions and probing questions, it was obvious that Mike was interviewing a company in trouble and that the senior executives were counting on the national sales manager to lead them out of difficulty. The sales organization was in disarray, sales people sold more lower-profit margin products because they were easier, order entry was in shambles, wrong products were shipped, filled orders were often not what the customers wanted, dealers were unsatisfied and not performing, and the sales force turnover eroded the customer's confidence and the company's effectiveness.

Clearly, the troubled company *needed* and *wanted* a "hands-on" sales manager like Mike who could turn it around and position it for further growth. However, given their cash flow dilemma, the company did not feel it could afford to pay Mike's salary demands.

Company Likely to Get

Although $45,000 is a fine offer for individuals growing into a territory manager's position or currently handling approximately $50 million in sales, given national salary range norms, it was too light for a $200 million company in trouble with eroding profits and market share. In Mike's favor, he knew the company could not financially afford to have the person in this role make a mistake or learn on the job. A person was required to hit the ground running, adding value immediately. The challenge is to respectfully and in a nonthreatening way point out that the person most likely attracted to that compensation structure would not be strong enough for the company's needs, although he or she may fit the compensation profile. You run the risk of portraying yourself as overqualified, but you can significantly minimize your risk by doing your

WORKSHEET 56
Profiling Your Offer

Complete each quadrant fully with your intent to develop counter arguments that justify a higher compensation package.

Salary Offer	Company Wants, Needs, Requires

Company Likely to Get	Optimal Offer

Note: You may reproduce this worksheet with our compliments.
Copyright © 1990 Robertson Lowstuter, Inc. (708) 940-4400

research on the company and by asking penetrating questions through-out the interview which support the need for a person like you versus one who may accept a much lesser salary.

Optimal Offer

The optimal offer represents that total compensation package you feel is appropriate for the company's opportunity and challenges, your credentials, and what other companies would be willing to pay. Your goal is to move the company from being out of synch with what they want, need, or require and the salary offer. You are trying to move them to properly align the job's demands with its compensation.

Seventeen Tips to Improve Your Offers _____

To help the decision makers or the recruiter safely explore this disparity and to make the shift, you (and Mike) should do the following:

1. Thank them for the offer. Be enthusiastic.

2. Ask them how they determined the compensation package. Express appreciation for the process and the "rightness" of the research.

3. Acknowledge that you feel the offer is not yet fully competitive, given what the company needs, wants, and requires.

4. Legitimize the offer. Acknowledge that the offer is valid given their cash flow dilemma and where they are with the talent that they have currently.

5. Gain leverage by highlighting both what the company *needs* (to be turned around), *wants* (strong commitment to hire the right person), and *requires* (seasoned sales manager with minimally 10 to 15 years of experience).

6. Briefly summarize your skills, abilities, accomplishments, capabilities, and fit for this job now and in the future.

7. Ask for feedback, "Do you think I could do the job?" "Is there anything that would make me unacceptable?"

8. Thank them for acknowledging that you could do the job well and you are an ideal fit for their short-term and longer-range plans.

9. Share with them the compensation elements and salary you are discussing with other prospective employers, which coincide with the ideal offer.

10. Ask for feedback, "How does this sound?" Pause, wait for a response. Now, if the decision maker starts to grab his or her chest

and gasp for air, you probably telegraphed a salary a bit too high. Short of having to administer CPR, you should smile and acknowledge that you, too, recognize a discrepancy between the company's offer and what you are finding in other companies as an optimal offer for an individual with your skills and needs of the company.

11. Help the decision maker to focus on the salient points of the situation by crisply summarizing the main issues which hopefully prompt them to say "YES!" Let's see how Mike Commons cuts through all the rhetoric with his target firm.

> MIKE: Clearly you need a person to help the company turn around, right?
>
> THE FIRM: Right!
>
> MIKE: You indicated that for every month in which the wrong person is in the job it is costing the company millions, right?
>
> THE FIRM: Right!
>
> MIKE: Based on what you and your team shared with me, I am stronger than the current national accounts manager?
>
> THE FIRM: Right!
>
> MIKE: So, if I was in place doing what needed to be done a month or two sooner (versus hunting for the person to fit the job at $45,000), I would more than offset the difference in your original offer and what I raised, right?
>
> THE FIRM: Right! [you hope!]

12. Reiterate that:

> **I do not see myself as overqualified, rather *fully* qualified for this position. While money is important to me, being in a challenging role is most important. As I may have indicated previously, I am willing to work with you on how we might structure a *total* compensation plan, not just salary. I would be willing to discuss a catch-up strategy, a percentage of the money saved or new sales generated, a hiring or sign-up bonus—whatever you feel is appropriate to keep your cash flow healthy.**

13. Express appreciation for the company's willingness to openly discuss the opportunities and challenges and the means to accomplish that through being flexible and responsive. ("Being flexible and responsive" is the subliminal message that they will, indeed, be open to increasing the compensation package in a timely manner.)

14. Ask:

- "What is the next step?"

- "Is there anyone else who needs to be involved in the discussion at this time?"
- "Would you like me to summarize our discussion and outline what I feel is a more competitive package?"

15. Prepare a summary of your discussion, possibly utilizing the worksheet format as the basis for your write-up. Before you share your worksheet or summary with your prospective employer or recruiter, you may wish to have someone whose judgment you trust preview the material. You certainly want to guard against language that makes it seem you are *demanding* versus *discussing*. Your best intentions mean nothing if your prospective employer feels you are overly demanding and disrespectful. Ideally, meet in person to go over the items, point by point. The next step is to mail it, but if you do you will not be able to observe the employer's reaction, a valuable source of data during delicate discussions.

16. If you must mail the letter, do so, with a word of caution: Before mailing the letter to the employer, call ahead and emphasize that the items outlined are discussion points based on your previous meetings and should not be considered as mandates or absolutes. This letter is intended to be a basis of further dialogue. Please note: If you have *any concerns* about being misunderstood, then *do not mail your summary*. It is far too easy for employers to agree to be open-minded about salary discussions before they read your observations. Handle this communication piece with great care, as it is very easy for the employer to reach the conclusion that you are too expensive. To emphasize the point that unless properly introduced, this letter could be a "deal breaker" . . .

Do not send the letter until you have discussed it with the employer or search representative!

17. Follow up very soon after the time when the employer should have received the letter; again, face-to-face meetings are preferred. Ask for feedback. Listen carefully and respond respectfully. This is a time to be very supportive of the prospective employer or recruiter.

Employment Contracts and Letters of Agreement _____

Employment contracts are formal legal agreements between an organization and a new employee which identify the terms and conditions of employment and the compensation and benefit package. Typically, employment contracts are reserved for senior executives or persons undertaking unusual, high-risk foreign assignments or consulting for a definite period.

If the organization does not provide an employment contract or confirming letter to you, you may wish to write a detailed *letter of agreement,* which outlines your understanding and acceptance of the offer. At the very least, you will be able to spell out the specifics of the offer in detail, including title, reporting relationships, base salary, bonus arrangements (if applicable), and any special compensation catch-up steps (with dates and dollar amounts). Ask, "Thank you for the offer and agreeing to these points. Before I make my final decision, I would like to see the offer in writing. Is that possible? When do you think you will be getting that out to me?"

Caution: Do not use the letter of agreement to gain things which you have not previously secured. Items still under negotiation can be mentioned in your letter but need to clearly be identified as still under consideration and in a preliminary stage.

Rules for Accepting an Offer

At this stage of your campaign, you have:

- Received an attractive offer (at least one) and perhaps effectively negotiated for more responsibility or more money.
- Expressed enthusiasm for the opportunity to be of mutual benefit and to contribute to the company's growth.
- Received a confirming letter outlining offer details.
- Evaluated this offer in light of other opportunities and your targeted career plans.
- Made the decision to accept the employment offer.

Because employment relationships are so personal, it is advisable to personally contact your potential manager or the human resource professional, whoever is appropriate, and follow these steps:

- Call your new manager first, accept the offer and settle any last minute details. If you feel comfortable doing so, send a confirming letter outlining the major elements of the offer.
- If your new organization asks you to sign and return the offer letter sent to you, do not balk. However, read the offer letter carefully, as returning it signed constitutes a contract binding on both parties.
- When in doubt, or if the stakes are particularly high, have an attorney review the letter for any issue which may be a problem if you and the organization elect to part company, hopefully not soon.

Rules for Rejecting an Offer

Most people would love to be in the position of having more than one offer to choose from. It is a heady experience, often described as scary, confusing, exhilarating, and "the best of all possibilities." However, you may have the dilemma of having only one offer for a well-paying position that you really do not want. What to do?

First, critically evaluate the offer in light of your short-term and long-term career interests, needs, and promotional opportunities, as previously developed. Second, determine what condition your finances are in—do you need to accept this position to keep yourself financially together? As distasteful as it might seem, you may need to accept an offer, knowing that it may only be on a temporary basis.

If the employment opportunity is not acceptable and your finances are OK, it may be appropriate to decline the offer. Communicate your decision on the phone (or in person), indicating your specific reasons. Do not reject a company's offer hoping that you can negotiate a better deal. If you want the job, say so, and negotiate. Only reject an offer if you are fully prepared to walk away from the opportunity with "no strings attached." *Before rejecting an offer,* you may wish to *talk it over with someone you respect,* then decide. Talk it over with your family members or close friends. Let them be a sounding board for you during this time.

After you reject a bona fide offer, be alert to a possible onslaught of conflicting physical sensations, feelings, and emotions. People who have rejected opportunities which were not right for them have expressed that they reexperienced the emotional ups and downs of their job loss. Although this experience was difficult, they also knew it was the correct course of action to take.

The Offer: A Checklist

1. How to evaluate:
   - By your current income and your value in the marketplace
   - By company comparison
   - With a total compensation comparison
   - With your *position selection criteria* as a guide.

2. How to keep your options open:
   - Buy some time with each offer.
   - Allow time to compare offers.
   - Request more time if you are anticipating another job offer.

- Ask to see additional facilities or key people in the company (possibly even board members or outside investors) so as to slow down the hiring process, enabling you to speed up other opportunities.

3. How to compare:
   - By base salary
   - By benefits
   - By bonus
   - By total compensation
   - By your career goals and objectives
   - By a simple ranking method

4. The confirmation:
   - Verbally accept the job.
   - Put in writing.
   - Stay in touch.

5. Your arrival:
   - Arrive on time.
   - Meet your new associates.
   - *Good Luck!*

> # You Don't Get
> # What You're Worth,
> # You Get What
> # You Negotiate.

LOOKING BACK
AND MANAGING
FORWARD

Ensuring Success in Your Perfect Job

STEP 12

Commencement—A New Beginning

Tired, restless, elated, deflated, energized, anticlimactic, relieved. These are common emotions at the conclusion of a well-run search. Now that the dust has somewhat settled on your search campaign and before you start your new career, contact those people who have helped you in your search and those firms with whom you'd like to continue to have some visibility. Here's also an opportunity to examine what you have learned and how you have grown.

Next Steps—Postsearch Strategy

One of the insights you might have gained during your search was the importance of networking with search firms, target companies, and personal and professional acquaintances. Do you recall Sam Donovan and his ability to generate a tremendous amount activity in a short time? After he was terminated the first time, we advised Sam "never to get caught with his data down." Jointly, we designed an ongoing contact strategy which fit his unique needs and geographic constraints. Granted, your situation will be different, but we recommend that you maintain contacts on an ongoing basis:

1. Commit to taking a contact (search firm account executive or professional colleague or friend) to lunch at least once a month. This will help you promote yourself in a nonthreatening manner and enable you to maintain your visibility appropriately.

2. Continue to be a networking source to others in need. Do you remember how gratifying it was to receive support from others when you were "casting about" for leads or even a friendly voice on the other end of the phone? Now it's your turn. We recommend that you make some time available for people who are trying to network with you. However, guard against overextending yourself by providing too much support, as you don't want to create the impression that you're carrying on your campaign.

3. Two to three weeks after you accept the new position, send a mailing to 50 to 100 contacts, including companies, search firms, and personal contacts indicating your changed status. For correspondence samples, please refer to "New Position Accepted" letters in Step 3.

4. Add value to other job seekers when they call—more than merely providing names. Inquire about the status of their search and don't be afraid to ask penetrating questions. Be a friend to a stranger. *Caution:* Do not "bowl people over" with your keen careering insights, no matter how correct they may be. Earn the right to volunteer information by asking what role the caller wants you to play—then provide your observations and recommended action steps which have worked for you in the past.

Growth Questions Designed to Unlock Answers

If you are interested in discovering how you could have achieved more at your previous employer, what you could have done differently, and perhaps why you didn't—great! This Step is for you. However, you may not be interested in going through this additional process of self-discovery at this time. That is fine, but we do recommend that you go through this process sometime soon. Answer the following questions candidly and completely:

1. What was the reason for your leaving?
2. What would *others* say was the reason for your leaving?
3. Why were you picked to leave versus someone else?
4. What things did you do at your former company to make yourself indispensable?
5. What things could you have done *differently?* Why didn't you?
6. What signs were visible that indicated the company and/or you were in trouble?
7. What did you do to protect yourself inside the organization *and* hedge your bets outside in the marketplace?
8. What did you gain by protecting your position? What did you lose?

9. If you did not do anything "protective," what did you gain by not taking protective measures? What did you lose?

10. If you could have been more proactive in your job search, why were you not? What barriers prevented you from acting?

11. If you were a victim of organizational politics, what can you do to stay out of the way next time?

12. What are your five-year career and life goals? Ten-year goals?

13. What experiences, on the new job and off the new job, will be instrumental in achieving your goals?

14. What specific action will ready you to achieve your 5- and 10-year goals?

15. How do you plan to keep your network alive and healthy and yourself appropriately active in the marketplace?

16. What are the top five responsibilities in your new job?

17. What are the top five challenges or demands in your new job?

18. Who are the greatest *proponents,* supporters, or advocates for you in this new position? Why?

19. Who are the greatest *opponents,* the people who will resist or challenge you the most. Why?

20. In what three ways can you contribute to your opponents? To your proponents?

21. In what three ways can these people and functions contribute to you?

22. What functions do you know least well? Who is in charge and when will you learn more about each one?

23. If you did not receive the kind of position, responsibility, or authority that you wanted on this move, what experiences are you missing? Who in the organization can help you gain that knowledge? What project or assignment do you need to gain the experience to qualify you for greater opportunities?

24. What is *needed* and *wanted* by your boss, your boss's peers, your coworkers, your subordinates (if appropriate), and other parts of the organization?

Starting a New Job—Your First Few Months

- Become a "consultant" in your new role, creatively problem solving and resolving conflicts or confusion.
- Learn how to *contribute value* to everyone with whom you come in contact. If you don't feel you are adding value, then do some research and figure out how you can help.

- Identify those individuals whom your function impacts and meet them. Get to know their needs, interests, and motivations. Learn about their roles and responsibilities. It is critical to your own success that you know what seems to work with your new colleagues.

- Do not talk much about how things were managed at your former employer, and do not be too quick to volunteer solutions which, at first glance, look just like something you encountered previously. If you don't stop and ask questions, you run the risk of being embarrassed by your incomplete recommendation.

- If you are replacing a person, you may wish to ask the following questions to key people:

  □ How did you view the other person?

  □ What was done well?

  □ What was not done well?

  □ If you could have had anything you want from this position, what would it be?

- Learn to gain support and endorsement of others (superiors, peers, and subordinates) by informing and involving them in your thoughts, feelings, ideas, and intentions. Do not confuse your need to use people as sounding boards with consensus decision making, it is not. Rather, strive to balance your need for information gathering with your colleagues' needs for a given outcome. Rarely will they expect more than that, and if you ask for their input, most people are pleased to support you. Involvement fosters commitment.

Signs That Your Company May Be Going to Downsize

It may seem odd to you that, having just begun a new job, you're being asked to look for signs that your company may be downsizing. However, given the nature of the changes in the corporate climate during the past few years, you can't be too alert to this problem.

Here are some of the things employees have reported seeing just prior to downsizing decisions in their companies. One or two may not mean much, but several signs appearing together could mean that you want to avoid major personal expenditures, bid to safer jobs, update your résumé, contact your network, and begin considering your employment options.

- Bosses seem distracted and under a lot of pressure.
- There is a lot of talk among employees about job security issues.

- The company is always "reorganizing."
- Needed equipment is promised but never appears.
- Company rejects ideas that might cost some money but which will save more.
- Preventive maintenance programs are dropped.
- There are frequent changes of plant managers or office people.
- Salaried vacancies are not replaced—jobs are combined.
- Corporate or division managers visit a lot more than usual.
- Open-door policies seem to go away.
- Bosses pick up job duties previously performed by their subordinates.
- Equipment is transferred out and not replaced by other equipment or with other products.
- "Difficult to please" customers are dropped.
- Large accounts are lost and not replaced.
- The company has recently been acquired by a new firm.
- There are no new products in a long time.
- Profitable customers are transferred to other plants.
- Night shifts and afternoon shifts are cut back.
- Research lab people in the plant are assigned to quality control duties.
- Research people are being let go or not replaced.
- Quality circle teams are deemphasized.
- Groups of strangers in suits are touring the plant.
- The word is out that the facility is not profitable.

Strategic Survival Plan in Your New Position

Take care of the company and the company will take care of you. Bring to the job, and convey to others, a sense of urgency about the task at hand.

Maintain some healthy emotional distance between yourself and the company. Work at remaining objective and professional in your approach to your job. Create a balance between your business life and your personal life.

Your future promotions will basically rest with your performance reputation established within your first 18 months on the job. Repeatedly ask yourself, "What's needed and what's wanted on the job, in the company, in my relationships?"

Don't be political. This can be permanently damaging. Therefore, refuse to discuss personalities and do not "take sides."

Always gauge shifting winds. Watch for changes. Be alert to new directions or trends or people in power. Become more known and visible when this happens.

Know more about your business and company than you need to know. This requires an inquisitiveness that won't quit. Read the company's annual report, the operating plan, and the financials. Ask about new products or new projects or programs in other departments. Learn how the company operates and become known to as many people as you can.

Always have a business or operational plan that you are working against and using to measure performance. If your goals are not being met, or have little chance of being met, then increase your pressure to succeed.

Review monthly what you have done. Measure your own performance against your own goals. Set next month's accomplishment goals. Give yourself a quarterly performance review. Be tough on yourself. Expect results, not perfection.

Status quo is death. Successful organizations expect action—all the time. Keep things moving. Make things happen. Do not sit on yesterday's successes.

No business will ever replace good gut instincts, personal courage, and a high sense of urgency! Be demanding, firm, fair, and genuine with others.

Everything you do will have a direct positive or negative impact on the bottom line. Prudence dictates performance—better performance.

Network constantly, both inside and outside your organization. Strategize ways to become visible within your industry and marketplace: Write a series of articles, volunteer for a high-visibility committee in your professional operation, or develop a speech and give it to conventions or trade shows, as appropriate. Become known as a facilitator of problem resolution and as a conduit through which search firms identify viable candidates for jobs.

Lastly, have fun!

BIBLIOGRAPHY

Careering

Beatty, Richard: *The Complete Job Search Book,* John Wiley & Sons, New York, 1988.

Bolles, Richard Nelson: *What Color Is Your Parachute? A Practical Manual for Job-Hunters and Career Changers,* Ten Speed Press, Berkeley, Calif., 1990.

Cotham, James, III: *Career Shock,* Donald I. Fine, Inc., New York, 1989.

Davidson, Jeffrey: *Blowing Your Own Horn—How to Market Yourself and Your Career,* AMACOM, New York, 1987.

Jackson, Tom: *Guerrilla Tactics in the New Job Market,* Bantam Business, New York, 1990.

Kanter, Rosabeth Moss: *When Giants Learn to Dance: Mastering the Challenge of Strategy, Management, and Careers in the 1990s,* Simon and Schuster, New York, 1989.

Kaponya, Paul: *How to Survive Your First 90 Days at a New Company,* A Career Press Book, Hawthorne, N.J., 1990.

Krannich, Ronald, and Krannich, Caryl R.: *The Complete Guide to International Jobs and Careers,* Impact Publications, Woodbridge Virg., 1990.

Lauber, Daniel: *The Compleat Guide to Finding Jobs in Government,* Planning Communications, River Forest, Ill., 1989.

Lucht, John: *Rites of Passage at $100,000+ . . . The Insider's Guide to Absolutely Everything about Executive Job Changing,* The Viceroy Press, New York, 1987.

Morin, William J., and Cabrera, James C.: *Parting Company—How to Survive the Loss of a Job and Find Another Successfully,* Harcourt Brace Jovanovich, Orlando, Fla., 1982.

Smart, Bradford D.: *The Smart Interviewer: Tools and Techniques for Hiring the Best!,* John Wiley & Sons, New York, 1990.

Sonnenfield, Jeffrey: *The Heroes Farewell: What Happens When CEOs Retire,* Oxford University Press, New York, 1988.

Tarrant, John: *Perks and Parachutes. Negotiating Your Executive Employment Contract,* Linden Press/ Simon & Schuster, New York, 1985.

Yates, John Alan: *Knock 'Em Dead Interview Questions,* Bob Adams, Holbrook, Mass., revised 1988.

Entrepreneurial

Axelrod, Norman D., and Lewis G. Rudnick: *Franchising: A Planning and Sales Compliance Guide,* Commerce Clearing House, Chicago, Ill., 1987.

Blackman, Bruce, and Jay Conrad Levinson: *Guerilla Financing: Alternatives to Finance Any Small Business,* Houghton Mifflin Company, Boston, Mass., 1991.

Boe, Kathyrn, *The Franchise Option: How to Expand Your Business through Franchising,* International Franchise Association, Washington, D.C., 1987.

Boroian, Donald D., and Patrick J. Boroian: *The Franchise Advantage: Make It Work for You,* National Best Seller Corporation, Schaumburg, Ill.: 1987.

Davidson, Jeffrey P.: *Marketing on a Shoestring: Low-Cost Tips for Marketing Your Products or Services,* John Wiley & Sons, New York, 1988.

Davidson, Jeffrey P.: *The Marketing Sourcebook for Small Business,* John Wiley & Sons, New York, 1989.

Diamond, Michael R., and Julie L. Williams: *How to Incorporate: A Handbook for Entrepreneurs and Professionals,* John Wiley & Sons, New York, 1987.

Eyler, David R.: *Starting & Operating a Home-Based Business,* John Wiley & Sons, New York, 1990.

Goldstein, Arnold S.: *How to Buy a Great Business with No Cash Down,* John Wiley & Sons, New York, 1989.

Greenbaum, Thomas L.: *The Consultant's Manual: A Complete Guide to Building a Successful Consulting Practice,* John Wiley & Sons, New York, 1990.

Levinson, Jay Conrad: *Guerrilla Marketing Weapons: 100 Affordable Marketing Methods for Maximizing Profits from Your Small Business,* Plume Publishing, New York, 1990.

Lindsey, Jennifer: *Start-Up Money: Raise What You Need for Your Small Business,* John Wiley & Sons, New York, 1989.

Lynn, Gary S.: *From Concept to Market,* John Wiley & Sons, New York, 1989.

Merrill, Ronald E., and Henry D. Sedgewick: *The New Venture Handbook: Everything You Need to Know to Start and Run Your Own Business,* AMACOM, New York, 1987.

Poynter, Dan: *The Self-Publishing Manual: How to Write, Print & Sell Your Own Book,* Para Publishing, Santa Barbara, Calif., 1986.

Shenson, Howard L.: *How to Develop and Promote Successful Seminars and Workshops,* John Wiley & Sons, New York, 1990.

Weinstein, David A.: *How to Protect Your Creative Work: All You Need to Know about Copyright,* John Wiley & Sons, New York, 1987.

Management Skills

Aguayo, Rafael: *Dr. Deming: The American Who Taught the Japanese about Quality,* Lyle Stuart, Secaucus, N.J., 1990.

Alessandra, Tony, Phil Wexler, and Rick Berrera: *Non-Manipulative Selling,* Prentice-Hall Press, New York, 1987.

Batten, Joe D.: *Tough-Minded Leadership,* AMACOM, New York, 1989.

Below, Patrick J., George L. Morrisey, and Betty L. Acomb: *The Executive Guide to Strategic Planning,* Jossey-Bass Publishers, San Francisco, Calif., 1987.

Benns, Warren: *On Becoming a Leader,* Addison Wesley, Reading Mass., 1990.

Coffin, Royce: *The Negotiation, a Manual for Winners,* AMACOM, New York, 1973.

Cohen, Allan R., and David L. Bradford, *Influence without Authority,* John Wiley & Sons, New York, 1990.

Cox, Allan: *The Achiever's Profile: 100 Questions and Answers to Sharpen Your Executive Instincts,* AMACOM, New York, 1988.

Cox, Allan: *Straight Talk for Monday Morning,* John Wiley & Sons, New York, 1990.

Crosby, Philip B.: *Leading: The Art of Becoming an Executive,* McGraw-Hill, New York, 1991.

DePree, Max: *Leadership Is an Art,* Doubleday, New York, 1989.

Fuller, George: *The Negotiator's Handbook,* Prentice-Hall, New York, 1990.

Gordon, Dr. Thomas: *Leader Effectiveness Training,* Wyden, Ridgefield, Conn., 1970.

Hyatt, Carole, and Linda Gottlieb: *When Smart People Fail,* Simon and Schuster, New York, 1987.

Larson, Carl E., and Frank M. LaFasto: *Team Work: What Must Go Right/What Can Go Wrong,* Sage Publications, San Mateo, Calif., 1989.

MacKenzie, Alec: *The Time Trap,* AMACOM, New York, 1990.

Senge, Peter M.: *The Fifth Discipline: The Art of Practice of the Learning Organization,* Doubleday Currency, New York, NY, 1990.

Thompson, David W.: *Managing People: Influencing Behavior,* MTR Corporation, Bannockburn, IL, 1986.

Walton, Mary: *Deming Management Method,* Putnam Publishing Company, New York, 1991.

Personal Development

Dyer, Dr. Wayne: *How to Be a No Limit Person* (Tape Program), Nightingale-Conant Corporation, Chicago, Ill., 1980.

Morrisey, George L.: *Getting Your Act Together: Goals Setting for Fun, Health, and Profit,* John Wiley & Sons Inc., New York, 1980.

Nightingale, Earl: *The New Lead the Field,* Nightingale-Conant Corporation, Chicago, Ill., 1988.

Panté, Robert: *Dressing to Win: How to Have More Money, Romance, and Power in Your Life,* Doubleday, New York, 1983.

Qubein, Nido: *Get the Best from Yourself,* Berkley Publishing , New York, 1987.

Qubein, Nido: *Positioning,* Nightingale-Conant Corporation, Chicago, Ill., 1989.

Robbins, Anthony: *Awaken the Giant Within,* Summit Books, New York, 1991.

Satir, Virginia: *Your Many Faces,* Celestial Arts, Berkeley, Calif., 1978.

Schuller, Dr. Robert: *Possibility Thinking,* Nightingale-Conant Corporation, Chicago, Ill., 1980.